IF THE G

IS GOOD,

THEN LICK

THE PLATE

By Loretta Barratt

MAPLE
PUBLISHERS

If The Gravy Is Good, Then Lick The Plate

Author: Loretta Barratt

First Published in 2024

ISBN: 978-1-83538-201-1 (Paperback)

Published by:
Maple Publishers
Fairbourne Drive, Atterbury,
Milton Keynes,
MK10 9RG, UK
www.maplepublishers.com

A CIP catalogue record for this title is available from the British Library.

Acknowledgements

I would like to dedicate this book to my mom, dad, and my daughter, Lillie.

I thank you for all the love and patience you have shown me on my journey.

****

As I move forward to the 'Ceremony of Keys,' I would like to thank my senior leadership team, life-long friends, and all the communities I have served throughout the years.

Contents

Author's Note

We Are All Leaders in One Way or Another

If the Gravy is Good, Then Lick the Plate

A Flavour of Me

Adding Depth to the Flavour

Adding a New Ingredient

Time for a Little More Seasoning

Becoming Head Chef

The Ceremony of Keys

First Serving

The Recipe for Success

The Interval

Second Serving

Refining the Recipe

Gravy Masterclass

All Aboard the Gravy Train

Appendices

Author's Note

"Why would anyone want to read a book about you?"

If you have taken the trouble to pick up this book, the question above is a fair one.

The first time anyone asked me that question was on a cold Monday morning in the middle of a Norwegian winter. I confess I was somewhat taken aback by the blunt response of my colleague when I first shared my desire to write a book. In hindsight, I realise she was absolutely right.

What I initially considered a cruel remark was one of the most honest and valuable insults I have ever received. You see, I am a firm believer that timing is everything, and, at that time, I really did not have a complete story to tell, not one that would have been much use to anyone anyway.

As I type these words today, however, I am a leader with significant leadership experience across the business and educational sectors.

Since I became a headteacher 23 years ago, I have taken two underperforming schools onwards and upwards. I have enabled both of these schools to become very progressive. Consequently, in 2004 and 2019, respectively, they became the first schools to be awarded Outstanding Status against the new Ofsted frameworks. At the time, achieving outstanding status against these new frameworks was perceived to be somewhat unattainable in the profession.

In addition, I have experience as an Ofsted inspector and external examiner for quality assurance of leaders. I have also worked extensively as a leadership and management consultant within the International Educational Sector at home and overseas.

With my proven record as a successful businesswoman and outstanding headteacher, I invite you on my journey of 'how it was done.' Hopefully, you will collect one nugget or two on this journey. Remember, one nugget could make all the difference to your leadership success.

Of course, these achievements have not occurred overnight.

I believe we are all leaders, whether it is simply of ourselves, the few, or the many.

We are all pupils from the moment we are born and follow different signposts in life to develop ourselves as leaders.

This book is the story of my journey from my early days as a pupil to a successful businesswoman in industry to an outstanding leader in many divisions of education.
You will gain insights into how I acknowledged outstanding leadership in both business and education has been utilised to transform the education sector.

It was on that morning in Oslo I was told no one would want to hear my story. This has now changed. The tide has turned. The difference now is rather than informing people that I want to write a book regarding leadership to help others, I have actually been asked to write this book.

The governing body of Dorrington Academy has invited me to share my leadership philosophy with you.

And so, as I so often say – timing is everything!

We Are All Leaders in One Way or Another

I invite you to accompany me on my journey to becoming an outstanding leader.

As a unique individual, first and foremost, you are a leader of yourself; from your first steps, you start to recognise signposts in life and make choices.

Meandering through life, as you grow, your role of leader may extend to the few or to the many, another choice.

Our vision of how we would like to live our lives as leaders continuously evolves; you will have many choices.

Mine is a journey where signposts have directed me through many pathways, with many diversions to accept and overcome. I have faced many challenges in pursuing my vision: to become an outstanding leader of many. I have always remembered, as a leader, my aspiration to make a positive difference to the many people I have encountered along the way.

Through this journey, I will take you through an array of experiences across both the business and educational sectors I have worked within. At each stage, you will be presented with the lessons I have learned. These lessons will enable you to reflect and choose to find a nugget or two to help you as a leader, in the workplace, or just for life in general.

Preparation is Key to Great Gravy

The title of this book is an analogy that relates to the choices you make in leadership.

As a leader, you decide if you will ever taste the gravy. Will you dip your finger in it, spoon it, slurp it, or, if you desire, just simply leave it alone?

I invite you to consider if you will be a leader who is successful or not. A leader who will take a strategically calculated risk or not. Are you a leader who is going to be honest with yourself? The choices you make will determine whether you are known as a satisfactory, good, or outstanding leader.

I share my experiences to enable you to face your fears, challenges, and change and recognise the right balance of pathways for you as a leader.

Please accept my apologies in advance if anything offends you. That would never be my intention. Instead, I hope you will allow yourself the odd smile, gasp, outright laughter, or whatever mannerisms you desire as you read on. It will help!

And so, to the first lesson, as your journey joins mine.

Lesson – Look out for signposts

We all occasionally recognise a signpost inviting you to open a door and choose. This will enable more informed opportunities for your choices, allowing you to successfully own and pursue your destination. You have already seen such a signpost and accepted my invitation; just simply by buying the book, a choice, your choice.

If the Gravy is Good, Then Lick the Plate

Apologies to my mother, who frowns at the title as in her words, "Oh dear, you would never slurp the gravy; you are a lady, and that sounds rather common." Of course, she is right. Mothers are always right, but I must confess I have done it, and the gravy tasted so good!

Talking of being a lady...

Yes, I have been raised to be one and constantly endeavour to fulfil this role.

However, if we are to acknowledge, "Ladies, do not swear," then it would only be fair at this point to admit to you that I also have a little bit of Lord Sugar in me, as on occasion, I say it just as it is.

So, if you combine a lady and Lord Sugar, you have a picture of me!

Not only have I slurped once in a while, but I have also needed, on the odd occasion, to swear many times. With this in mind and the potential for it to happen to many of you out there, I offer you one of my top tips for leaders:

Top Tips – Always have your own private space

You MUST have your own sanctuary and office, if circumstances permit, and never share one with your deputy leader.

Your office is your sanctuary.

You can go into your office with total freedom and without fear of judgement, swear to your heart's content!

Believe me, you will have many a 'f**k it' moment with a b*****ks thrown in for good measure.

Remember, your office is for your safety, and a therapy room is just for you. Without my office, I would never have become an outstanding leader.

Is the Gravy Calling you?

Picture yourself at a dinner party at someone's house or a restaurant, and the meal you have is so good. I bet it is the gravy that makes all the difference. It is simply divine and lingers in every part of your mouth, forcing you to put your tongue on autopilot.

It is so satisfying that you miss the keywords in conversations, your mind instead fixating on how good the gravy is.

Suddenly, you face a dilemma. Your eyes are drawn downwards to an empty plate except for oodles of gravy. You feel your eyes pulsating and your pupils expand as your gravy infiltrates your brain, asking, "Do you want to taste just a bit more, or are you going to miss the opportunity and just leave it on the plate?"

You hear the gravy calling to you. You know you want to taste it, but you resist, so the dilemma begins!

Do I dare try to savour it again?
How could I do it?
Is it acceptable?

Is it appropriate?
What can I get away with?
Will I be judged?
Is it etiquette?
If I do, will the hosts invite me again?
If caught, will my reputation be in tatters?
If caught, will I be remembered as 'the one who did the
*   unthinkable?*

As these questions race around your mind, you become aware of the others around the table having the same internal battle. You look around the table and recognise all the signposts, everyone's pupils enlarged, all looking downwards, inaudible questions, followed by nonsensical answers and inevitable pregnant pauses. It is a collective Oliver Twist moment for sure. You all want more!

Yes, the signpost points to the gravy asking you to 'Come this way.'

Lesson – Own your choices

When faced with a dilemma, you must remember it is very easy to follow the crowd or wait to see what somebody else does. As a leader, you must be true to yourself and trust your judgement.

So, What do you do With the Gravy Left on the Plate?

Choice

You could just leave, with regret, the gravy enticingly on the plate. Accepting it is simply there to stay, untouched; wasted.

Choice
You may look for leftover bread to dunk and soak it up.

Choice
You could reach for the teaspoon, even the desert spoon.

Choice
Oops, you could accidentally knock the plate over your hand and then go to the toilet to lick it off.

Choice
You could suddenly get animated in conversation with the person on your right (the left too obviously) and with utmost delicacy and discretion slide your finger around the rim of your plate nearest to you.

Choice
With grace, you nonchalantly, take finger to mouth to just simply remove it, especially as your serviette is conveniently under the other person's chair and it would be rude to disturb.

Choice
You could offer to take your plate to the kitchen and when no one is looking (especially if your partner is there) just go for it and have a good lick.

Choice
You could be really clever, go back to fetch more plates and pick up your handbag. The one with your go to water bottle inside. When you get to the kitchen, you, with haste, empty water

bottle and with urgency, pour the gravy off all the plates into the bottle. Casually, you place the bottle back in your bag. On arrival back home, you have a slurp, putting the remainder in the fridge for the next day. As you know, it will taste even better the next day and you do not want it to be a one-hit wonder.

Choice
In the event of recently having had your bag stolen, enter the kitchen, armed with the plates full of ounces of tasty gravy, put your head in the recycling bin and attempt to find a suitable gravy receptacle. A water bottle would be ideal but anything with a closable lid will suffice.

As you have no bag, you will need an excuse to go outside for some air, allowing you time to strategically hide your contraband gravy ready for the great escape. Your hiding place needs to be secure, discreet and convenient to escape with at the end of the night. An obvious choice is in your car boot. You may not have a car, in which case you could consider concealing the gravy in the nearest flower bed, hanging basket, behind car tyres or in the safe arms of a friendly garden gnome, job done!

When you get home and the great escape has been successful, follow the method outlined in the previous choice.

Choice
If in a restaurant, escaping with your gravy is a little trickier. You could just save yourself the trouble and ask for a takeout, as the gravy was so good, it would be a tragedy to waste such good gravy.

Then, the same routine applies when you get home, a slurp, and saving some in the fridge for tomorrow.

Lesson - Consider all your choices carefully for the situation that you are in
'Timing' is of the essence for all situations and pre-planning will always pay dividends.

Lesson – Always be prepared for a great escape
Do not go bull at a gate, take due diligence when pouring the gravy into your receptacle.
Try your best not to spill a drop, take extra care to avoid spillage and waste.

Lesson – Always be prepared to explain your actions

Keep your explanation simple.
Stay calm if caught red handed extracting the gravy from the dinner party.
Do not act in haste as it could cause long term consequences that could be avoided.

Example
You are caught in the kitchen.
Simply and calmly explain you were so concerned that if you had poured the gravy down the sink, it could potentially cause a dreadful blockage and smell, leading to long-term health and safety consequences.
Explain how you have personally experienced this in your own kitchen as you pull an exasperated face. Hold your nose in

disgust whilst explaining how the smell was simply putrid and expensive to fix.

Take care to convey to your host that pouring their gravy into your bottle, is absolutely, no trouble for you, as you have solved this issue before and would hate to see them suffer a similar fate.

Then, nonchalantly walk off with an air that this favour is an everyday occurrence.

How you choose to take the leftover gravy indicates what type of leader you are now and what you could become.

Remember, the choices you make determine the potential leader you are in life. What do your choices say about you as a leader?

From the choices below, which one resonates with you now? What would you choose?

Choice – You never taste any gravy because you do not like it. Likely Outcome – You are not a leader of others.

You may never be a leader of others; if that is okay with you, then fine. It could be that the time would never be right because you are content with what you have already tasted and will settle for that. That is all acceptable, understandable, and perfectly okay.

Choice – You want the gravy but will never permit yourself to taste it.
Likely Outcome – You are Consistent.

Everything you do is potentially nondescript, same old same old, no impact, mediocre standards, rarely remembered-leading to problems, discontentment, and underperforming.

You will never realise your potential as a leader.

Choice – Dunking the bread or using a teaspoon or tablespoon to collect the gravy.
Likely Outcome – You will unlikely be appointed to a leadership role of the few or many.
This is an absolute NO for a leader of the few or many, not acceptable standards in the public domain.

As a leader, you set the standards and expectations for those you lead to follow. You must always lead by example.

Choice – You convince yourself you are happy with the gravy you have had.
Likely Outcome – You will be a Satisfactory leader.

You will be in safe hands - but you will always just be that, in safe hands.

Despite wanting the leftover gravy, you choose to leave it on the plate time and time again. It could be because the occasion is simply inappropriate or you just do not have the courage or imagination to take it.

You will only realise your full potential as a leader if you do not stay in your comfort zone.

**Choice – You live in the hope that the leftover gravy
accidentally finds its way to you. You always apply a potluck
approach.**
**Likely Outcome – You will be seen as a 'Chancer' leader,
relying on outcomes by accident.**

Without a doubt, you always rely on outcomes to come about
by accident because you fail to apply a strategic plan to take the
gravy. Then, as a leader, you will enter the danger zone. You will
be seen as a dangerous and ineffective leader. You will
potentially lead your organisation into a downward spiral.

Chancer leaders tend to only stay in one leadership position for
a short time before they move on.
They never stay around to see the outcomes of their policies
and practices. Consequently, they are only successful in the
short term and are often known as the one-hit-wonder.

A leader who relies on being a one-hit wonder moves around –
until they are eventually uncovered, luck runs out, and this type
of leader runs out of steam.

Ultimately, you are recognised as a totally ineffective leader
without staying in power, potentially creating problems in the
process.

**Choice – Strategically plan to take the leftover gravy every
single time, in whatever way suits you.**
**Likely Outcome – You are the Egotistical leader. It is all about
you. This type of leader is worse than the Chancer leader.**

This type of leader is often classed as an arrogant risk taker and
does not know how their actions negatively affect people or
situations.

This leader wants to avoid recognising the importance of balance and timing. The leader, classed as a Chancer, has no clue and relies too much on luck. Here, the egotistical leader is more dangerous because they consciously calculate to take risks ALL of the time for simply their own gain and not the greater good.

This leader strategically plans to take the risk every time and is a dangerous liability to any organisation. Being nothing but a risk-taker will likely bite you in the short, medium, or long term. Consequently, you may be dismissed as a leader and highly unlikely to regain a leadership position of any credibility.

The establishments you lead and manage are likely to come crashing down.
Choice – You sneak a wipe around the rim of the plate every now and again.
Likely Outcome – You are a Good leader.

You are also like a safe pair of hands, but occasionally, you may gather the confidence to take small risks.

This choice may enable a leader to take further strategic risks at a later date and thus potentially become an outstanding leader.

Choice – If you strategically plan to take the extra gravy to the kitchen and put it into the bottle when the 'timing' is right.
Likely Outcome – You are an Outstanding Leader. You are a leader with a vision who plans strategically, reflects appropriately, and takes a balance of calculated risks, thus resulting in positive outcomes, which define you as an outstanding leader.

You have a well-balanced strategic plan to take the extra gravy when the occasion is appropriate. Sometimes, your plan comes to fruition, and you enjoy the leftover gravy successfully.

Other times, although the gravy tastes good, you decide it is time to rest as you are satisfied with what you have already tasted.

On other occasions, despite a carefully calculated strategic plan, it fails or you simply abort due to unknowns that affected your plan. Unknowns that you merely could not have foreseen.

You reflect and analyse what and why it went wrong to move forward confidently to try again when the next appropriate occasion presents itself.

You stay undeterred for the future.

I am a leader who adopts the final choice. I adopt a balanced, strategic approach to taste the leftover gravy when the time is right.

Your leadership style will doubtlessly evolve over time. Reflecting upon my career, I realise I am a leader who adopts this latter choice. I am always willing to enjoy the gravy, but only when the timing is right. I have always been inclined to think strategically but my confidence to do so has developed with experience. It would be impossible to share all of my stories and experiences throughout my career. However, I hope those I have chosen to share with you will give you useful insight and encourage you to reflect upon and develop your leadership style.

Food for Thought

As you read this book, I invite you to revisit these choices. Maybe your choices will change over time as you evolve as a leader.

Lesson – To be an outstanding leader, you need to be open-minded.

Never go into leadership if you have a closed mind and are never prepared to try the gravy. This would be irresponsible and unfair to the people you lead.

Leaders with closed minds to new learning, skills, knowledge and understanding will find it difficult to recognise what ingredients makes a good gravy in the first place, never mind what a good gravy tastes like!

As a consequence, you will never value the difference the gravy makes to any meal. Obviously, as a leader you will decide whether it is right to take a risk or not. However, when you are responsible for preparing future generations, can you really afford to never try the gravy? Ask yourself, would that be 'Right?'

Importantly, an effective leader should not constantly focus on taking risks, there has to be a balance. If you are a constant risk taker, you will fall foul and even those successful risks of the past with their fabulous outcomes could potentially be marred by that one risk too many, a failed leader.

A leader, who plans strategically, will adopt a balanced approach to know if, when and how to taste the gravy. This type of leader will have the opportunities to maximise their potential and the establishments they lead and manage.

A Flavour of Me

My values have always guided me and have formed the foundation of any success I have enjoyed as a leader. If you are going to fully understand my values and principles, it is only fair that I tell you a little about me as a person.

Every Leader was Once a Pupil

Long before I stood at the front of a classroom, I was a pupil myself. It is often said that your school days are the best days of your life. In my case, that simply was not true but I still learned many valuable lessons along the way.

Without doubt, I am blessed with wonderful parents who have always been there for me and thank goodness they were because I hated school. I was a child who sucked their thumb which resulted in goofy teeth by the age of five. In addition, possibly as a result of watching TV too closely, I had a terrible squint. This resulted in having two eye operations. I distinctly remember the experience of forcing myself to consume bowl after bowl of plums and custard at the Children's Eye Hospital before each operation, this scarred me for life. However, the fabulous pair of red rollerskates my mother gave me after being discharged, just about outweighed the terrible hardship of digesting those plums. Thanks to the unflattering combination of goofy teeth and newly acquired glasses, I can honestly say, with my hand on my heart, my school days were a nightmare.

I distinctly remember one day at secondary school, when a weasel of a boy pushed me to the limit. He had picked on me one too many times and this occasion was the straw which broke the camel's back. I could feel my blood boil and my inner strength rise as I lunged instinctively for the hood of his parka coat, detaching it in one swift movement. That moment of madness saw me banished to Mrs Maundrel's needlework room all afternoon where I was tasked with sewing it back on. Not an easy task I can tell you.

Despite the cuts on my finger and the lack of empathy from Mrs Maundrel, I can honestly say I have never regretted what I did. To be quite frank, it felt good and, in my opinion, he deserved it. However, over time you will be pleased to know that such rash decision making is no longer part of my philosophy, as it only ever leads to a short term fix – he was still a weasel.

It was in fact the diligent work of a wonderful dentist that enabled me to abandon my braces at the age of eleven. I suppose I should also begrudgingly thank the bulldog of an optician, who shouted at me every week when I visited the eye hospital. For ten years, she demanded I strengthen my eye muscles by pulling levers on a machine to force an image of a parrot back inside its cage. Finally, with my sight restored and my teeth straightened, I was discharged, no more glasses, no more braces.

As I approached my second year in the sixth form, studying A level History and English, according to my mother I started to blossom into an attractive young woman.
I think my mother's observations were correct as it seemed that the Head of Sixth Form demonstrated a sudden interest in me. Every afternoon registration, for some odd reason, she found it necessary to stroke the back of my hair whilst calling the

register. She even got her French class to pray for me when I took my driving test. However, she maybe gave the game away when she chose me to be Head Girl in year thirteen.

What a moment!

What a turnaround. The joy in this achievement did not last as I found out I was only picked for looking good in a suit, not for my academic intelligence and social skills. This disappointment was exacerbated when I walked into a buzzing foyer to see a crowd gathered around a poster studying something that had peaked their interest. My fellow pupils were all eagerly paying ten pence for charity, a lot in those days, in order to have a guess at naming the mystery pupil in the photograph.

It was not until I forced my way to the front of the crowd that I realised the picture they were so amused by was in fact my year seven photograph. My transformation over the years had certainly been considerable as not one of them correctly identified the shy and goofy girl who was now their Head Girl. They raised a lot for charity but I simply could not believe this spectacle had been organised by one of my own teachers, who ironically, was no oil painting herself. The sound of her laughter, alongside my peers, was like a knife being driven through my heart. That moment has never left me.

Lesson – Never misuse your power.

That was the day I learned my very first leadership lesson. A person in a leadership position must never ever misuse their power, as one action or word can have a long-lasting effect on anyone.

As a leader, I remind those I lead to think carefully about what they say, not to abuse the privileged position they hold, and never ever misuse their power. Children, in particular, are fragile and have long memories.

Some Lessons you Cannot Learn in School
Successful A level results...time to decide what to do.

Off I went to work for an international estate agent, selling timeshare from St Martin's Tower, overlooking Birmingham's famous Bullring Market, leading and managing their travel department. I was poached within 3 months, to lead and manage a travel agent bucket shop in Birmingham's Bull Ring.

A bucket shop, for those of you that do not know, was legal but specialised in cheap airline seats all over the world.

Every Tuesday, I boarded the six am train to Soho London, queuing to grab the list of cheap seats released at ten am. Once I had obtained the list, I made a quick phone call back to the travel agent bucket shop with my international flights secured at bargain prices. My sales list was guaranteed pride of place on the travel pages of the Birmingham Evening Mail that night...boom! Once published, the seats sold, sold, sold non-stop!

I could secure you a ticket to anywhere. From Benidorm to Barbados, Venice to Vegas. My ability to secure a bargain resulted in plenty of commission and a never-ending supply of cheese and eggs from market traders keen to stay in my favour. Click, click, SOLD! I loved it. Unfortunately, six months later, on a busy Tuesday morning, the police barged through the crowds and within minutes the travel agents were closed. With no deals left to offer, I found myself buying my own cheese and eggs.

Apparently, the owner had done something not so legal elsewhere and served time. Swiftly moving on, I embarked to my uncle's hotel in Torquay to help out in his first season. Shattering, but fun. Also had a quick innocent fling with my cousin, and yes, my mother found out about those two kisses! Oops.

When the summer season ended, I went off to university. I spent the next three years in a tracksuit studying a great course, 'BA HONS IN LEISURE AND RECREATION' specialising in popular culture. Right up my street as I loved sport.

I had a wonderful time, too many adventures to share, but I will boast that my dissertation got published in the library entitled, 'The Conceptualisation of Leisure Counselling in Contemporary Society'. Apparently, according to my professor as the honour was announced to very hung-over students, I was ahead of my time.

Actually, he was right. My dissertation predicted great change in the workplace, changing attitudes to the work ethic and highlighting the importance of quality leisure time with regard to mental health.

In particular, it suggested the challenges of our times today and the changes in the workforce alongside the diminishing work ethic, unemployment, early retirement coupled with the challenges of mental wellbeing.

It highlighted the potential growth and importance of leisure counselling as we would enter a time when we would need to adjust to a certain change in a culture of thinking in the 21st century.

Overall, I emphasised how people could adjust to this change through leisure counselling. My work predicted how we would need to be counselled on the significance of having leisure in our lives to help people develop their self-worth and sense of identity.

Furthermore, it advocated the importance of leisure time, no matter if we are in work, unemployed, retired or stressed. It highlighted how leisure time should be valued. Not only for those who needed a work / life balance but for those who no longer went to the workplace for whatever reason.

Thanks professor for the acknowledgement.
Graduated, now what?
My parents loaned me £1000 and challenged me to double my money in three months by Christmas.

This is where I got the name of 'Arthur Daley' - The Wheeler and Dealer.

I bought end of lines from a variety of wholesalers and hit Wellesbourne market in Stratford. This is a great market, still thriving today. For those interested, plenty of fakes!
I sold everything from thermal socks to Christmas paper. I even tried my own pork roast stall, constructed largely thanks to the DIY skills of my ever-supportive father. The latter was a disaster. I mean who could have predicted on the day I launched it that it would be the hottest October day on record. No one wanted a hot pork roast! Competition was fierce too. Who would have predicted that a luxury, state of the art 'pork roast on tour' juggernaut would roll into town and pitch up next me, let alone the full-blown fight that erupted in front of my stand and scared everyone to death. Despite my pork roast remaining intact, to this day, I have never been able to face a pork roast again.

On a positive, as it is essential to stay positive in adversity, my unusual line of mismatched pairs of odd sized, fluffy slippers proved a hit with the punters and I doubled my money overnight.

After completing the challenge set by my parents, I secured a job selling mobile phones when they were designed like bricks. Interestingly, market traders became my top customers. Wherever my career has taken me, I have always felt a strong affinity with market traders.

After my probation period of 3 months, and with my sales through the roof, the director rewarded me for my impressive sales figures with the keys to the company's lovely black Manta GTE. Gosh I thought I had made it! I learned many useful lifelong lessons whilst working here.

And so to the first. I recall an embarrassing moment. It began with me moaning constantly to our loyal company mechanic Dave. I was desperately trying to convince him there was something wrong with my beloved company car. There had to be a fault or something dead lurking beneath the bonnet because there was what one could only describe as a putrid smell of cabbage! Despite Dave's best efforts, no fault was ever found, no dead animals, nothing. However, much to my frustration, the smell got worse and oddly stayed with me constantly. I found my colleagues in the office giving me a wide berth as the repulsive stench followed me wherever I went. It was not until a friend, not to be mentioned, solved the real problem – ME! She proceeded to reveal, over a glass of red wine, the way to rid myself of the stench was not to wear plastic shoes whilst driving. It has been leather ever since!

Very soon, I found myself relying once again upon the loyal world of market traders. It is remarkable how often the relationships I have built throughout life, especially on those markets, have underpinned my success. Most importantly, the market traders taught me to appreciate the importance of valuing the individual, irrespective of professional or status. It is important, as a leader, never to look down on an individual or think you are superior just because you have a bigger chair. People can often fall into the trap of measuring their success by material possessions. Ask yourself, do you think that you are more successful than others if you have a bigger driveway, bigger white lions at its gates, a bigger car or the bigger chair in your office? You may think so. However, through my interactions with the market traders, I learned very early on such possessions are superficial. You have to really work hard and hope people judge you on what you do, not what you own.

Whilst selling phones once again, I appreciated the world of the market traders.

I remember one occasion at the NEC, selling car phones at an exhibition; I strategically placed myself by the men's toilets.

I stood in the pathway of a stocky guy in a brown, sheepskin jacket. Just as I attempted to give him my patter he stopped and said, "Grab me on the way out, needs must!" I waited, and he re-entered the hall a happier man, he simply gave me his business card and said, "10.30am Monday, be there."

I did as he requested and arrived in Mold at 10:30 am the following Monday morning.
Wow, the place was unbelievable, stables, race track, barn conversion after barn conversion and one huge workforce.

As I tried to navigate my way through the maze of barn conversions, I heard his voice long before I set eyes upon him. He was bellowing certain orders, with creative terminology, to his workforce and then called me into his office. I was not there long. Within moments, we were marching towards his car and my initiation began. An hour and a half later, I found myself selling duvet covers behind one of his Liverpool market stalls. I clearly passed his challenge and as a result his loyal customers were soon informed that I was the only woman to buy a phone from. I travelled up and down the M6 North for many months, he virtually owned all Manchester and Liverpool markets.

Once all the market traders were kitted out with mobile phones, he introduced me to the world of car traders and auctioneers in the North. He respected that I sold on negatives so I did not waste anyone's time. I sold according to their needs and at a competitive price. Not necessarily the cheapest but what I sold them was fit for purpose and mutual respect followed.

As I struggled to find a backstreet car auction in Manchester, I rerouted to accommodate a pressing call of nature. I found myself pulling up at a fairground, a very famous one. Never one to miss an opportunity, I scouted for the biggest caravan and asked to see the man in charge. Never ever underestimate how fabulous the caravans they live in are.

I sat waiting in his caravan and chatted to the three formidable women who were sitting looking at me with an air of suspicion. A rotund man with a twinkle in his eye burst through the door. Without hesitation, I quickly informed him what I was selling and then asked if I could go through everything with his wife. She smirked.

This was a moment where I followed my gut and recognised his wife was the boss. Oh, and yes, she was!

Again, we built up mutual respect. I had endless orders and every time I was paid with bags of fifty pence pieces. I never counted the money in front of them, 'that simply would not do,' business was built on trust and respect.

I learned a lot about people and their values. Most significantly, to judge situations with care and to never, ever have the audacity to think you are better than the next.

More sales, more sales.

I managed to crash the lovely black Manta GTE twice on the M6 whilst changing my Anita Baker cassette over. It was a good job, but after twelve months it was time to move on. I hold fond memories from this period and I can proudly say I sold a Panasonic handheld phone to a very famous music mogul but still loved the market traders the best!

Next, I applied for a job at TSB bank selling products. The advert said applicants aged twenty-eight plus, but I ignored that.

One month later, aged 24, I was selected as the youngest woman to be employed in the sales executive position. Interestingly, I was one of three women in a workforce of three hundred and fifty men. I was handed another set of keys to another company car, a slightly underwhelming red Rover, and off I travelled to Andover for my training.

On arrival, I received a phone call from my line manager in Solihull. He warned me not to be awarded the training course gold pen or I would not last. Quite frankly, I had no idea what he was on about.

Four weeks later, I was travelling around three branches and selling was good. Soon, I was off to the annual sales conference. It was announced I would be awarded one of the three Saturday branches in Birmingham. At that time, Saturday branches were rare and sought after. So rare in fact they enabled you to treble your earnings. The joy of this news was shared in front of three hundred and fifty men, dazzling in designer suits. Aromas of Armani aftershave, that would disguise the smell of any cabbage. My joy was quickly dampened by what I can only describe as a headless chicken sitting on a volcano (not sure where that one came from!)

A voice suddenly erupted, exploded actually, from the back, "She is shit off a shovel."

I was clearly struck off the heckler's Christmas card list, but I was trebling my money so the sting of his outburst was soon forgotten. Fortunately, I was earning enough to buy my own Christmas cards and address them to myself. And that is when I understood the term, 'the green-eyed monster syndrome'. A term still very prevalent today sadly. I can honestly say without doubt this was the unhappiest time in a job ever, I hated it. It was cutthroat, full of anxiety and the highest pressure ever and it left you so empty.

As I handed over my resignation a year on, the line manager at Solihull smiled and said, "I warned you not to come top of the course and win the gold pen."

However, not every experience was bad. One particular fond memory was with a customer in Oldbury. I had to do a home visit - she wanted life insurance.

I walked in armed with my 'Black Country dictionary', as they have their own lingo. I was trying to learn it not solely out of respect but also to have a remote chance of understanding what was being said. As soon as the door opened, a massive bulldog wrapped his legs around my right leg rather excitedly. Dragging the dog on my leg, I entered the coal shed.

Well actually no it was not; it was their living room which was plastered with Elvis pictures and coal, so much coal. I sat on my briefcase and when offered a hot drink, I informed them that I didn't drink hot drinks. I made it my rule when selling, to strategically decline any offer of a hot drink. It often saved time and embarrassment.

On this particular occasion, we talked of our love for Elvis and they insisted I borrowed two of their videos of Elvis to return on my next visit. Rather, sticky video cases.

When I returned, the dog was there again to greet, lovely. I sat on my case and noticed how the lady of the house looked very serious; then it all suddenly made sense. Her husband entered the room wearing his marvellous 'Elvis cloak'. They both stood up, looking at me with nervous anticipation, "Now Loretta, we have given it much thought and we really like you and want you to join us on our Elvis convention weekend."

'Oh crikey oh reilly', I started to panic, I mean I loved Elvis, but not that much.

I sat and wondered how I could get out of this predicament without causing offence. I slowly got up, held them both and said, "I am so honoured that you have asked me, but I would only disappoint you as, although I am a fan, I come nowhere near to the love you have for him and it would be wrong to come, an insult to you both." This honest approach resulted in a warmth and mutual respect for each other. Honesty is the best policy in situations like this.

Sadly, for them, I did not sell them anything. It would have been wrong, they simply had no money. So, I decided to pick up the briefcase, stroke the dog and bid them farewell. Their love for each other, and Elvis of course, would be good enough for them. They popped into the bank to tell me all about their convention, salt of the earth and I loved them for it. Christmas cards were exchanged.

As hard as this part of my career was, it changed my outlook on many things. I think this is where I truly learned what empathy for others really meant and how fickle life can be. I understood the saying for the first time 'you are only as good as your last sale'. I had watched many sales reps crumble under the pressure, they fell into the trap of living beyond their means. The finance industry encourages you to spend, spend, spend and this creates the pressure to earn, earn, earn. This is not good for anyone, especially when some just cannot find the strength to stop.

It was a very valuable time and I am forever grateful for the experience but gosh I hated it.
I learned that earning lots of money does not necessarily bring with it fulfilment or happiness. As hellish as this job was, it opened my way of thinking and doors of opportunity.
Importantly, I did gain many valuable insights about myself and people.

Lesson – Every pound has the same value, irrespective of who you are and what you do

- Never be too quick to judge others.
- Money and material possessions do not necessarily equate to happiness and fulfilment.
- Do not fall into the sand traps on the golf course of life.
- You are no better or worse than anybody else.
- Honesty is the best policy, even if it makes you uncomfortable.
- When driving, never wear plastic shoes as it will be the quickest way to lose friends.

Adding Depth to the Flavour

Leader of My Own Business

Throughout my previous ventures, I saved and saved to have enough money to set up my own business. By now, I had come to realise I am not a woman who really likes to be controlled. Instead, I am someone who likes to have the freedom to be creative in the workplace. More bluntly, I enjoy having a licence to be a bit of a free spirit which allows me to think outside the box. Creative thinking, I have found always maximises the efficiency and effectiveness of opportunities as they present themselves.

'Barratts' importer of dried flowers for retail and wholesale was my new business venture.
This time it was a family affair. Courageously, my father left his job as an engineer, and my mom joined as a somewhat noisy silent partner. She is an amazing woman who had a successful job in the antique and jewellery trade. My mother is a true lady that maybe, if born at a different time with today's opportunities, would have been a woman famously known for her creativity. Like many gifted women of her generation, she was simply denied the opportunities that we take for granted today.

In spite of this, she was admired by many. I was always impressed when she told me of how a very senior executive of Marks and Spencer would be chauffeured from London to Birmingham, just to be served a fine collectible piece from her.

Her creativity is second to none, her window dressing was breathtaking. Although her talent is in a league of her own, I am thankful that maybe a little of her creativity has always made me think outside the box, which makes the difference between a good and outstanding leader.

So, together as three business partners we were 'Barratts' together. We hired a Luton van and travelled to Amsterdam armed with papers enabling us to acquire our free samples of dried flowers and ferry them back to England to trial in our new business. The paperwork enabled us to go through the green channel as we did not need to pay any duty on free samples. It was legal!

The journey started well, until it hit us there was a possibility of missing the ferry. Not enthused, my father put his foot down a tad too much. As a bend approached us a bit too fast, we ended up ploughing wildly through a field full of hay, missing a telegraph pole by mere inches. Oh, I remember it well, my mother and myself did a remake of the film 'Planes Trains and Automobiles' screaming with our fingernails embedded in our chocolate eclairs.

With a sigh of relief and a hefty dry-cleaning bill, we eventually re-joined the tarmac again. We screamed with joy with no sound apparently, no backcombing of our hair was necessary that day. My mother and I both sat rigid staring at the sign 'Dover Ferry port two miles'.

Meanwhile, my father simply started to whistle. Something he is good at and proud of. In fact, he has been congratulated for his whistling by people from all walks of life. He even received a merit award from the children whilst doing a stint as caretaker at the school of my first Headship.

After the arduous journey, we arrived in Amsterdam. We had fascinating tours by growers, who helped cram free samples of dried flowers into the back of our van. Excited to have almost accomplished our mission, we headed back to the ferry port for our return crossing to England.

I will never forget the moment on that ferry as I glanced at my parents fading in and out of consciousness as we approached Dover. You see, this was out of their comfort zone, they never really understood how we could drive through the green channel with a Luton van full of dried flowers without paying any import duty. Despite constantly reassuring my parents that the paperwork was in order and everything was legal, they were so new to such entrepreneurship, they never quite believed me.

Remember, my parents were of a different generation, something I relate to more successfully now, especially when I look at the 'youth' of today and doubt their actions and choices. As we approached, I saw the enormous neon sign flashing vividly for the green lane, 'this way if nothing to declare'. Once more, I reminded them if we were stopped, to tell the officers we had nothing more to declare than a carton of cigarettes and a bottle of whisky. "Oh yes, LORET," they mumbled in uncertain unison.

As we approached, I must admit I even now started to feel a tad nervous, silently praying our accountant had given us the right papers for the green channel. When we slowly edged forward to the barrier thinking, "Phew nearly through," out of nowhere, a rather impressive man stepped in front of the van, his extremely large hand signalled us to STOP.

As I casually pulled up, I quickly reminded my parents what to say again, "Carton of cigarettes and a bottle of whiskey." A barely audible, "Ok," was the reply.

Within seconds, his commanding voice enquired, "Anything to declare?" As I turned to my mother for her practised reply, I was aghast to see her tongue hanging out and her eyes closed. No words.
The immaculate customs officer politely asked what was in the back of the van, with such confidence, I said, "Free samples of dried flowers," In hindsight, I probably handed over the paperwork too eagerly.

As I was escorted to the customs offices, an elite team of sniffer dogs eagerly descended upon the van with Mom and Dad inside; determined to uncover a stash of illegal substances embedded within the boxes of dry flowers.

I was questioned for what seemed a lifetime. The chief officer, with a well-practised air of authority, turned to me and said, "Where is your health and safety certificate?"

Now, luckily for me, I do believe in the spirit, and on this occasion, I believe they were looking out for me. With confidence, I adamantly informed him how this was not actually a requirement for dried flowers. In response, he wryly smiled and said, "Just checking you know your stuff," and with that he wished me good luck with the rest of my journey.

I cannot remember how I got back to the van but as I mustered the energy to climb back in the driver's seat, I could not help noticing the odd smell of cabbage coming from my left. Yes, my mom and dad were unconscious and no plastic shoes insight.

No words were needed and we followed our instinct straight to the nearest pub. We pulled over, ordered two whisky and dries plus a diet coke, sat and took a hell of a gulp as we finished in almost unison.

As the adrenaline wore off and the whiskey hit the spot, I told them about my interview, my mother turned to me and said, "How on earth did you know about the health certificate?" "Research, mom research," I replied. Truth be told, this was one of life's lucky guesses. I have no doubt mom knew I had not got a clue what I was talking about.

On the last leg of the journey, mom turned to me, slightly recovered, "We will never ever do that again Loret, promise?"

"Promise Mom."

Dad, pretending he knew we would be alright all along, now broke out into another of his trademark cheerful whistles.

We always had deliveries by courier after that. I was always so impressed as this huge container reversed down the cul-de-sac at seven am once a month. Needless to say, I lost more Christmas cards as neighbours were not so impressed as me. On reflection, this calculated risk was perhaps somewhat naive, why on Earth did I think that we would not be stopped in a crammed Luton van returning from the drug capital of Europe, Amsterdam?

Business went well. We set up a retail outfit in Worcester at the Shambles market. By now, you may be starting to see the recurring theme with the markets and the significant role they have played in my life.

I would recommend to you, from experience, never have a retail outlet which requires the customer to climb stairs, you cut out at least a third of your customer base. No offence to anyone who lives in Worcester but the residents tend to window shop. They look and admire, yet do not spend.

We cut our losses and pulled the shutters down on this retail outlet when we realised the stench of cheese from the cheese specialist below engulfed our outlet, even the dried flowers wilted.

As somebody who is always willing to turn adversity into opportunity, we decided to expand our dried flower wholesale business: it now incorporated supplying our product to retail outlets, big agricultural shows and private display work.

We supplied many retail outlets including a very famous shop. I declined to supply Marks and Spencers as they wanted us to supply everything too cheap.

Marks and Spencers think you should be grateful to them to even sell your product and you know by now 'that simply would not do.'

Perhaps our most memorable customer went by the unforgettable title of 'Knobs and Knockers'. We had spent months preparing to supply flowers for the director of the company's private estate.

Eventually, months of work culminated in the day of delivery. Proudly, we placed them strategically in each room of the vast estate. My mother and I stood back and admired the fruits of our labour. As we went about our work, we counted no less than five people painting the walls of her ladyship's kitchen. There was not a tin of emulsion or a roller brush in sight. Instead, they were equipped to paint the vast kitchen wall with the sort of fine brush you would reserve for an intricate watercolour painting. They looked very p****d off, especially as the director of the household watched their every minute stroke, mmm not a good sign!

When it came to pay our invoice, I remember the pompous woman laughed in a way which would make Cruella Deville shudder. She refused to pay and wanted them cheaper. I detected the painters stopped mid stroke in anticipation of my next move and my mother swayed and held onto the fine kitchen table, terrified as to how ferocious my response might be.

Well let me tell you, I think I shocked everyone by not responding at all. I said absolutely nothing and calmly asked my mother to get back into our Postman Pat van. I quietly collected every flower arrangement and placed them in the van whilst deliberately ignoring her attempts to antagonise me further.

Once I had placed the last arrangement in the van, I turned to Cruella, 'mutton dressed up as lamb' and in a clipped tone with a warm but forced smile said, "Has anyone ever told you where to stick your knobs and knockers?"

With that parting remark, I calmly turned on my heels to find the painters giving me a guard of honour to the doorway. In honour of my victory, her long-suffering team of decorators raised their minute paintbrushes as one, saluting me with admiration, they were impressed. They had clearly waited months, if not years, to see somebody finally put this dreadful woman in her place.

'Barratts' truly was a family affair and my Nan was the undisputed Queen of our brass irons filled with dried flowers production line. She was a wiz at knocking them out, producing hundreds every week. They sold well at the markets. As soon as they hit the stalls, queues were guaranteed.

Talking of my Nan, she came with me to all the big shows. At Gatcombe Park when we sold to royalty, my nan did not quite understand that royalty do not carry their own money. As the bodyguard reached to pick up one of my Nan's famous brass irons without offering the required £13.95 by way of payment, my Nan took offence and proceeded to chase our Royal member to the water jump. There was a right royal standoff which was only resolved when one of the bodyguards discretely coughed up the money. Nan was buoyed and returned to her stand to resume business as usual. Thankfully, the waiting queue had observed Nan's business approach and were stood with money ready.

Who would have thought a simple brass iron not only paid the bills but opened doors to lifelong friendships? I made mine in the Asian community. Mr Singh, was my main supplier of the brass. Too many stories to tell you. I met not only him but many other wonderful people during this time. Mr Singh enjoyed nothing more than finalising the 'deal' over an extremely sweet tea. I still have the odd tinge of guilt today about killing the plant in Mr Singh's office. Whenever he left the office to check on my order, I would discretely empty my sugary tea into the nearest plant pot. Little did I realise, I was slowly drowning his beloved lucky bamboo as we haggled over the buying price.

Returning to Nan's capacity for telling it like it is. I had bought, from China, a juggernaut full of beautiful Christmas hanging balls (now behave). Of course, we pretended they had been delicately handcrafted and sold them as such.

One Sunday at a Christmas market, my strategy was to flog the lot. In order to achieve this, my tactic was to hang one in a prominent position and then I educated my nan. "Now Nan, do not forget if anyone asks if we have any more, just say, 'Oh I am not sure I will go and check for you', no one wants to buy something too common."

Anyway, we had four hundred to flog so busy, busy. What a line! As the day wore on, nan, a great sales woman, basking in the amount of sales, forgot the plan. A lovely woman drooling over our display of products said, "Oh you only have one Christmas ball left, would you possibly have another?" My nan, overexcited at her mounting commission, said, "Of course my dear, we have about one hundred and seventy around the back." Obviously, no sale there then. "Oh nan," I said exasperated, but I still loved her.

I must confess to you, I have a lot of her in my makeup.

I have inherited her traits of frankness, honesty, directness and sometimes just simply saying it as it is.

Of course, these traits do not always go down well but you will find it is often the best way. You must remember constantly going around the Wrekin can often create confusion and sometimes can cause more harm. Not to mention getting yourself into too many pickles. The business carried on for a good 15 years but not with me in it, even silently!

Although she was unaware, my nan gave me the ingredients to add further depth to the gravy. Were it not for one of Nan's characteristically direct interventions, I would not have made the move into teaching. She had an ability to get the timing just right.

Well you see, I had a partner who was used to getting what he wanted. He was charismatic, wealthy and many were attracted to this. Ironically, me however, not so much and Nan was the only one to pick up on this.

One sunny afternoon, he unexpectedly called in to our busy, buzzing workshop whilst my nan was beavering away with her brass irons. A conversation occurred between my partner and Nan, a conversation I am glad I was not present for.

Anyway, in his arrogant way, he apparently flippantly said to my nan, "Well Marg, how do I get Loretta to marry me then?" Distinctly unimpressed, she sipped her tea, not sweet, and irritatingly informed him, "Look, if you have not got her by now, you never will, so don't be silly," and carried on nonchalantly sipping her tea.

Nan was right by the way. When the time came, I turned the marriage proposal down. You can meet someone promising you the earth, yes, he was so wealthy I probably would have never had to work, as he repeatedly told me, but you have to have an inner strength in life to be true to yourself. Whether in love or the workplace, if something does not feel right, then do not do it!

The break up. Painful, yes, and further exacerbated by him asking for every present back that he had given me throughout our relationship, shirts from many a concert, CD's, you name it. So, thank you to my mother because as we boxed everything up, we sent it off with a brass iron for good measure. Dad just whistled with relief in the background, cut himself a wedge of cheese and admired his brass irons with renewed vigour; he could not stand the man!

After turning the proposal down and much soul searching, I wanted to carry on having the courage to be honest about all aspects of my life. You see, in times gone by, I thought about being an actress but above all else I wanted to not only be a teacher but a headteacher; who makes a difference. After voicing my intention, the PGCE place was booked and my parents bought me out of the business.

Although I left business and the Bullring behind, the spirit of those markets will never leave me. Yes, I really was Arthur Daley in business. And I loved it!

Lessons

- Your family is important - always.
- Health and Safety must be the number one priority - always!
- Do not be frightened to try something new; you might be surprised at the outcome.
- Everyone wants to be respected.
- Careful when you are driving.
- You are only as good as your last sale.
- Sometimes luck can help - but it would be a mistake to rely on it; it will eventually come up to bite you.
- Do not ever under sell yourself for a moment of glory. You must value yourself and think short term fixes are not necessarily the recipe for long term success.
- Always remember most people with old money treat you well, but the nouveau riche, including lottery winners, suddenly think they can look down on you as they are somehow superior. I think not! Never be looked down on ever.
- It is important to remember that no one is better than anyone else just because they have fame or more money than you. One-pound coins have the same value for everyone and your money is as good as the next.

- Be to the point. In time, people get used to directness and believe it or not people may respect you for it. Of course, not everyone, but hey ho.
- Always be polite when you are doing business. Mutual respect is at the heart of success. Working for yourself is rewarding but it can be very demanding because you never cut off from it. Despite this, if you want to have a go at business yourself, you should
- Accompanying the hard work, you may have numerous moments of laughter, tears and cheese just as I did. I did learn so much.
- In life, if you have a nagging feeling of 'this does not feel right' be brave and have the courage to move on: you will never be fulfilled! This is as true for love as it is for business. There will be a reason for the nagging feeling; your gut feeling. There is a reason why you feel as you do. You might not understand it immediately but trust your gut instinct. One day, along your journey of leadership, you will reflect and be thankful you left it alone!

A Recipe Handed Down the Generations

Before I finish this chapter, I want to just take you back to my first job, it is important.

I was 14 and it was my first Saturday job at a well-known milliner in town. The owner was known as 'the Duchess of Birmingham'. Mrs J was pure elegance in every way, a prominent figure in the Jewish community. She petrified me. At

10am on the dot, I would check the mirrors were polished, her chair was ready and I stood to attention as I could hear the tap, tap of her walking stick striking the pavement.

The saleswomen shouted, "She is here," and, with full military precision, I opened the door for her.

Her style was immaculate and she graced a turban every Saturday. As she settled into her seat and surveyed her kingdom, I was immediately dispatched to the Rackham's food hall, which in those days was something to savour (House of Fraser now), to get ¼ kilo of Kenyan coffee fine to medium blend.

After a few weeks, I graduated to also preparing her morning snack, a Granny Smith apple cut in equal proportions. The thought of slicing those segments with military precision still makes me break me out in a sweat!

She trained me initially on how to serve bridesmaids headdresses. Over the next few months, I mastered it and did well. She then promoted me to sell the 108's a straw hat, very popular and a must at £13.99.
You must appreciate this was no ordinary milliners, it was for everyone but the rich and famous came. We will not talk about Hollywood stars. The job taught me both the importance of 'the art of discretion' and 'how to exaggerate' where necessary.

Being creative with the truth is essential. At times, there is the occasion when it is necessary to say to the customer, "Yes, the hat, it frames your face madam," even if, truth be told, said hat would have looked better worn by Johnny Depp.

You have to respect, everyone has their own taste. Sometimes you may just need that sale but always accept the customer is always right. If the customer loves it anyway, what is the harm. Somethings are best left unsaid.

Ascot season always clashed with summer bridesmaid's mania. I cringed everytime the overzealous saleswoman would step forward if she spotted someone 'not easy on the eye'. She had a terrible habit of judging people on sight. She would scurry to the front door and turn away anybody who she felt was beneath the standard of the shop, taking pleasure in reminding them, "This is not a look around shop Madam." God knows how she did not get bopped, but she did not and they left. Some would tell her where to stick her hat, others would be so upset and embarrassed they just left immediately.

I always remember thinking I would never treat anyone like that but maybe some underperforming teachers over the years might disagree!

Back to Mrs J, over time she took me under her wing, I think she liked me. She would click her fingers and we would descend into the basement. Thousands of hats, and I mean thousands of hats, filled every part of that building, all stored by colour, size, shape and price of course! She knew where every hat was, unbelievable, an absolute expert in her trade.

One day, a regular, wealthy customer came in, usually she was only served by Mrs J. To my astonishment, Mrs J clicked her fingers and instructed me to serve her under her supervision. I instantly froze with fear. Recognising this, Mrs J simply touched my arm, smiled and said, "You can do this." I spoke to the lady to ascertain her requirements and without further ado, I laid the tissue on the counter. It was essential to lay the hats on, but laying the tissue was an art form in itself.

I remember to this day how my hands trembled when I descended to the stairs to pick her three or four hats, never anymore as that would confuse the customer. My legs seemed to be reluctant to move. After what seemed like an age, I ascended the stairs and meticulously laid the hats in front of her, one by one.

Strategically, I placed the hats on the customer's head. With my little finger protruding slightly to the right (very important) I tilted the hat over her right eye, an absolute necessity to frame the face.

Mrs J observed my every move and every word.

Without Mrs J's intervention, the customer was delighted with my recommendation and proceeded to buy the beige felt trilby hat with the most enormous peacock feather on the side. It was my most precious sale ever, £79.99, and I felt I had finally made it as a saleswoman.

"Well done dear, now I will have a coffee and Granny Smith," said my mentor. We never spoke about the sale again but I have never forgotten how great that sale felt; an achievement for sure!

Over the next three years, I extended my hours to include school holidays and she mentored me in so many lifelong skills. I learned everything about colour, what suits people, how to serve people, profit and loss. Three of the most valuable lessons she shared with me were the importance of giving people the time (regardless of how much you had to give), to take an interest in people and most importantly recognising that having an 'Eye for Detail' will make all the difference in every aspect of your life.

Mrs J gave me the best training in my life. Yes, I only earned £2.50 and after plucking up the courage to ask for a pay increase after two years' service, she took two months to inform me that I had earned fifty pence increase. Although I would be lying if I said I was not disappointed at my fifty pence rise, I was. But when I look back now, I should have worked for Mrs J for free, well not quite free!

Understanding respect was at the core of everything she taught me and, above all, she instilled in me the necessity for a strong work ethic.

I have never forgotten every lesson she taught me.

Furthermore, by actually having the privilege to work for her, I understood the importance of recognising there are experts in different fields and you really cannot put a price on the importance of working with an expert.

I love respecting and admiring experts and many have helped me through my leadership career.

And I have sought many.

But for now, I thank you, Mrs J.

Lesson

- Do not be afraid to seek advice from experts in their field, none of us can be experts in everything. The mistake people in leadership often make is they feel it is some kind of weakness to seek advice from an expert.
- You cannot always open doors by yourself.
- If you do not seek advice from experts on your journey to reach the highest standards of achievement, I guarantee you will never maximise your opportunities to make a difference to those you lead!
- Open your mind and learn from everyone you can. You will be more skilled and knowledgeable for this and ultimately, so much more successful.
- Do not be too proud or worried to ask, maybe you have not got the qualities to be an outstanding leader if you do not!
- Collaboration and learning from people who know more than you are the keys to being a successful leader and manager no matter what the profession.
- In education, we are fundamentally teachers and we lead learning establishments so we should always strive to keep learning but everything comes with a health warning.
- Resource and take the time to seek out the right experts.

- Do not be fooled, there are always those people out there that think they are an expert, but they can often be deluded and are just not quite the expert they think they are. Be brave, to say, "No, I have found someone that may suit better," even if it is uncomfortable.
- Some think it is an easy option to move from leadership, to say they are an expert in this and that.
- Others may think that it could be an easier route when leadership has got a tad too tough to move on. They are now an expert.
- Others may simply have been unsuccessful as a leader and reinvent themselves an expert. Beware of this type of expert.
- Do your research, invest in the right expert, they may not be the cheapest, but, it is the quality you want, so, no short cuts here. Always think value for money and are they right for me? It will pay dividends.
- This leads to me to remind you of the importance of surrounding yourself with a team that possesses skills maybe you have not got. You will see this in the way I structured my leadership at Dorrington Academy.
- Sometimes people do not need to know what you really think, even if it would give you great satisfaction to do so. It is not worth it, and remember you are better than this as a leader!

Adding a New Ingredient

PGCE is TOUGH training in one year!

Three weeks in college and back on the road, this time in my own red Ford Fiesta GTE (Chicken Licken was my car's name, in fact all my cars have been called this, God knows why). My daunting first teaching practice awaited.

Suddenly, World War Three started. "Who the hell is in my parking space?" Not a pin dropped. My blood drained as the realisation struck me that in my haste to be punctual, I had parked Chicken Licken in the space reserved for the Headteacher.

I felt like I was taking my last steps to the guillotine as I stepped forward towards the voice, keys in hand, to admit it was mine.

The rest of the staff cynically looked at each other with some amusement, as if to say, she won't last.

I gathered myself to stand outside the Headteacher's office. Suddenly, from the other side of the door a booming voice bellowed, "I hate PGCEs."

Mm, two minutes in and he repeated that again to my face.

I was not deterred but it was not exactly the start I wanted.

Nearly the end of the first week and the regular unknown 'bug' that all schools encounter, hit this school. The teacher I worked with, admired very much by the larger than life head, got the bug!

The headteacher, perspiring slightly, due to staff shortages and no supply (he hated them too), pounced towards me like a silver back gorilla.

He looked me up and down as I clutched my hundred centimetre rulers. Measurement is always a safe lesson, easy displays, looks good and the children love it as they get to be so active.

"So, are you up to it?" he gruffly asked.

Not knowing what I was answering to, out of fear I just replied, "Yes."

So, I found myself teaching year 4 full time for five weeks. This good experience, culminated in getting a fantastic reference and he succumbed to say, as I left the visitors car park, "I take it back about PGCEs, there is always the exception." Knowing how this Headteacher was not a man to give compliments lightly, (unless of course you were the year 4 teacher) I was thrilled.

Chicken Licken and I drove directly to the pub to celebrate. We were off!

The months flew by. Before I knew it, I embarked on my final teaching practice. To my surprise, the headteacher lived on a barge. No offence to anyone living on a barge, but I was amazed at how she lived comfortably on a floating barge given her colossal stature. I knew she disliked me immediately, my size ten red suit obviously offended.

I remember thinking, how on earth would I survive eight weeks of her in what was already considered to be one of the toughest schools in the city.

My fellow student was 20 years older than me and winged it, by her own admission, on to the course. She was petrified with nerves and she admitted that she felt out of her depth. I decided we needed to stick together, as I observed an awful boy put a needle in her cup of tea, her name was Janet.

We lived close to each other and we had a pact that we would get each other through each week and go straight to the pub on a Friday night to therapeutically help each other to face the next.

I can tell you, without those Friday nights, we would not have made it.

Quickly realising what we were up against, I knew I had to go the extra mile to win the respect of the children. I suppose this way of working has never left me, much to the dismay of others.

I think trying to gain the respect of the Headteacher was simply a non-starter. She was one key short of a lock regarding her interpersonal skills.

After our second drink on our first Friday night having survived the week, I informed Janet we would build a fairground for the next seven weeks and it would blow the bulldog (that was the head) away. Janet was forever grateful.

Whilst building the fairground, again, I learnt about the importance of health and safety, especially as I hired an electric saw for the project.

Bulldog never saw it in operation but the Ofsted inspector did. He never mentioned it, I do not think he cared for the bulldog either. It was the longest eight weeks of my life. The landlord of the pub took pity on us by week three and reserved a table for us for every Friday night.

The time came to call in favours. A few men from Janet's not so little black book as well as mine got us a team to help build this fantastic fairground for the children, with all rides actually moving. The kids loved it.

Bulldog really gave me an awful time, crushing me at every opportunity. Even the staff, who had been their donkey's years, took pity.

Finally, on the last day of the teaching practice, we launched the fair and I was observed for my first job as a newly qualified teacher (NQT).

We passed, but not just passed, we were the only two in that year to pass with a merit!
To my surprise, as we packed our cars with our resources and of course some of theirs, (well you just have to don't you) I was staggered to see Bulldog approach my car.

I thought 'oh s**t,' she has seen me take those Pritt sticks, I am in for it.

You see, the Headteacher never came to see our fairground launch, unlike the rest of the community, so she had no idea we had made huge, permanent holes in her stage for our rollercoaster, or did she?

Holding my breath, I thought I was in for it. Janet quickly got in her car and shouted meekly, "I will see you there."

As she waddled up to me, Bulldog looked at me silently. She stared before begrudgingly offering me an unexpected compliment, "You are natural, you will go places," and that was the last I ever saw or heard from her.

The only thing I must say, she loved the children and she was dedicated, but you just cannot gel with everyone.

As I arrived at the pub, despite Janet obviously being absolutely over the moon that we had not only survived but had received a merit. She looked nervous and drank her gin a little more swiftly than normal which is saying something.

Quizzically, I looked at her and asked her what was wrong. Silence, another gulp. Janet turned to me and sheepishly confessed, "Please don't think I have lost the plot, but Bulldog offered me a job there and I have accepted."

"What the f**k Janet!" was my instinctive thought but then, after a few gulps of my own gin, my heart melted when she continued to justify her choice with, "Look Loret, who is going to employ me in my late forties? Amongst other things I am expensive."

I got it, but I was terrified for her voluntarily returning to that soul-destroying school but if she was happy, so was I.

We were an odd pair with little in common but we had bonded in adversity and really cared for each other.

We celebrated our survival far too much but we did not care.

Janet phoned me the next day to inform me she could not go to college to get her merit certificate on the Monday as she had been very ill on the Friday night after our celebration. She proceeded to throw up and professed to not knowing how, but the toilet seat had fallen on her nose and she proudly was now in possession of two black eyes.

I did persuade her to collect her certificate on Monday, concealer is a great thing. We were over the moon. Merits with jobs.

I need never have worried about Janet, she stayed with Bulldog and her two successors.
Janet became a fabulous SENDCO and I loved her for being my partner in crime. You must remember, we learned from each other. 'Janets' you will find have their own story to tell. I often chuckle at my Janet's but her stories stay only with me - I promised!

Lesson – Never Underestimate a Janet

- Health and safety must always be the number one priority, even if you are planning to live on a barge.
- You cannot gel with everyone.
- Never underestimate the quiet colleague, I call them 'Janets'. They may not shout about it but they will always have their own skills and stories to share and you can learn a lot from them. Very often you will find the quiet Janets can be the best!

The Taste Test

Summer 1991, I was lucky to be offered several NQT posts but I stuck with my first offer, a catholic school in a challenging area for many reasons.

I loved it. So many stories to tell but too many to share in this book and some would get me into trouble. I am still friends with the Headteacher of this school today so the less revealed the better.

I worked hard, got promoted quickly and took on many areas of responsibility and initiatives.
I learned in the first week of teaching the value of pots for pencils in the middle of the table and how to set up a real community newspaper in my second year (that nearly killed me 3 times a year).

I will not forget the day a cocky girl, who proceeded after me telling her off to open her legs and pee blatantly in front of me, arms folded with a look, as if to say now what the hell are you going to do about that!

To this day, it still makes me smile. I simply asked her to sit down. I carried on teaching, leaving the pee on the floor until after school. It helped that her father was an Elvis fan; as you now know I am too. I knew she was defiant and had a lot to learn. Some things are simply best ignored to be dealt with sensitively later.

My first staff meeting simply blew my mind. Can you believe we spent an entire hour discussing whether to mark books in green or red pen - seriously!?

To somebody with my business background, this simply seemed a pathetic waste of time.

Without wishing to sound arrogant, this is the moment I knew I wanted to be a headteacher. Sometimes honesty is the best policy and the red and green pen saga is what did it!

I vowed to myself that when I became a Head, I would not be talking about whether to mark in green or red pen. I have, however, been known to spend two training days discussing with staff whether we should dress as gnomes or scarecrows for our upcoming community day. After two days of deliberation, we decided we would do both.

Together, We are Stronger
One of my happiest times was being promoted to be in charge of community initiatives. This post has been one of my most treasured to this day.

The Camps

I organised two camps for mothers only. The first was themed after the Julie Walters film 'Wearing Pink Pyjamas'.

Twenty-five women and staff hit Ashbourne in Derby. Leaving was delayed as I had to get a mechanical problem fixed on one of the minibuses before we left.

After fixing the minibus, I arrived back to pick up the moms and found the caretaker shifting eight bin liners of empty cans. Oh, what had I let myself in for.

I had planned the weekend for weeks with pre-visits and persuading my mother to do cauldrons of spaghetti bolognaise laced with a beverage or two (god that went down well. Thanks mom.) Every team activity and challenge, and of course chicken and chips at the local pub for our first night, had all been meticulously planned.

The whole weekend everyone had to stay in pyjamas. It was just amazing, emotional, funny simply a memory engrained in my brain until the day I die.

Outcome:

- Three hours before returning, they did not want to go home.
- Two divorces as some moms realised they had other destinies.
- I was at Good Hope Hospital when one of the bungee straps snapped and tore the side of my eye open.

One of the best initiatives I have ever done.

Two years later, it was time for the sequel. Same moms, plus more, headed to Capel Curiq in Wales. The theme this time was the, 'Baywatch babes on camp'. Everyone had to camp, wash in the stream and sing for their supper. There were numerous challenges, laughter and tears. Just simply exhausting but just so great.

I must highlight two things.

Firstly, when I moved onto the Deputy Headship, one of the wildest mothers on the camps was asked if she would join the community team on a part time basis and carry on my good work – she is still there today. These camps were instrumental in leading the community and breaking down barriers to teaching.

Secondly, I received a phone call from the police one week after the second camp asking me to go to the station. Thinking it was one of the moms winding me up, I told them politely, goodbye. One hour later, the head appeared in my classroom to inform me that she had received a call from the police and that I had to go to the police station. I remember thinking what on earth was going on? Well apparently, there had been a murder in the pub we frequented at our Baywatch Babes camp and the police wanted me to help them with their enquires.

Imagine my embarrassment when the police officer presented me with a compromising photo of myself in a blonde wig and swimsuit in order to confirm my identity. I will never forget it for the rest of my life, my face was nearly as red as the swim suit.

Over the years, I have been contacted several times regarding this murder. My fellow 'babes' have since told me it was eventually resolved. They had it on reliable sources that two men went away for the weekend, apparently best friends, and the one murdered the other, rolled him up in a carpet and rolled him down stream. Mmm well who knows the real truth, but I do remember I did not account for that in my risk assessment!

These camps enabled me to fully understand the importance of teamwork. There was no way I could have organised these camps on my own. I may have had all the ideas, planned, prepared and managed but I needed a team to help me make it happen.

Arranging these camps really installed three key significant factors that are incorporated into how I lead and manage:

- Collaborative teamwork.
- The importance of humility in everyday life.
- Bringing out the talents of others and developing them.

I had:

- People who lent me all the tents and marquees.
- People who made a huge barbecue tray for a pittance.
- My mother making the infamous spaghetti bolognaise.
- A wonderful trophy man - still in business today and I still use him - who designed all my award certificates and trophies at cost.
- Companies who gave discounts on food, tickets, instructors for activities, the campsite and so much more.

- A pub landlord who provided great pub food and closing time in the early hours plus karaoke and darts.
- A free loan for three minibuses.
- A whole team of family, relatives and friends that helped me set camp up early.
- A team of staff that volunteered to come with me and take part in the community initiative.
- A farmer who rented his cottage for a quiche Lorraine.
- A head who had the confidence to let me do it.

The list goes on.

All activities challenged everyone in some way as we rock climbed, took to dry ski slaloms, canoed, cycled, abseiled, sang, completed cave expeditions, camped and orienteered to the pub.

I remember on the first camp some moms never made it to the pub. The wildest mother was the one who we found sitting on the same starting rock four hours later. She told us she had problems reading the map and had ended up in the same position she started in. When she arrived at the pub by car for her chicken and chips, I simply said, "That will not do". The mothers on the other hand, used to sniffing out bulls**t from the Outer Hebrides, were not so forgiving.

The activities were taken seriously. Everyone understood this was a competition with certificates and trophies to be won but fun was still essential.

Irrespective of age, everyone likes a certificate of congratulations.

Positivity, regarding achievements, no matter who or what age you are can have a lasting influence leading to positive life-changing outcomes.

On these camps, I witnessed these mothers transform from frightened, fragile individuals to strong women ready to take a chance. This was life-changing for me as a leader and as an ordinary person.

After each weekend, no one really wanted to go home, including staff. We were a crowd of women from all walks of life that by the end of it would always look after each other. There was a bond and it remains.

We speak of breaking barriers down to help parents come into school and approach teachers for help in aiding their child in education. These weekends, overnight, tore down those barriers! The community group even expanded and we set up courses for the moms to retrain to re-enter the workplace.

So, let me assure you, these camps were special to many people.

Teamwork was always at the core of these initiatives.

These weekends played a crucial part in helping me to create my vision for the future. I was determined to be a headteacher that created inclusive communities.
Thank you to everyone who helped me and of course, 'The moms'.

Two Key Factors:

- This is where I first introduced the motto for my future as head at Dorrington Academy, 'TOGETHER WE ARE STRONGER.'
- Importantly, Mrs J's training came into its own. I appreciated the importance of the eye for detail when organising these camps.

Through my headships, you will see community is at the heart of it. I advocate that working with your community is fundamental to any organisation's success.

I have always invested in helping members of the community learn new skills and for many it has opened doors to new careers. Many have become teaching assistants and gone on to teaching. Bringing out hidden talents in anyone, child or adult, is a passion of mine. It is a key feature of my leadership.

Lesson – Collaborative Working

- Collaborative teamwork is the key to success and greater achievement.
- You will never be successful if you think you can do it on your own.
- If you ask, you may be surprised how generous people can be.
- Always give rewards - everyone loves them, even if they do not tell you.
- Lasting friendships can be forged if you make the effort.

- Inclusive communities can break down barriers to maximise progress.
- If you make the extra effort to have fun in the workplace, progress will be accelerated.
- Risk assessments are vital for any trip.

A Kick in the Teeth and Rain Check

The hardest lesson in this first teaching job, but probably the most valuable even though it nearly broke me, occurred on the last day of term before a well-earned summer break. The head had been unbearable for some weeks and everyone was waiting to see who would be in the firing line, everyone stayed clear!

Two o'clock on the last day, I was called to her office

Fifteen minutes later I left, totally heartbroken.

The head simply ripped into me in a way no trade union would allow today but that was then. Bearing in mind, I had worked my socks off all year. I never left much before 7.30pm except for a Friday.

In the office that afternoon, the head proceeded to carry on with her budget, whilst informing me I get up everyone's nose and I am not liked. She called me something else too, although I can't repeat the word. As I exited her office, I remember telling her to look in the mirror and she would find the definition of the word looking back at her. I left two hours later for the summer holidays, totally confused and broken.

I had a dreadful summer, planned to leave the teaching profession but as you will see, I did not. Instead, I returned for the new academic year. I just carried on and waited. Oh yes, when I put my first request in for another job, the head tried to hold my hand and apologise but I snatched it away, still hurting.

I reflected over the next twelve months and actually she was probably right. I worked so hard I showed others up who did not want to work as hard as me. So, quite rightly to them, I was a pain in the butt of humanity! I get that now, but at the time, it was a hard pill to swallow.

Over time, I kind of forgave this head because actually she cared for me and I her. It was a strange relationship but a treasured one. As I drank coffee at her house, going through my presentation for my first headship interview, this time when she held my hand I did not snatch it away. She explained her motives for that terrible day and of course I understood very early on in my headship why she did what she did. Years later, I totally got it!

I spoke at her retirement farewell and expressed that she simply had a dedication and vocation to give children the best. Very few heads could follow. She sent me my usual Christmas card this year and we will catch up soon.

Another memory, was when Professor Brighouse (he is a 'Sir' now) a worldwide renowned expert in education, spent a morning with me teaching English together to sixty pupils. Yes, sixty, in the hall for twelve months. You will appreciate this was a massive task. Building work was going on and needs must.

Professor Tim Brighouse, is an expert for sure and one to be respected. I was a little scared that day. As of course I wanted it to go well, but I certainly was not intimidated, I rarely am.

I certainly had respect for such a knowledgeable man that day and I loved it. He taught me many valuable lessons that have forever stayed with me and without doubt have helped me on my journey.

One disappointment, he had dirty scuffed shoes, and laces always undone. Now that was unnecessary, no eye for detail, I thought. I was so wrong here; he actually did have an eye for detail, but shoes were not important to him, so many other things were.

I made an exception due to his brilliance and I suppose professors are professors and can be eccentric, quirky and often scruffy. Essentially, appearance is unimportant to them as they get so absorbed in their subject and they certainly have no time for tying shoe laces. Interestingly, he did have a young attractive blonde woman as his wife so I heard, but that may be just a rumour. That did not surprise me. He was rather captivating as a professor of education; but as a headteacher today he may be challenged in different ways in these changing times
A headteacher is generally not seen as a professor and standards of appearance are essential if you want to instil the highest standards in staff's appearance and pupil's uniform. So heads, clean shoes please!

Tim and I crossed paths a few times in my early leadership and he taught me many things. He asked me to do a few bits of research, mainly concerning how we teach underperforming boys.

One that sticks with me most is when he shared a coffee with me and he spoke about energy zappers, something I now look for everyday as a head.

He informed me an energy zapper are those staff who constantly moan and are negative. His advice was that you simply must let them go, as they have a downward spiralling effect on everyone else and ultimately the education standards of our children. So get rid! We will revisit this at Dorrington Academy.

Thank you, Tim, I mean 'Sir Tim Brighouse.'

It was 1997, I was appointed Deputy Head. There was a big school community send off from everyone. Well nearly everyone, you cannot win them all.

The farewell was all very overwhelming, all a bit too much really. I will never forget it. I felt totally humbled!

Lesson – Collaborative Working

- Have consistency regarding marking children's work. Prioritise the importance of helping children know how to progress. Do not spend too long deciding the colour of the pen you will mark it with…. total misuse of time.

- Manage your time effectively and productively, what outcome do you really want?
- Nurture NQTs, now known as ECTs.
- Organisational classroom management is key to good teaching.
- Some things can be dealt with more effectively later.
- Decide if you want to be outstanding in all you do, then accept you will upset people along the way.
- Always have a mentor, someone you can trust who will not be offended if you listen but ignore their advice, as you ultimately must make the decisions.
- Take the opportunity to work with the odd professor who is more than an expert.
- Always have clean shoes.
- You cannot always get things right first time.
- Take on a challenge, you may be surprised with the outcomes.
- Forgive.
- Be humble occasionally.
- Have fun in your job.
- Dare to take a risk and be creative, you may be surprised.
- Love and embrace your community.
- Learn from a valuable professor even if they have scuffed shoes; they maybe a 'Sir' one day!

Time for a little more seasoning

It is important to have a range of educational experiences to fully respect the challenges of our peers. So, from a school in a challenging area, I secured a position as Deputy Headteacher in a school with completely different challenges and a very different community.

The application was not straightforward and had a twist the most imaginative could not predict. Common practice in the catholic sector is to put the headteacher of your present school and the priest aligned with the school, as referees. This is exactly what I did.

I knew the deputy head position would attract much interest, so great care was taken with the application.

Several weeks passed without any correspondence. I was summoned to my current headteacher's office who informed me she had received a telephone call from the priest who was the Chair of Governors at the school I had applied for. He informed her that the governors had made the decision to re-advertise but they were keeping my application on file. With a tinge of disappointment, I accepted their decision.

This tinge of disappointment swelled very quickly as the headteacher advised me that if she was me, she would go and see the priest who had written my reference. This was because the Chair of Governors had said to my head that they all found the reference rather odd.

Looking at her expression, my whole body instantly flushed with anger; what on earth had he written in my reference?

My head allowed me to go to his house immediately. His attire and full English breakfast, indicated he certainly was not expecting me. With some trepidation and awkwardness, he let me in. Actually, he did not have much choice as I had virtually knocked the door down. I made my way into his lounge before he digested his bacon!

I remember it like yesterday. I looked him straight in the eye and asked him what on earth he had written in my reference to create a potential problem; especially as I not only worked my butt off, but I had just trained the children for an important sacrament only that month and was a Eucharist minister.

His awkwardness initially led to him blabbing through a load of waffle. Undeterred, I told him to tell the truth. What came next was quite astounding and pathetic. He informed me he had indicated his concerns about my catholicity as I did not read in church on a Sunday.

What followed was a sermon from me; "Forget the Ten Commandments, this is my
commandment to you, 'You shall not lie,' otherwise like Moses you will see the light and
then there would be a parting of the ways." This shamed him into apologising and resulting in him confirming he would contact the priest (the chair) from the school I was applying to and change the reference. As a penance I left him chanting verses of the 'Hail Mary' as for me I went home and had two Bloody Marys.

Yes, you must appreciate I did not read in church and quite frankly, I never had any intention of doing a reading in church, and to date I have not. Well, maybe just a little sermon when I got carried away at the Christmas production in the church of the school of my first headship. I think I was on a high with the gospel choir and the drum kit I took in (but more on that later).

Eventually, after my reference was rectified, the interview day arrived. Twelve people were on the panel and the competition, as I predicted, was competitive. When I got the call offering me the job, I was thrilled.

What I did not bargain for was finding out why the priest had originally tried to sabotage my application. It transpired that his agenda was more focused on another female candidate, to whom he was 'exceptionally' close. My application was a potential threat to her getting the job. I can only assume she was exceptionally enthusiastic when it came to reading in church.

Yes, let's leave it as exceptionally close. He left the priesthood strangely not long after and I believe travelled into the sunset and, overtime through the catholic community, he asked for my forgiveness periodically for many years after. I simply say one must move on, simply not worth bothering with, life is too short. Moving on, sometimes we just have to put things in their box with the lid firmly on at times and I had a job to do and he was of no relevance.
I was busy as deputy head, changing policy and practice, upsetting a few whilst exciting others and that was just the first week.

A month in, I had a surprise visit from the local authority adviser who informed me I was selected to be in the first cohort to study for the National Professional Qualification for Headship. Quite perplexed as I had just started being a deputy, she informed me that someone above, the powers at be, had been watching my progress and wanted me to apply. The process for this first cohort was rigorous, we were the guinea pigs!

A day in Dudley followed with all sorts of tests and leadership group tasks. Strangely, from the selection to the final assessment, I was always grouped with men. I think they were fascinated as to how I would interact with them. Perhaps they spotted something in the psychometric testing.

We were told successful candidates would be invited back the following week for a formal feedback interview and told whether they had been accepted or not on the course. Armed with our four-page psychometric test results, I went off with a male candidate to the nearest pub for a quick read.

To amuse ourselves, we decided rather than read our own first, we would swap and read each other's. I soon regretted that, as he bellowed with laughter. Enough was enough, as his laughter turned to pure hysterical antics, I asked him impatiently, "What on earth?" it said about me.

It took forever for him to regain composure and then with glee he told me, "To summarise, it kind of says you would make a good head as you could be a bit of a b***h if pushed. but you would need a good PA." I was horrified, as I hate that word that rhymes with itch, it makes me shudder.

Finally, I seized the document and read their conclusions for myself. I discovered, upon reading it, that basically it said I would have no hesitation in making those hard decisions when needed. My fellow candidate had clearly put his own interpretation on their words but he was right, I would always need a good PA.

He then asked me to summarise his. I did not hesitate for a second before responding, "Basically, it says you are weak and you will be crap," say no more.

I was called back the following week. A sleek tall gentleman in, well I suppose one would simply describe it as a 'neat grey suit' smiled as I sat down. He fixed me with a stare as he leant back nonchalantly in his chair and said, "I have been so looking to seeing you again, now tell me do you actually like men?" Well, I was staggered and asked what on earth he meant by that. He elaborated and explained that in all the group leadership tasks I had annihilated all the men in the group.

Without doubt, I went crimson but you will be pleased to know I managed to compose myself before answering that, yes, I did like men, but I did not feel they should necessarily be picked to be a leader just because they wore the trousers. Especially, when the men in said trousers were spouting a load of crap.

He roared with laughter and told me he would enjoy watching my career as he handed me the letter to begin my course at Warwick University.

For the next year, I had absolutely no social life; it was a sheer hard slog. All training for this qualification was at weekends and

you were told if an assessor puts their hand on your right shoulder you have failed and must leave the course immediately. No stress there then!
My leadership style was described by the assessors as a cross between an activist and pragmatist with the ability to reflect and apply appropriate theory.

Over the year, assessors were very clever mixing the group's dynamics. One particular weekend was actually dreadful, I really struggled. So much so, when it came to the presentation, I found myself staring into the projector, only stirred back into the present by a hand on my left shoulder. Phew yes, I said 'left' shoulder.

I was absolutely mentally shattered; the two days leading up to the presentation had been gruelling. You see, they had put me in a group with leaders who had a reflective /theoretical style and I simply found it frustrating and totally mind blowing. The word compromise was taken to the limit, poor decision making and lack of progress. Christmas cards certainly had no place here. I have no doubts they were as frustrated with me like I was with them.

One year on, with an overwhelming sense of relief, I drove to my assigned assessor's office with my eight finished assignments. Each one was like a dissertation; I had put my heart and soul into it, all bound and pristine.

I actually stroked them before I handed them over, I felt so proud.

The assessor swivelled round to reveal a garish outfit that would not have been out of place in a circus tent. With absolute disgust, she grabbed my assignments and threw them to the other side of her office. As I stared at them sprawled along her office floor, I felt the breath of her anger, as she spluttered, "Well if you think I am going to read all of that you are mistaken," and promptly asked me to leave. Driving home, I choked back the tears. My only consolation was that I had photocopied them, and importantly, I had actually also produced summary documents. The summaries I took to her the next day. Realising I had made her life significantly easier, her demeanour was transformed. Oh how friendly she was then.

On reflection, I concluded that actually I was proud of my full documented assignments. Without the detailed analysis and findings contained in them I would not have maximised my learning opportunities, knowledge, skills and understandings and certainly not been able to do a summary of them.

Interestingly, the NPQH today, with all respect to those who have taken it in the past few years and those who are presently doing so, is much like a summarised version compared to the full version that the first cohort undertook in 1998. I do not think the summary is good enough. Candidates today will never understand the relentless pressure which that initial cohort faced of trying to balance the pressure of this gruelling course with their existing jobs. It truly prepared us well for the realities of leadership.

Top Tips for Leadership Group Task

Having passed all the documentation, it was time for my final assessment day. Yet again, I was surrounded by all male candidates. I wondered if this placement was mischievously arranged by my friend in the grey suit.

First up the group leadership task.

A noble HR gentleman in the business sector, highly sought after in his profession at the age of 78, taught me: always, if possible, get in first in any leadership group task with your idea as you immediately get marks for leadership. He also said if you do not get in first, sit quietly and really read through the task and accompanying documentation until you find the hidden nugget everyone else has missed, as there is always one, the very small detail.
First task and I got in first. Tick. Done!

Second task, of course, I was pipped to the post. Obviously, they were rattled that I had gotten in first in the previous task. It was quite amusing hearing their perspiration plop on the table, as the four guys braced themselves to blurt out a word first when the assessor banged the table for the discussion to commence. While they jostled to be the first voice heard, I calmly scoured for the hidden nugget. My distinguished HR adviser had highlighted this possible scenario. He explained that their eagerness to impress and competitiveness to be noticed would potentially lead them to overlook a key detail that I could use to my advantage. They will be so eager to get in first they would have missed the nugget.

Imagine the scene. With one-minute left until the assessors called time for discussions to begin, I found that nugget. The nugget beamed to the back of my retina as it registered in my few brain cells. The boxes of bent nails, yes, this would affect everything!
Marks for eye for detail. Tick. Done!

Four pm, I was totally knackered. I went for a drink with the men to celebrate, we had passed. I did say I liked men and that is all you are getting on that score.

NPQH in Hand, Last Leg of Deputy Headship
This school had different pressures to my first one and I quickly learned both were as challenging as the other; just in different ways.

I had a good partnership with the head. He was a genuinely nice man, highly respected in the catholic system and I respected him and very much enjoyed being his deputy head.
He had a good command of English which rescued me when he checked my first headteacher application. You see, I must have had early menopausal brain fog and had misused the word 'exacerbate'. If he had not picked it up, then I absolutely would have had no chance of being shortlisted.

He was an ideal head for me to serve as a deputy.

Thank you, Paul.

The children were great.

I was always teaching year 6 and judged to be an outstanding teacher. This led to lots of filming of me teaching the children for the local authority to support current thinking such as 'Assessment for Learning'. Some training videos were available locally, nationally and internationally. If you look hard enough, you may come across one or two today especially with 'Assessment for Learning' still being a key component of effective teaching. In fact, when I worked in Norway, to my astonishment, they used the video there. It was a bit uncomfortable, gosh the camera never lies does it?

It is not just the teaching staff who contribute to the running of a successful school. The dinner ladies at this school were fabulous; they helped me run the rounders team. Oh yes, we were passionate about rounders. We always excelled and with that came envy, disputed decisions and often the referee banning me from the coaching area but don't worry no one messed with my dinner ladies.

I loved them dearly and we stayed in touch for many years. We had such laughs. Thank you, dinner ladies.

I was also in charge of the choir. Without doubt, if he had heard me sing, Gareth Malone would have tapped my right shoulder and sent me home immediately.

As a deputy head, you have courses galore. One in particular, was when I was selected to do a year-long leadership and management course for catholic schools. I was shocked to be invited. Only six people from England, Ireland, Scotland and Wales. I arrived paralysed with fear, dreading the thought that my lack of experience of reading in church, never mind singing, would be found out again. I need not have worried. On that first morning, I struck up what would become a lifelong friendship with the course leader, a formidable nun, who just went by the name 'Sister'. I still do not know her first name to this day.

Sister literally did not know how to walk, she ran everywhere. Her vocation coupled with her work ethic was a sight to be seen. She very quickly found out I could not speak or sing any Latin. She taught me the art of lip syncing; you can imagine how quickly I liked her. My lip syncing talent has saved me in many a school assembly over the years.

The course was exceptionally demanding as well as enlightening. One weekend still makes me laugh. In our second year, yes it was long, I left sister very disappointed!

You see my mother wanted me to sell one of her solitaire diamond rings, it would be no exaggeration to say it was one fine rock. I was so scared to leave it anywhere so I put it on my ring finger for safe keeping. Anyway, thinking nothing of it, I was busy preparing a presentation on the 'second coming' when suddenly sister burst out in song, no not in Latin. She sang "the hills are alive, Loretta you are getting married!" She nearly cried with joy. I think she liked me. Well obviously, I told her the truth and she was totally gutted. Sorry Sister.

Sometimes during your life, you cross paths with someone special and Sister was. She was so honest, clever but oh so shrewd and became my mentor for a while.

As you know by now, I tend to speak as I find even if you are a nun or a priest, but still with respect. On one occasion, Sister just seemed to constantly break out into a sprint and I said, "For god sake Sister can you just take a walk? Slow down!"

Her reply was a beauty, "Think that is what we call the pot calling the kettle black Loretta."
Point taken, she was right, I was working at a pace myself then. We did laugh together as she gave in to accept a cup of tea. She went on to greater things, Director for Education at one of the colleges in Oxford. Sister wrote my reference for my first headship, with many others as they wanted at least 5 (honestly).

This remarkable woman gave me a very useful piece of advice for my headship.

When I got my first headship, she telephoned me and said, "I have one thing to say Loretta, if you need to pass on a message to staff that you know will not go down well, get your deputy to do it whilst you stand behind the door and listen." Her advice was sheer brilliance and one that I have followed many times. Thanks Sister.
There were one or two valuable insights I gained through this deputy headship and would be amiss of me not to share them with you.

First insight. The day Margaret Thatcher resigned. I was disgusted at her treatment by her own fellow pack; now you must be patient. I did not always believe in every policy she implemented but I had admiration for her. A true leader. She wanted this country to have a prominent place in the global landscape; and I felt that should be respected.

Before the revelation taints some of your views of me, I would like to inform you that I did march in London for Arthur Scargill's miners' strike and I was part of thirty who broke into the Education Offices in London protesting the educational cuts. We were escorted out by the police and even made the news, well radio news.

Nevertheless, I will not apologise to you for feeling disgust at the shambolic and fickle way Mrs Thatcher was treated by her own fellow MP's. I despised the sheer backstabbing by her fellow MP's and the cowardly way, in my opinion, her successor hid away and waited in the wings with an apparent toothache before jumping into her seat while it was still warm.

Funnily enough, many years after this particular PM was himself replaced, I had a brief encounter with this man in a farm shop witnessed by my mother. We watched him walk in and literally spend approximately fifteen minutes caressing one brown egg. He just stood there caressing this egg. We watched with total amusement as he continued to analyse every aspect of it. Meanwhile, his bodyguard shuffled his feet. For obvious reasons, he pretended not to be there, out of embarrassment rather than the line of duty for sure. We sympathised, who would want to be a bodyguard for this egghead?!

He did not buy it and moved to the next tray to pick up the dick egg (sorry, typo, I meant, 'duckegg'). We were certainly not going to wait around whilst he examined that one.

We stood outside and howled with laughter. Now, was he thinking of the past as he lovingly looked at that egg, we wondered? Then again, when we look at his impact as a leader, he may just be, 'WET, WET, WET, as Mrs T would say!

As I fought back the anger at Mrs T's treatment in the staff room that morning, an established teacher took me to one side and said, "Can I give you a piece of advice dear? Never, ever, discuss politics in school if you want to get on." One thing for sure, discussing politics with colleagues can potentially further deplete your Christmas card list.

That advice I have never ever forgotten.

The second insight in a nutshell as deputy, was that it suited the head teacher of this school for me just to get on and lead the necessary change. You must remember, people do not really like change but sometimes it is needed for progress. Often, when you implement it, you ruffle people's feathers and they can get a negative impression of you.

This all changed the day my dog died. I had to go home and have two days off school, I was so heartbroken. On my return, a teaching assistant, who lived for her cockatiel, came up to me and said, "We all thought you were hard and that has changed now."

Two weeks later, the staff put up a poster of the 'Adoptathon Dog Event', it was for me. I said to everyone, "NO!" I did not think I was ready for another dog but I was first in the queue that Saturday. The staff welcomed Katie, my cross Labrador. They were overjoyed and suddenly loved me. They adored the pictures of Katie that I put on the staff notice board, but were not so keen on the new playground duty rota. How fickle life can be. As the breaktime bell went, so did my newly acquired popularity.

Food for Thought

You could find this a useful conversation point when you are sitting at the dining table whilst you contemplate what to do with the extra gravy.

Draw circles of all different sizes and look at them.

Now, ask yourself, are they the same?
Discuss.

The answer is YES. They are ALL circles, they just look different. Now, look at a number at schools and ask yourself, are they the same?
Discuss.

The answer is YES, they are. They are ALL schools whose purpose is to give children the best education. They just look different!

Lesson

- Sometimes things happen that you would never predict, be it religious or not. Always try and keep the faith that the truth will prevail in the end.
- Just put some things in its box with the lid on and move on - forgiven maybe but not forgotten.

- A psychometric test describes you in a particular way and opens doors by identifying areas for you to develop. My male friend in the pub, like us all, had areas for development in leadership. He worked on them and is a man that children loved. He had empathy and was a good head. As for me, well you can decide at the end of the book.
- Who cares who wears the trousers, totally irrelevant. If you think someone is talking nonsense, it may not always be appropriate to say so. Always ensure your facial expression does not give the game away. I continually work on mine.
- We should simply appreciate we all have different leadership styles and what works for one does not necessarily work for another. As the saying goes, "If we were all the same, the caravan sites would be full."
- When you are preparing and writing documentation, it is important to appreciate the needs and the audience you are writing for.
- There are times when a full document is necessary to plan strategically, as you need to really drill down into data, interpret and explain how you will address your findings.
- Importantly, full documents, if to be shared with different audiences, can be put in a shorter summary document to help the reader quickly ascertain all they need to know from your full detailed analysis.
- Never produce any documentation or plan unless it will make a difference with a positive impact,

otherwise it will be a total waste of your time and everyone else's. And it is very Annoying!

- Beware of people in garish outfits unless they are part of a circus.
- Your private office is exceptionally important. You can rant at breaking political news and cry all at the same time and no one will be wiser; without being left with egg on your face!
- If possible, work in different schools before your first headship to expand your understanding and perspectives of different educational establishments. This is not essential if you work in a large establishment; as you will get many opportunities to widen your perspectives.
- Assessment of any organisation is key for progress.
- Always be prepared to learn from others with experience. Unless you really know they are totally useless!
- Do not be a deputy leader, unless you have the mindset and ambition to lead the organisation. It can be a very challenging role.
- When filming, never wear red - not flattering and adds on pounds!
- When filming, remember the microphones that are attached to precarious positions on your body are always turned on.
- As a leader, it is essential to remember that every member of staff should be valued. They all have an important contribution to make.
- Do not judge a book by its cover.
- Strategically and wisely, use your deputy leader.

- Always get someone to proofread everything you do and I mean everything.
- Never lead the choir if you really cannot sing a note. If you cannot sing, you simply cannot sing, even if you are a deputy leader.
- Never talk about politics in the workplace and always have a TV in your office. It is important to keep up to date with the news and the weather (especially anticipated snowfall). But, more significantly, the TV will become your new best friend. You can talk to it about anything; it will not judge you for your politics or answer you back. An added bonus, it helps fill the gap of loneliness.
- You must be prepared, it can be lonely at the top.
- Recognise the perceptions of you will change constantly. People can be fickle; but accept it as part of the job, do not take it too personally. You will get used to the daggers in your heart. Trust me the pain subsides. It might not totally go away; but it subsides!

Becoming *Head* Chef

I vividly recall attending a course listed as 'Aspiring to be a Headteacher' course.

I could not believe it when the adviser informed us we should expect not to be successful in gaining any headship position until we had been for at least six interviews. I thought, what a load of nonsense. If you are right for the job, then you should be appointed. Mmm quite naive of me.

I soon found out in those days you joined something called a 'round'.

A 'round' was a group of deputies applying on the current circuit for headships. I am delighted to say this is not the case these days thankfully.

Maybe people have come to their senses or maybe it is to do with not so many people applying for headships.

First Application
As I was deputy in the catholic sector, I was expected to continue in the catholic sector. I was shortlisted for my first position. For two weeks, in preparation I found myself talking to the wall, myself or anyone who would listen. My ten-minute presentation was timed to within the last few seconds by a very patient friend.

During this two-week period, interestingly, the priest, who was the chair of the new school, visited one of my referees regarding my application. You must appreciate that on this occasion this was nothing to do with not reading in church. He wanted to know if there was anything this referee could say negative about me as apparently my references were very good indeed. The answer swiftly came back, "No nothing." So, he left. This revelation did not come to light until after the interview.

With my gruelling preparation complete, and my presentation firmly in my briefcase, I was ready. So, you can imagine my disappointment when on the day before my interview I was taken aside by yet another priest who was not to be questioned. He told me the interview was a foregone conclusion and I was to just go for the practise. I cannot write down my immediate reaction but I think by now you will have a good idea what my face looked like and what my fruitful terminology was as I talked to wall that night. This was well and truly a 'f**k it' moment. I decided to throw my hat in the ring and give it a shot.

The interview day was a long day including an assessed lunch with governors and some staff. At the end of the day, we all sat together waiting for the door to open and the successful candidate to be ushered in to the panel to be told the good news.

It was obvious who was going to be appointed from the moment we arrived; let's just say the candidate sitting like a peacock gave the game away. There is only so much small talk you can make in these situations, and to be honest, we all just wanted to get out of there. Except Mr Peacock of course, who I think actually took forty winks whilst waiting!
I even ended up talking about last season's Manchester United results, I did get desperate.

The time just ticked on, on, on and on.

Phew, at last the door opened and I thought, great, Mr Peacock will be called and then straight home for a glass of wine. Yes, I was right on that, home for a glass of wine, but to my surprise, so was a bewildered Mr Peacock. As we exited, we were informed the panel needed longer as they could not make a decision and we would be contacted later that evening.

With this unexpected turn of events, and the realisation that actually this was not going to be a clear-cut decision after all, it dawned on me that I did not want the job. I simply did not feel holy enough and I knew I was not the right leader for this particular organisation.

I desperately pulled the car over. Sitting in the car, I did not glow, I broke out into a sweat of fear, and I pathetically started to speak to the window screen. I recall asking it, "What if it is me who has thrown the cat amongst the pigeons?" No response came and I recall screaming, "No please no, I do not want it."

As I connected all the dots, my fears were exacerbated as I started to wonder why the clerk to the panel had thrown herself on my bonnet and asked for my strategic booklet for the school. I scraped her off and naively, I handed it over.

Half a bottle of red wine and four hours later at 8pm, the phone went. The priest, who was the chair to the panel, blurted, "Oh Loretta, I am sorry." But, it did not stop there. He continued, "Sorry, sorry," gosh the apologies went on. With relief I assured him it was actually totally fine with abit too much elation in my voice.

8.25pm the phone rings again and the priest's familiar voice said once again, "I just want to say sorry again." I reassured him again, I was totally fine. It is not often the unsuccessful candidate is required to console the chair of the panel.

10pm and, oh yes, the phone goes again. At first, I really could not decipher who it was. After catching the word bless, I answered, "Oh it's you father." I think he had a sherry or two, but just a guess, it could have been three or four. He continued to chant his well-practised apology, "I am so sorry, so sorry, you understand so sorry." After counselling him again, I finally got through to him I was more than happy with their decision.

Two weeks after the night of apologies, I received some interesting feedback. The adviser of the panel contacted me unexpectedly when the time was right to confirm that it was me who had thrown the curve ball to the panel. Thank god they never caught it! Oh, and the governors were grateful for the plan for the school. Mmm, 'you're welcome!'

Second Application
Candidates consisted of three men, two women, and just a small selection panel of seventeen! I nearly fainted.

After the first five minutes, I should have left. Three male parent governors made it clear they wanted a man. Now, you may wonder how I know that, well they simply said it to my face. I really am not sure why I just did not pack up and go, but I had spent hours on my presentation so onwards I thought, let's just sock it to them.

After the presentation, I got a migraine. I had never had one before and had to lie down in a hotel nearby until my afternoon interview.

During the interview, a full argument broke out amongst the panel of seventeen. Exceptionally embarrassing, the adviser's mobile went three times. If she had bought it off me, it would have had a silent mode! The other female candidate following me had a full-blown argument with the panel. I think at one point she even threw her briefcase in anger as she was that livid!

At least all of us candidates got on with ease, except for the arrogant gent from London, who had his tie undone exposing his hairy chest, and you guessed it, scruffy shoes. Not that I have any problem with hairy chests, but I do with ties not properly worn for an interview. And you know how I feel about scruffy scuffed shoes. Standards!

The smarmy adviser came in and called for 'Tom Selleck'. Well, that was not his name but right now that is the only hairy chested gent that springs to mind, sorry Tom.

One of the candidates got to his feet and said, "That's it everyone, come on let's go." With one last hurrah as we made our way out, we turned to the adviser and said, "Mate, you will find the guy you are looking for at the corner shop buying a mars bar." This is totally true, and we all laughed and left. The other female candidate, still simmering with the after effects of her earlier rage, made a wonderful hand gesture as she passed the room where the panel continued to argue. Let us just say, she did not use her thumb.

The chair and several other governors of the school resigned that night. I know as the chair was the head of my first school! She could not speak to me for quite a while due to embarrassment at the total shambles. 'Tom Selleck', who got the job, lasted about five weeks. He just left, probably for another mars bar at another corner shop.

Third Application
"Inner city school, was it for me?" I asked myself as I reread the advert.

I went to have a look.

Oh no. I walked in and within a few minutes I really knew I wanted this headship. I just loved the whole sense of multiculturalism that oozed out of its walls. The children just captivated me immediately. It needed a lot of work; the picture of the pope had seen better days for sure and the issues that would be left behind by the present headteacher, a nun who the community loved.

I can honestly say I was nervous as the interview date drew near. You see, I just wanted it so bad. The night before the interview, I got a call to inform me that due to reasons they could not divulge, the interview was cancelled and was to be rescheduled. No explanation, but they would be in touch.

You can imagine what the hell I was thinking this time. No words, no actions, more wine.
Three weeks later, the morning of the interview, I felt sick with nerves. My ritual of not speaking to my mother before an

interview was quickly broken, I could not find my earrings. This would simply not do so I dashed to my mom's to get hers as she had the same pair.

I picked up my friend's red Astra estate. What relevance is the car you may ask?
Well, after the look around visit at the school, as I was on my way out to my car, this year 5 boy chased after me. He broke out into a rap,

> 'Hey miss if you come again,
> they will have the wheels off that,
> in less than ten'.

After much consideration, approximately 3 minutes, I decided if I was called for an interview, I would borrow my friend's car and leave my BMW Z3 safe at home.

I was last on the schedule to be interviewed. I made my way through heavy, lunchtime traffic and renowned road works. As I meandered my way, literally, to the interview, an unknown event presented itself. You get used to these unforeseen events in leadership; so maybe on reflection, this was to be a test in itself.

The event occurred as I was approaching the bottom of the road where the school sat. I suddenly found I could not see. I tried pressing my nose against the window screen and I still could not see a bloody thing. I thought I was going blind with nerves but then the smell hit me and the flames danced through the bonnet. S**t the car was on fire!

I flung open the door, grabbed my briefcase, abandoned the car and ran and ran and ran to the school only to be met by a previous candidate just leaving. We had encountered each other many times since that day in the pub when we laughed at each other's psychometric tests. He was on 'the round' with me and Mars bar man, the infamous Tom Selleck. Today, my friend was my marathon man. Shouting for help, I grabbed him and said, "My car is on fire! Can you go and sort it and I will meet you at the bottom of the road later?" Do you know, he did not hesitate, he just totally collapsed with laughter as I carried on running.

He shouted, "Watch out for the guy who mumbles on the panel. I could not understand a f**king word, a total nightmare." Oh great, I thought as I carried on running. I so much wanted this job.

As I walked into the interview room, before I sat down, I had to apologise for smelling of burning rubber! At least it was not a cabbage. In hindsight, I think they cut it short as I literally stank so bad.

Despite the stench, the interview went well. I was asked to describe how I would do an assembly about a red teapot. The mumbling governor; oh my god his mouth moved but nothing came out. It was on the third attempt I finally got it. You see, he was an accountant and he wanted to know how my business experience would benefit the school. Oh, I instantly loved him!

At the end, I am sure the nun opened the door to the car park too quickly, but maybe I was imagining it.

Looking for my car, I suddenly realised it was on the drive at home and then gradually my heart rate slowed, my brain started to work and I came back to planet Handsworth. As I glanced around, I saw marathon man standing with his thumb ups at the garage at the bottom of the road. How convenient was that, a garage at the bottom of the road. In the taxi on way home, I phoned my friend to tell him about his car and how he needed a new hose or something blah blah; the engine was pretty knackered.

I tell you I could have gone ballistic when he casually answered, "Oh that yeah, I knew it was dodgy just had no time to fix, I am getting rid of it anyway." No words, No words!
Apparently, according to another candidate, the reason for the delay of the first interview, was it had been reported to the authorities that the chair of governor's wife had been shortlisted for the job. No more to say, a new chair had to be appointed.

You will soon see I was also appointed. Before we move with trepidation to this 'baptism of fire', my first headship; we need a brief step back in time.

Another important Saturday and holiday job was at Marks and Spencer in Birmingham, whilst studying for my degree. I started in the warehouse, then the dress department, and progressed to stocking the food department for extra money at 5.00am. It was a great job. As a student with little money, I stocked up on food both in the canteen and at the end of the day.

All staff could buy any food that would soon be past its sell by date. Everyone queued and I mean everyone. I still do not know to this day why I always grabbed the egg custards instead of the expensive joints, but all my friends back at college were more than happy with egg custards. Nineteen pence for a packet of three. Bargain. We were all happy for any food then; yes, I was popular on a Saturday night!

By the time we graduated, we all looked like an egg custard, I was about two stone heavier. I am not so keen on egg custards today.

Over time, I had the honour of being promoted to Customer Services. One particular Saturday, whilst merrily working away, I was asked up to the manager's office. A hush went over the counter; what did this mean, was I in trouble?

As I brushed the egg custard crumbs from my uniform, I sat anxiously across the desk from the highly regarded Mrs Criton. To my surprise, she asked if I would consider applying for a graduate position at Marks and Spencer for personnel management.
I read the signpost and I grasped the opportunity. After one year of rigorous interviews, I beat off tough competition to be selected for the final two-day assessment panel in Leeds.
The competition was cut throat. We were under surveillance as soon as we checked in. It was a superficial situation as we were under constant scrutiny. I was watched every minute by assessors: when eating, through tasks and socially throughout the evening.

There were twelve candidates, several Oxbridge graduates and me from sunny Birmingham.

After the first day, the dreaded board game came out. I chose not to play the board game as it seemed a set up. A very overconfident graduate had suspiciously brought the board game with him.

Obviously, he had played this game many times before, well that took interview tactics to a new level as far as I was concerned and I was not buying into it. So, I chatted merrily away with others. Suddenly, there was a hush from the left. Frustratingly, it appeared that no one playing the board game could get a specific answer. Mr Overconfident, the board game owner, who was no fan of mine after I beat him on an earlier leadership task, shouted over, "Oh I am sure Loretta will know this." He repeated the question and everyone looked at me; thinking with a tad too much enthusiasm, could she answer it? The tension whilst people waited for my answer was 'very still'. The one strong female assessor looked over with sympathy at the predicament I found myself in. I delved into days gone by 'David Edmunds', I answered nonchalantly. "What the hell," gasped my fellow competitors.

To this day you must appreciate, I really did not know where I got the answer from; but I do remember the wonderful look the female assessor shot me. Oh, she was bemused; think she liked me.

My final interview at the end of the two days was testing; another female assessor led the interview.

Weeks later, I was called again to see Mrs Criton. She explained, it was not the done thing for her to speak to me about the decision regarding the final selection process; but as she had recommended me, she wanted to tell me herself. I did not get an offer.

I was absolutely devastated and she knew I would be. She looked at me and said, "I should not say as it is not our policy but I want you to understand in years to come, you will be glad."

I simply could not see it then and again she knew it. The pain was terrible.

She proceeded to inform me, I was the lead candidate regarding strategy and social skills, but after much deliberation, the selection panel had decided I was not a 'yes' woman. She explained how M&S needed 'yes people', as we were too busy and simply did not have the time to train graduates who questioned too much if it was a good idea to display the female bras and pants in the men's window.

Of course, in hindsight, she was totally right. I am not a 'yes' woman and quite frankly bras and pants in the men's window display 'simply will not do'.

This rejection hurt but was invaluable at the same time. Well I can say that now but at the time it hurt a lot.

Thank you, Mrs Criton,

Lesson

- It is always best to practise for a presentation to an audience prior to the real thing. Once prepared, practise, practise, practise, it will pay dividends. Expect to be nervous as it will give you an edge.
- When you walk into an organisation for a position, if you genuinely do not see yourself there and the organisation is not right for you, then do not apply. You are wasting everyone's time, as well as yours.
- Never believe people who tell you how many jobs you need to apply for before you are likely to get one. Ask yourself why would they be saying this? Was it simply the case for them?
- Always apply for a role with total conviction.
- In all honesty, if you do not take the opportunity to visit and research the organisation prior to applying, you should not be short listed in my opinion. How do you really know if the organisation is for you? This goes for any job position.
- Things happen for a reason.
- Always be ready for a curve ball; these can really throw the cat amongst the pigeons.
- Always leave the panel a summary of your presentation but not the detail of how you would do it. Let whoever is appointed do their own work not yours.
- Take the decision, if negative, with grace. Life can be a very, very small world.
- Accept sometimes it is who you know, not what you know. That is life I am afraid, and let us not pretend. It really is a total waste of your time and emotional energy to get caught up in this.
- Never give up.
- Check the mode of transport that you intend to use to get you to the interview is reliable.

- If it is a ten-minute presentation, then that is what it is, not eleven.
- Rejection hurts for sure. Annoying as this saying is 'it was not meant to be'. Sometimes rejection is for reasons we will never ever be privy too, do not waste energy on trying to figure out why.
- Panels rarely give you a second thought when you have left as they have their own lives to get on with. So, you just get on with the next one.
- I would never appoint a candidate wearing a tie half way down to the chest. They would probably just gulp the gravy at the table, then probably belch whilst raising their right leg without a care in the world - no thanks!
- I do not care less if you are a 'mars man' or a 'marathon man'. It is more a question of are you right for the organisation? And importantly, is the organisation right for you?
- Sometimes it actually takes life experience to realise you did not get appointed for totally the right reason and you are happier in the long term, it just may not feel so at the actual time.
- Time is a great healer.

The Ceremony of Keys

The 'Ceremony of Keys', metaphorically, is a process in any organisation when the outgoing leader hands over the keys to the incoming leader. The 'Ceremony of Keys' is challenging for the outgoing leader as well as the incoming one in any organisation.

'Respect' is the key during this change over.

On a blistering hot July day, Sister, the retiring head of the school where I was to embark on my first headship stood by the picture of the Pope. Now, do not get confused, this sister is not my inspirational mentor Sister I have spoken of before.

Sister performed the 'Ceremony of Keys'. This well-established ritual required her to remove the key which was on a chain around her neck and place it in my palm. When she handed me the key, it appeared to be physically stuck between her long, thin, bony fingers. I was left with no choice but to yank it from her grasp.

Phew, first hurdle over with.

Twenty-three years on, after being appointed to my first headship, I now appreciate the emotion behind the 'Ceremony of Keys' and it is one that all aspiring leaders should respect. Naivety and hunger to make your mark can blind any new leader on the day your predecessors perform the 'Ceremony of Keys.'

So, This is for All My Predecessors

Every leader wants to make a difference and move the organisation forward in their current arena.

All my headship predecessors successfully made their mark and that, without any question, must be respected.

But, time moves on. Constantly changing landscapes and challenges present themselves and for whatever reason a new leader takes your place one day, it is inevitable. The challenge is how we leaders cope with passing on the keys. And, as I approach my retirement, do not be in doubt my next 'Ceremony of Keys' will not be easy either. I will miss it, as much as it is time to.

It would be disingenuous not to admit I do not want my successor to be better than me.
Yes, successful but not better!

We all have different ways to prepare for the eventual handing over of the keys.

One consolation, it appears not so brutal as it is for our Prime Ministers who have the office locked as soon as they announce their resignation. Nevertheless, soon enough you cannot unlock the doors.

And so, I now fully appreciate, as the lock is being slowly turned, as I approach once again the 'Ceremony of Keys', how my predecessors may have felt.

I am not one hundred percent sure of course, what my predecessors think of me, as I can only surmise from what I have heard through the grapevine and at times their actions. It would be fair to say, not much has been complimentary; sometimes the drums at the grapevine ceremonies have burned too brightly to be totally ignored.

But You Must Understand, I Get it!

My predecessors worked hard and were successful but it is the letting go that presents a major adjustment and adaption.

Anyone who has held a position with power will find this a challenge.

Leaders will always get plenty of criticism. You just do not need it from your predecessors but maybe human nature makes that too much of a challenge for some. I respected my predecessors, but I probably doubt that they believe it. Through both my headships, I immediately made changes in the short, medium and long term to schools my predecessors had themselves put their heart and soul into and that can hurt!

As a newly appointed head in each school, I was employed to make change. To make the schools progressive; to change a culture of thinking in an ever-changing world both locally, nationally and internationally. And that is a simple fact.

Have respect for your predecessors' tenures always but with that comes with a health warning to any future leaders.

As a leader, you cannot shy away from making changes if they are needed. I am not talking of change for change sake, that would be a mistake.

When change is needed for growth, then it will be your downfall not to proceed due to an emotional draw not to offend your predecessors. Do that and you will fail.

Yes, if you have empathy for predecessors, it will be hard but who said leadership was easy.
I only hope my next successor, just gets on with carrying the journey onwards and upwards and does not need their own 'Ceremony of Keys' for some time.

So, thank you to my predecessors, I did respect you, and I hope I have the empathy required to give respect to the incoming head which sadly my predecessors have never shown me, even to this day!

'What hurts you makes you stronger'. I hope so, I am sure I will be judged for that too but as the saying goes, 'that's how the cookie crumbles.'

Lesson

- Respect your predecessors.
- Accept they will not necessarily be in your fan club and you certainly will not be on their Christmas card list but there are the exceptions.
- Carefully evaluate what to sustain and what to change for growth.

- Do not be drawn to address what your predecessors say negatively about you. That is a lost cause, a battle you do not need and you certainly will never win. Some draw battle lines as soon as you are appointed, well before the 'Ceremony of Keys', and it is not always personal but sometimes it inevitably is.
- Just get on with your job and do what you were employed to do.
- You were not employed to make friends, although at times that is a bonus, you are employed to give the organisation the best. So, do your job!

First Serving

Once the Ceremony of Keys was complete, I arranged with the governors to spend a small amount of the holiday preparing for the new academic year. Invitations were dispatched to family and friends and then I arranged for an industrial sized skip to arrive.

I am partial to having a skip onsite and for those cynics, 'NO' I am not ready for the scrap heap yet.

The replies came in; my team was ready!

I had tried to prepare them for what was to come. Sometimes no matter how much you prepare someone for what is coming, seeing is believing and so I introduce you to 'The Pritt stick culture'.

The day began at 8am. I watched as the team meandered through the school, taking it in. I waited with anticipation for their opinions. We collectively decided to look in every nook, crook and cranny to find any resources and complete a stock check.

As I listened to their chorus, I heard, "Pritt sticks here...more here...more here... hey more here!" Then Aunt Mary added in exasperation, "Honestly how many elastic bands do you need? Pritt sticks here...more elastic bands." Maureen would then shout, "Guess what I have found?" In unison we shouted back, "Pritt sticks".

As they sang the 'anyone got a Pritt stick?' song, I had another mission to do, quietly, but that was my business. I scheduled a 10.30 meeting in the staff room. Tea, coffee and cakes. Food is a must to keep the team happy.

We meet and I have quietly completed my first mission, but you need to have patience before I share this with you.

Maureen and Aunt Mary reported to the team that in total the following has been unearthed:

- 58 boxes of 24 Pritt sticks, equating to 1392 – checks still ongoing
- 88 boxes of 100 elastic bands equating to 8800 – checks still ongoing
- Paper - 455 reams of 500 sheets equating to 227500 sheets of paper – checks still ongoing
- Paper clips - lost count
- Paints. 10 boxes of 6 paints in each colour. 12 colours in total equating to 720 in total – checks still ongoing.
- Coloured paper - beyond us in our time frame
- Paint brushes - beyond us in our time frame
- Science equipment - beyond us in our time frame
- Maths equipment - beyond us at this stage
- Pencils/coloured pencils - silence
- Exercise books …"Do you mean worksheets?" said Maureen
- Pat – "No Maureen, exercise books," - confusion- as there were so many worksheets!

Scene 1: Drink tea and make a plan
Mom: We need to gather all in one room
Me: Agree, everything needs to be audited in logical order

Pat: Yes, we need to gather everything first, as best we can, in any spare room available
Dad: I will be in charge of filling skips *(no one could fill a skip strategically like dad)*
Maureen being a teacher is still in shock, needs more tea.
Mom: Where is Keith?
All: Sizing elastic bands
Maureen and Aunt Mary are on the Church community board in Coleshill parish- a very significant parish as it is the head office for the diocese - yes, I have connections. Both stare in disbelief at the number of bibles.

It took fifteen days to gather all resources to a temporary central place and to count and log them all. Some staff paid a visit - just to have a nose.

On a day, when we all reached a pain barrier, we recalled over more tea and mom's sandwiches how we had observed a senior member of staff in the school for the last three days just walking literally over us as we tried to sort all of the coloured paper.

Scene 2: Finding Keith
Maureen: Not once did she even pick up a sheet, she just walked over the sprawled sheets
Mom: This is not going to be easy, LORET
Dad: Where is Keith?
All: Still sizing elastic bands

I reassured my mother the adviser who appointed me said they needed a trouble shooter as things needed sorting. So, do not worry! I was getting the picture.

Scene 3 – Still looking for Keith

Aunt Mary: *echoing from a distant corridor.* More Pritt sticks
All: *Roar with exasperated laughter*
Pat: **!?**!?**

No words I can repeat. Pat was a secondary PE teacher. She had a sharp tongue and it kept us all entertained, especially as fatigue set in - thanks always for that Pat.
Dad: Who put the huge piece of wood at the bottom of the skip and put the rubbish on top? I could have used that to build the sides up
Everyone gave an 'I dunno' shrug
Me: *Glancing guilty at the dirty mark on the wall where the old portrait of the Pope once hung* - Too late now dad just carry on.
Maureen: Where is Keith?
All: Still sizing elastic bands

As fatigue was setting in, mom's sandwiches were a Godsend. No one beats mom's tasty sandwiches and god, did we needed them. Thanks mom!

Three skips later, we sat exhausted and happy with what we had achieved. I lost half a stone. Every cloud!

Alarm on. I turned the key for now and locked the door. It was four days until the new academic year and I had my first assembly as head to plan.

Scene 4: Keith located

We got to our cars
Mom: Where is Keith?

All: Oh s**t, he must be still sizing elastic bands
Me: I will go turn off the alarm
School reopened, found Keith, ordered him to leave it. He did not argue for once.

Keys in lock again - all headed home.

We achieved just a little order but it seemed a tall order. Gosh we were tired, but we did a great job. A plan had been devised for the redesigning of a few rooms on a planning sheet. We had cleared an old classroom to allow for the construction of a huge resource room.

Nerves steadied as I had made some order. The vision started to appear and the strategic plan was in process.

Thank you, to my first team who have stayed with me through the good and the bad, 23 years on in fact, and we have reminisced over every New Year's Eve gathering.

Lesson

- Collaborative teamwork - you will only achieve so much without it - **not much.**
- Get your hands dirty and get started.
- Never ask anyone to do something you are not prepared to do yourself.
- Always complete a head count before setting the alarm.

Headship - September 2000 to April 2004

September 2000 -The local authority made it clear the school needed improvement.
April 2004 - We were the first school to get outstanding against the new Ofsted framework.
In 2004, we were named in the top fifty schools by David Bell in parliament and received an award.

So How was it Done?
To be frank, I cannot tell you every step and every turn, there are far too many to share.

As leaders, we always need to prioritise and so I have picked out some significant turning points for you. As you continue, remember this was my first headship, a one form multicultural inner-city catholic school and it was a place to build; to add more layers of flavour to the gravy. A dash of this and a sprinkle of that enhanced the base of the gravy. As the gravy thickened, I acquired the skills, understanding, knowledge and abilities needed for what I have achieved at Dorrington Academy.

Many lessons. Many successes. Many mistakes.

So, to the night before my first day. Pat and I are lifelong friends, yes, that is her category. I believe you have friends for a reason, a season or for life and Pat is one for life. The night before my first day, Pat came to mine for our traditional gin and tonic. Oh yes, even then we were ahead of the trend.

Tradition was always to have a gin and tonic before a new half term, term or academic year and that night tradition prevailed, especially as Pat was moving away from secondary PE to special behaviour units.

Pat, over the years, became highly respected in special needs and reintegration for children that need it.

She has established many life friends. You see, my 'Pat', as I call her, is rare. A good one who never forgets; nothing to do with her fetish for cards for every occasion, that's another story, another time.

No, she is just a good friend and she did not let me down that night. After a good gin and tonic, we embraced each other as we said goodbye, no words, just a hug as we set off to our new challenges.

Lesson

You need a good, loyal friend, who will not only be your critic, but also the person you can have a long drink and a laugh with, and maybe the occasional tear and rant, without judgement.

First Day

I set off. New suit, new shoes, new briefcase and new second hand car, a 'Grand Cherokee', now mess with those tyres if you dare!

Tactically, I planned a training day, an absolute must for new leaders. I spent the morning with the staff talking through my overall vision for the school to become an outstanding community school. I explained how there would be change and discussed the outline of how I envisaged this taking place. I explained my stance on the importance of a learning environment, teamwork and community to break down barriers. I explained how I would observe, get to know the school's existing community, policy and practice and that together we would put together a full vision so collectively we would own it.

I informed them that pennies make the pounds and I liked value for money. You can imagine their delight as I emphasised there would be no more waste as I embarked on discussing, how to my dismay, the horrendous amount of unnecessary resources I had found to date. I detailed the plan for having a purpose designed resource room, nothing fancy but purposeful from floor to ceiling with health and safety ladders by the end of the first half term. This was a first proposal for the Governing Body.

Taking a direct approach, I told them all I was fully aware that the entire community did not want Sister to leave and understood their apprehension of a new broom, but this new broom had arrived and my bristles were primed and ready.

Before setting them free to prepare for the following day and have a much-needed gossip, I informed them that my door is generally open, but when rarely shut, it will be for a reason. I explained it would be a journey with its ups and downs for sure but together we could achieve the best for the children. It was their right to have the best.

Lastly, I explained how I will always listen but to not be offended if I ever say, "Well yes, I have not only listened but actually heard you, but we will still do it my way."
On that note, in silence they left. I distinctly remember one woman saying, "God she is direct isn't she," whilst the others were saying a few Hail Marys. The looks just said it all. "Welcome," mmm.

You must always remember it is important to start as you mean to go on. If direct is your style, then do not pretend it is not.

As they scampered away, I shut the door of my office and breathed. Seconds later, the phone rang. Paul my first head, always told me the first phone call as head is the hardest to pick up. Irrespective of the amount of calls you have dealt with as deputy, as head, you are on your own. You are the head!

With a deep breath, I picked up the phone. The secretary definitely did not want me there, she lived in the parish and she loved Sister and only Sister would do. So, as I picked up, I just got from her in a flat as a pancake tone, "Call for you," and a click, click. I introduced myself and waited for the caller to speak. Almost not breathing, I was relieved to hear a familiar voice, "I got you ha ha it's me, Paul."

Oh, the relief, a friendly voice. It was short and sweet, "You will be fine and I am here if you need me." Thanks, Paul.

I do not know where the day went but I spent some quality time with the deputy. She was not to be underestimated in a quiet way and staff loved her, so did Sister. I believe the feeling was mutual. Common thread of the day was that no one would BE LIKE sister. I remember driving home thinking well, who wants to be!

First day, first assembly, an absolute total disaster.

Staff loved it for all the wrong reasons. As well planned as it was, I did not bargain for the annoying persistent wasps that invaded the hall. Despite zapping a few, wasps that is, you just sometimes have to admit defeat.

At lunchtime, whilst booking a wasp removal team, I could hear a real commotion. Before I could get out of my office to assess, there was an almighty bang. The force knocked me back as my door ripped open. What I can only describe to you as a cross between Fury and Tyson stood in front of me. This brute had smashed my door down, leaving it hanging off the hinges. In no uncertain terms, he threatened me with, "No one will be like Sister so watch your step." Stunned to the spot, I watched him belch and leave.

I staggered next door to a desperately depressing office to find another Mary, the admin/finance/receptionist/secretary, smirking gleefully at her computer with amused satisfaction. I asked her who that delightful gentleman was. With total disinterest, she continued to stare at her screen. She flippantly, as if she was telling me what was on her shopping list, responded, "Oh him, he is the biggest drug dealer round here," - lovely!

I made myself a strong cup of coffee and decided upon my next initiative: to improve my front of house; the school office; reception and security.

Lesson

- Security systems for your reception area are essential.
- Front of house has got to be right. First impressions count and they will be the key team for any head.
- Head's office must have a strong door.
- Start as you mean to go on, irrespective of the welcome.

For the rest of the day, I observed as much as I could. I spoke to children, dinner ladies, cooks and the caretaker. Exhausted, I contacted contractors for a new door and to obtain quotes to construct the resource room.

I really was just like a headless chicken, skating on thin ice. So, I set about setting up a timetable to interview staff to assess what they liked about the school, what they would change and what they wanted for themselves. I also set up a pupil's survey and went out on the school gate at the end of the day to speak to parents.

The Gate at the End of the School Day

Oh dear, I stood there with an over exaggerated 'hello' smile on my face. I had a few nods, and a few replies to my hello but the rest huddled in groups. They observed and glanced me up and down, certainly not admiring my new red suit and new shoes, to the whispers in the breeze, "Come back Sister, come back Sister, come back Sister."

Not deterred, I drove home, had a large glass of wine and spoke to my family and friends. Reassurance was given and as Scarlett O'Harra said in Gone with the Wind, "Tomorrow is always another day."

I ploughed through the next couple of weeks and established my expectations regarding punctuality and attendance. This letter led to the governor's wife obstructing me on the school gate and telling me basically what she thought of that in no uncertain terms. Once again, I was transported back to the market place with this woman swearing like a real fisherman's wife.

One Friday afternoon, a member of the staff with an ear to the community, who I think liked me, informed me there was trouble at the inn. A particular group of moms were setting up a meeting at the local pub that evening to get a petition signed by as many as possible to get me dismissed. Upon hearing this, I slowly got my coat and umbrella and made my way out through the kitchens to the gate. Going that way, the ring leader did not see me strolling towards her; she was so animated that she could not digest the signposts from her comrades who were trying to let her know that I was standing behind her. I listened as she spewed, "Let's face it, Sister was on the gate every night,

it's just not on. She's got to go and then we can get sister back."
As she started to hand out flyers for the big sign up, she sensed
an eerie uncomfortable silence fill the air.

Trying to look unfazed, I just simply said, "As you can see, I am
here on the gate, is there anything I can help you with?"
Immediately stunned into silence, all she could do was just
grunt.

I asked her if she had a spare flyer whilst reaching out and
helping myself to one. The grunt became a pathetic murmured
snarl and so I turned slowly to the next parent and wished them
a nice weekend and another one and another one until the
front of school was empty.

Guilty as charged, three out of five nights I was on the gate but I
was far too busy to be there every night, so I arranged for the
deputy to be on the gate the two nights when I could not be
there. Armed with a glass of wine as I sat exhausted with friends
at home, we all wondered if the meeting was in full flow. As the
clock struck eight, Pat raised the flyer and we all raised our
glasses. Not the best weekend, but I still was not deterred.

Monday morning came and it was business as usual. Knock
knock, my source pops her head in, "Apparently no one turned
up for the meeting except for the infamous 5." We smiled.

Lesson
- Management needs to be visible every morning and
  evening. Often many potential problems can be
  nipped in the bud by doing this.

- Stay calm when you are faced with adversity.
- Recognise, when the predecessor was so apparently loved, emotions can tend to run high.
- Remember, the importance of 'timing'.
- You are not going to be accepted overnight.
- You will be in cloud cuckoo land if you think you will be welcomed by everyone, or actually anyone initially. You are unknown and maybe not wanted.

First Governing Body Meeting

The governors wanted change and I was the woman appointed to make the change. It was their decision and I was hopeful the governors would be positive this journey of change had begun.

I presented three initiatives to be passed, plus the proposal of a new governor, who was sitting in the staff room just in case they agreed to hear his application. An experienced governor strategically picked by me. The three proposals were as follows:

- New resource room.
- Drummer from Ronnie Scott's to teach the children how to play the drums. He was brilliant and could take thirty at a time once a week, sheer genius and up to date with all latest songs.
- Advert for secretary.

How stupid of me to be so optimistic! It turned out the Chair was very close to guess who, my beloved predecessor. The Chair immediately went into a tirade of how she objected to my style and threw out objection after objection. Her outrage opened the floodgates for another governor to start his rampage, culminating with the governor of the wife who told me in no uncertain terms where to go over punctuality.

This governor proceeded to race through his memorised speech, that obviously had been dictated or shall I say drummed into him by his wife. He had learned it well but he could not look me in the eye. It was this straw that broke the camel's back. Passionately but calmly, I informed them I was here to stay, the school needed change and we all had a duty to work together to make it happen.

I asked them to reflect on their shameful behaviour and that of some of the parents. I stated, "If we are to believe the teachings of Jesus Christ are at the heart of this school, then it is time to show some respect, not hypocrisy. I am moving this school forward. Sister has gone!"

I stood up and told them I would give them fifteen minutes to reflect.

From past experience, this amount of time was just the amount of air I needed, a slow smoke of a cigarette actually. Yes, I did enjoy one in those days, and the cook's private hiding place suited me just fine.

I recall so clearly as I closed my eyes, slowly took a puff and said out loud, "God this is a baptism of fire!" On return, my plans were voted through and my experienced candidate for governors, who had sat patiently in the staff room, presented his application and was accepted. He became the new chair.

One governor in particular, chased after me after the meeting and profusely apologised. Of course, he did not speak for his wife just himself. Well that was a start! I felt sorry for him, as he was an intelligent man who got caught up in the snowstorm and lost his way. More about how to deal with snow forecasts later. I woke up the next morning with renewed vigour. A page had been turned, apologies had been received and, although we all accepted changing a culture of thinking would take time, we would try and move forward together for the children and its community.

The morning after, as I wedged my door open, there was just more thing to do.

I would say my next action was by mutual agreement, it would never have worked.

It was clear as muck, I knew after the first meeting. She was not a fan and grieved for Sister, yes, my local authority advisor. After one pathetic point too many, I just gave her one of my, 'that simply will not do looks'. That was enough for her to snatch her scarf and I assume (not that one should assume) run and have a catch-up cup of tea with Sister and tell all. Yes, Sister was still discreetly scurrying somewhere in the community.

I will always recall her parting words as she left the office that morning, "You are just not Sister are you?" This was the only thing in our short working relationship we agreed on. I simply replied, "No, I am not!"

I contacted the local authority that morning and was given a new school improvement adviser. He was to be a companion for a few seasons and was just what the doctor ordered.

Over the next few years, we developed great respect for one another and he was my mentor in later years too and actually I was for him.

I was within minutes of making it to half term when the dreaded phone went. To my surprise, Mary my admin/receptionist was actually enthused for once. She informed me with childlike excitement, "His Grace's office on the phone for you!" What literally!? I had met the new Archbishop for Birmingham four weeks earlier at the first Catholic Headteacher Conference.

Now, I must break off a little to elaborate on this first encounter with the Arch.

I attended my first Headteacher's Catholic conference. I carefully decided what to wear. I settled on the three-piece lime, green woollen suit. Nervous, yes, I was. As I walked in, I got a coffee, glanced around and noticed a free seat by five female heads nattering away. I took a deep breath and headed over. I said hello and asked if the seat was free. No reply, just a half-hearted nod, so I sat. As I sat, in unison, they all got up. Yes, all five of them walked away to another table. I will never forget that sinking feeling, ever. I could barely lift the coffee cup, trying to control my hand not to show I was deeply wounded. Deciding what the hell I was going to do next, I suddenly felt a hand on my shoulder. Not really wanting to look up, I heard a familiar friendly voice, "Do not worry about them, get your cup and come over to us." It was Paul, head from the school where I was deputy, just in case you have forgotten.

I loved Paul that morning.

Paul knows me well and he was not surprised after the Archbishop's opening sermon that I discreetly made my exit. A full day there, not a chance!

As I drove back to school, I just kept recalling the group of dreadful gossiping women constantly looking over from an in increasing growing crowd of female heads. Then, it dawned on me. Obviously, they simply did not like my lime green woollen suit.

Lesson

- Do not wear bright lime-green woollen suits.
- Allow yourself to be rescued every now and again.
- Always clock the discreet exit route out of a conference hall.
- Accept there is nothing you can do about gossip so, do not waste your energy on it.
- Always smile at any person of importance when they are speaking at a conference, they will think you are listening.
- As a leader, when you leave an organisation for whatever reason, have the professional respect for your peers to cut your ties and allow your successor to do their job.

On that journey back, I thought about conferences. I recalled the one-day conference two weeks previous that was not so bad. Yes, you will always get the heads that all know each other but this was a big conference, for not just heads, but heads and deputies all over the city. So, at such large conferences, there will always be someone like you, desperately hoping deep inside that they will find someone to talk to.

At this particular conference, I selected my workshops carefully and I enjoyed them. At the last coffee break, I just sat down. I never wear the obligatory identifiable name badge, anonymity has its uses.

Chatting away to some deputies a small confident women with a slightly overdone shaggy perm joined us. Thinking we were all deputies, she was in her element and her chest started to protrude just a tad more, not that I was really looking but you could not dismiss the shadow across the glass table. She did the rounds, ascertaining which schools we were from and having revealed mine, the glass table went into total darkness. Gesticulating wildly, she declared gleefully, "Well, I have heard the new head there is a right B***H." (rest rhymes with itch).

"Mmm," I replied.

"I mean, she has replaced the stations of the cross with modern versions. Building a resources room apparently. Staff and parents hate her, don't they?"

"Mmm," I replied.

Yearning for more she continued, "So how long have you been there?"

I paused for a moment, "Oh now let me think, not long, about 7 weeks." The light on the glass table suddenly reappeared as she sank slowly back in her chair. There was a hell of a pregnant pause followed by a blubbering, "Oh god you are the new head, aren't you?"

I smiled at her with pity as she squirmed, "Mmm," I replied. This time when I got up, my new-found friends followed.

Lesson

- Do not always wear name badges at conferences, shove it in your pocket. You minimise the chance of the speaker spotting your name and asking you a question plus unexpected bonuses.
- It is not too late to learn.
- People always surprise you.
- Preparation is the key.
- Progress should be embraced.

Mary put the call through. A man with a very distinctive Irish accent, rather mellow actually, informed me he was, Josh the Archbishop's secretary. I thought this was lovely. Finally, we were breaking down barriers as male secretaries were starting to become the norm.

"Hello, Josh," I said using my warm, welcoming voice.

Excitedly he declared, "I have great news." Surely, not to inform me of the second coming? I thought, oh NO, NO, I should be so lucky. He proceeded to inform me, "Your school has been chosen to be the first school at which the new Archbishop Bishop will perform the Sacrament of Confirmation for the children. This is a great honour and it will be a tremendous occasion with many dignitaries."

My voice quivered as I enquired, "Why us?" Obviously, I knew it was not to do with me or was it? He explained, "Well actually, you are both new to your posts and the church in the school parish is seeped with history."

I cannot really recall much else of the conversation, except he said he would contact me after the half term break. Just as I was about to put the phone down, I heard Josh say, "Oh one more thing before I go….the ceremony will be all in Latin." As I put the receiver down, I reached for my Latin dictionary to look up the translation for 'Oh f**k.'

I shared the news of the Archbishop's visit with all the staff before they broke up. Bearing in mind the community had not embraced me, it was amazing how the staff reacted to the news. "This is the best half term ever," one shouted. "Praise the Lord," another chanted. And one even enquired, "We will have to find that picture of the Pope and hang it in pride of place!" Good luck with that, I thought.

As I gathered up my keys and briefcase, I noticed a 'post it' on my desk; it was from admin/secretary Mary.

I picked it up. It had a number on it for a 'Latin tutor'. I laughed and realised maybe there was more to her than meets the eye.

Yes, there was, and I sensed the tide was just turning oh so so slightly.

New Half Term

Contractors were on site, a trader known for his good work. Andy, and his labourer Dave who was a person of short stature. They were fabulous, got on with the job and joined in our dressing up days for charity; good community spirit. They did a great job with the resource room, maximising every single space. One funny moment occurred when a Year Two child went up to Dave and said, "Hey Mister, is the reason why you are so small is because you don't eat your carrots?"

Lesson

Never underestimate a child.

I appointed a new, larger than life secretary who changed all our lives for the better. Within days, the transformation was remarkable. Suddenly, the front of house was now an inviting place where everyone wanted to be and all were very welcome. Yvonne and Mary, although extremely different, gelled and Mary became happy. She grew in confidence and accepted my invitation to be trained as a fully qualified bursarship. She was meticulous, good and very kind hearted. Mary opened up over the years, Yvonne unlocked the door. They were a great team and became my confidants.

Yvonne had a love for food, like me, well a bit more than me to be fair. The staff room was revamped and the kitchen became a feature. If you could not find Yvonne in the office, she was in the kitchen cooking surprise lunches. She was naughty though. She hated getting up off her chair to open the window to press the button to open doors to visitors. One day, she arrived late, hair not so coiffured. She was a lady of stature and loud, but spoke very well.

That day, like many, she looked rather pleased with herself. Without further ado, she produced a contraption out of her bag. We waited. When the day's first visitor arrived, to my utter surprise, for the first time Yvonne said, "Do not worry Mary, I will get this." In shock, we watched as she performed as if she was the 'cat that got the cream'. She reached 10 cm to her right side and the contraption flung into action. It grew longer and longer. Ping! She pressed a button and suddenly a knob came out of nowhere, then with a feminine touch she placed the knob on the button and hey presto the door opened. Yvonne had not moved an inch!

Yvonne had three chair replacements and two more knobs on her contraption by the time I resigned, but I never had to replace the carpet. Yvonne would swivel on her chair to the filing cabinet. If she could have scurried into the kitchen on it she would, but she always got up for Ofsted and dignitaries.

She became the clerk to the governors, a strategic move of mine - a winner, they liked food too. Yvonne could blag her way out of a brown paper bag. She even broke down barriers with the 'drug dealer'. She found out he liked fishing and funnily enough so had I when I was growing up (that surprised you didn't it). Having gone fishing with my dad for many years, as part of his father's fishing club, I certainly knew a roach from a barbell and a gudgeon. So, overtime, the drug dealer and I had found a common interest to break down barriers and fishing unlocked the key to him being on my side. Yes, I had won him over. The downside was I never did persuade him to abandon his dirty grey, tracksuit. A win nevertheless and one that paid dividends! Thank you, Yvonne and Mary.

Lesson

- Your front of house team is key for creating the right impression of your organisation.
- You want to be welcoming and professional (as much as you can), first impressions count.
- Front of house have their ears to the ground and trust me, all leaders need an ear to the ground.
- The office knows everything.
- They protect you.
- Importantly, they are your team, your very own team. Yes, your deputies are your right hands but the front of house/office staff are your real team, just for you.
- There is an etiquette you create with them, one of trust. You can share a joke, talk about most things, cry, laugh and they lift you when you need it and believe me if you are happy, then you do a better job.
- Take time for people, you may be surprised how they can help you break down barriers in your establishment.

The Archbishop

Both Marys, of course, would not miss it for the world. Yvonne thrived on the spectacle of the day. Not a shred of nerves, unlike myself. So much work had gone into the preparation for the confirmation ceremony.

The ceremony went perfectly; well almost. I invited many people from the community who I wanted there, some had shown such kindness after our first turbulent half term. To remind you, the first half term can be summed up like this, Sister and the school community not quite ready to 'cut the biblical cord' that had held them together.

I decided to invite an elderly man, Tom, who always attended the weekly school mass, he loved the drums too. He was always so pleasant and never failed to touch my arm as he left, a reassuring touch that said, 'You are doing ok.' Strangely, some members of the community were extra friendly to me as we approached the time to send out the invites. I do not care for fickleness, some people will always be that way, and 'that just will not do'.

Do not surround yourself with fickle people. You do not need these type of people. Accept there is a good possibility they will always trash you in the Ofsted anonymous survey and there is simply nothing you can do about it, no matter how hard you work, how happy the children and staff are, they will just do it.

They try to be clever, hoodwink you sometimes, but trust me their true colours shine bright again and again. Do not take it personally, it is their problem. It may just be down to not liking your suit, car, job, hair or they maybe just unhappy and being

aggressive is in their makeup. Just accept and leave it alone, they are not important in the bigger picture.
The 'fickles' did not get an invite.

As I gazed at the altar transfixed, I was so so glad I had time to remove the full-size drum kits that Steve my drummer, lead drummer from Ronnie Scott's, (think I mentioned that before, oh well) had got me for a bargain price. The church, in my opinion, had been crying out for a drum kit. We needed to celebrate and I found an ideal spot on the altar. The weekly masses were great. The children played the drums in a way that would give Ringo Starr a run for his money. We all belted out the hymns, including me; no one cared that I could not sing a note.

Even though some staff would not admit it, they loved it. Unfortunately, I cannot say that for the priest. He was not too keen on me. I think I frightened him, well actually I know I did, and that was never my intention, but he needed to be managed. No more to say.
Yvonne had organised an unbelievable buffet for one hundred and fifty guests. She was quite aware I wanted to avoid the Archbishop at all costs and so keenly kept him circulating with Josh in tow.

I think his 'Grace' knew I was doing my best to busy myself and soon, I knew the time would come. Yvonne, her hair that night looked fabulous, carried herself so well. No matter how many sandwiches she offered him as a distraction, eventually I saw her, plate in hand, direct the Archbishop towards me.

Knowingly we smiled at each other, my well-practised, "Good evening your Grace," to my astonishment flowed naturally, as if we had met many times before. All was going dandy, when suddenly he pointed to one of the many pictures on the wall, yes there were many modern and old. Please, I thought do not let him ask me what scripture the picture was related to. He continued to point and said, "Tell me Loretta what is that picture of?" His friendly familiarity threw me. Despite staring at it across the hall for what seemed an age, nothing came to mind, I went blank.

I laughed nervously for forgiveness and simply said, "Honestly, I have not got a clue, your Grace."

He really laughed out loud and said, "I know you don't, well let me tell you." Oh gosh here it goes, I thought, he is going to find out next I have never read in church. Mercifully, he just turned to me and said, "It is a picture of the Birmingham Bull Ring, do you know much about the Bull Ring?"
I cried with laughter and said, "Well your Grace I certainly do and I could tell you a few stories about my early career in the Bull Ring but maybe not." Oh, I was suddenly overcome with fear that this 'simply would not do'. I had let my guard down.

How could I have forgotten I had put the picture of the Bull Ring there? Thankfully, he was relaxed and intrigued as he said, "Well I like a good story and I reckon you may have a few to tell." How did he know?

Suddenly, not so confident, I just smiled and with that he turned to Josh. They had a quiet chat and his Grace turned to me and said, "Please accept my invitation to AFTERNOON TEA AT THE

CATHEDRAL Thursday next, 2.pm and you are welcome to bring a guest."

I knew he sensed my total utter fear at the thought. Remember, you can only wing it so far until you are uncovered. He smiled and I accepted. Like an Exocet missile I zoned in on Yvonne just about mustering the words, "Office NOW!"

My invitation was soon the talk of the whole community. Everyone was keen to know who I would take to tea. Yvonne, endeavouring to be subtle, repeatedly wondered aloud, "I wonder what his sandwiches are like?" even when we were counting the dinner money. Of course, taking Yvonne would be a safe bet, but that would not be fair to Mary, and I would always consider myself fair although some may dispute this. I noticed staff were working later than usual and we were inundated with parents offering to hear the children read. Remember how I feel about fickleness though!

I knocked on the door and passed over my invite, it was absolutely the right decision. New suit, new shoes, hair done with extra care and a visit to the dentist for the hygienist's touch of magic clean. My guest looked so refined, sitting in the taxi clutching an old briefcase. Josh greeted us. As he left, I looked around to see the Archbishop standing there in a M&S jumper. I know it was, as I had only just bought my father one, wine colour as we referred to it then, although now it would probably be referred to as an aubergine or just plum. Anyway, I digress, he said, "Welcome Loretta."

"Hello your Grace, please let me introduce my guest, Tom."

Tom was simply in awe. I touched his arm, this time it was my turn to reassure him that all would be ok. I felt absolutely fine. You see if the truth be known, I am not really scared of anyone, sometimes a situation but not a person. I always wanted afternoon tea with the Queen, oh I would have relished it, just a good chat and putting the world to rights. Anyway, it was not the Queen, it was the Archbishop and I was going to enjoy it.

He apologised for his attire and he asked if I would prefer for him to change, "Oh no your Grace you are just fine as you are," (looking back, too familiar. Oh well!)

We had a lovely afternoon. Photographs are always useful to get the stories going and Tom had brought many of the parish through the years; he treasured them and they were important to him. When Tom perused the bookshelves of his Grace's lounge, his Grace and I put the world to rights. We certainly did not agree on everything and maybe I got too brave at times but there was a mutual respect. I think he probably predicted we would disagree on many things but we also agreed on many things too. We encouraged each other to be open minded and to recognise the importance of looking at things through different perspectives.

Remember, not only listening but hearing is key to learning. I learned many things that day. His Grace thought it was a shame I was no longer offering 'cheap bucket flight seats', he may have need for one or two. I assured him, if he got the call to the Vatican, I still had contacts.

"Bye Vincent oh, sorry I mean your Grace," gosh that was tooooo familiar. I do tend to call people by their first name, even staff, as I often can't remember their surname. And when I cannot remember the first name, well the children are sweethearts and if adults, they just have more intonation given to the start of the sentence as if I know their name "WELL HELLO THERE." Revealing that I did not read in church would simply have bored this man, he understood many things from many perspectives, and I liked and respected him. As Tom and I walked to the taxi, I took a moment to look back and give him a final wave. He smiled and he looked up to the sky. Yes, he had gotten the measure of me.

Tom, turned to me in the taxi back to school, this time he held my hand and said, "Loretta, thank you, I will never forget this day – ever." Our eyes glazed over, we did not speak for the rest of the journey, just held hands.

I often reminisce when the 'Cardinal' is on TV. I always smile and then remember what an opportunity I was given. I learned so much that day, many things, yes, but mainly about myself! Thank you, 'Your Grace'.

Lesson

- Go and visit the Bull Ring; it has much history, useful for a conversation at the dining table, remember a small 'nugget' can be handy.
- Know your pictures and the story behind them.
- If you are putting on a function, do it well, good food always.
- Do not always play safe, challenge yourself.
- Respect people with different views, as long as the

views are not hurtful or to the detriment of others.

- Do not fear people in authority, just respect them and you will be respected too.
- Sometimes we do not want to make the effort to learn new things. If you do not make that effort, opportunities might pass you by.
- Recognise there are some good, humble people out there that are probably wiser than you.
- Show kindness; it costs nothing.
- Try your best to know as many names as possible especially the children's.
- Someone who knows Latin well can always tell when you are miming!

The Recipe for Success

The Strategic Plan

In 2000, this was an underperforming school. By 2004, it was outstanding and was named in parliament as one of the top performing schools in the country.

The crucial factor in achieving this remarkable transformation lay in the strategic plan and the manner in which it was executed. I can only summarise here, as there is far too much to write in this book. You may want further elaboration, but that is for the another chapter.

Following the summary, I will delve deeper into the specific fundamental aspects that played a crucial difference on the journey to achieving 'outstanding status.'

To Summarise

From the outset, I set out clear, high standards of expectation for children, staff, parents and the community. The vision was for the school to become an outstanding community school with respect for the community at its core. A school who went out into its community and brought its community in to achieve the highest standards of achievement for all.

A school that instilled values of respect at every level, irrespective of age, status and culture. Most significantly, our primary purpose was to focus on the development of the whole child. Every child was expected to leave our school confident in who they are as unique individuals.

The Strategic Plan

I always use three headings for the School Improvement Plan:

- The Learning Environment
- Teaching and learning (you may want to call this Learning and Teaching)
- Leadership and Management

Every year, each of our initiatives fell under one of these categories and were accompanied by an action plan that encompassed costings. Underpinning everything was the need for quality not quantity. We had a strategic timetable, including an aspects table, which was completed and adapted each year for five years in advance.

Its aspects referred to everything, from day to day organisation, to teaching and learning.
Collectively, we decided what we wanted to 'park and drive', what to monitor, what to prepare and what to develop. We adopted the paradigm shift theory to our practice. Sometimes, unknown factors affected the plan which caused us to take a different route to achieve our vision. However, the vision never altered. We simply adapted. If any factor appeared as a potential threat to our plan, we embraced it and turned it into an opportunity.

The strategic plan consisted of short, medium and long-term plans. Each was set and reviewed each year. Outlined below is my approach to conducting short-term, medium-term and long term plans.

Short:
• Assessed the children
• Acquired an understanding of the children, their needs and next steps required for improvement
• Surveyed policy and practice
• Full audit of every aspect of the school plus interviews with all stakeholders
• Following audit and evaluations, revising, planning and implementation could begin
• Devised the strategic plan with stakeholders so they also had ownership
• Ensured the strategic plan always drove the budget
• Ensured the School Development Plan, budget and CPD was aligned
• Adopted the paradigm shift to all our plans
• Arranged an event quickly for the community, children and parents
• Built relationships with governing body and assigned them to areas of monitoring
• Sourced services of experts from different fields
• Appointed key front of house staff and reorganised day to day organisation
• All existing contracts were analysed and benchmarked. If necessary, they were cancelled and renewed more competitively elsewhere to ensure fit for purpose at the right price

Medium
• Established learning environment strategic plans. (The learning environment is a passion of mine and is fundamental to how I organise and run a school- I am known for it! More on this element later as it is essential.)

- Introduced assessment for learning to every aspect of lesson planning as it is at the heart of effective 'learning'
- Staff devised new marking scheme that was relevant, had a purpose, was concise and not time consuming with little impact
- Set the children by ability for core subjects
- Prioritised Early Years for a total overhaul of practice and policy
- Action plans - for initiatives we were driving each year
- Redeployed resources including staff to maximise the efficiency and effectiveness of resources
- Relevant CPD that supported the strategic plan
- Updated policy and practices
- Constant 'thinking outside the box'
- Staffing structure revised
- Employment of new staff and supporting underperformance
- Capability for staff who I could not turn around to deliver expectation of standards
- Investment in teaching assistants
- Invested in performance management for all
- Utilising outside expertise

Long
• Adding depth to the above • When the inside environment was finished, we developed the outside learning environment - all the playgrounds equipment to support learning and, installing a new astro turf pitch to expand sporting opportunities in school and community • Revisited all existing practices and policy to allow for further initiatives, refinement and depth • Constantly 'thinking outside the box' for creative ways to motivate higher expectations of achievement for all • No room ever for complacency

- Constant monitoring and evaluation to ensure we were the best that we could be
- Constantly examining the political, economic, social and technological fields to keep abreast of changing landscapes both locally, nationally and internationally that could affect our vision
- Always looking at how these changing landscapes could be a strength, weakness. opportunity or threat to our strategic plan
- Underpinning this continual analysis, consider 'what is working?' what is not working?' why is it not working?' and ultimately, 'what are our next steps?'

Let me remind you, when I first looked around this school as a candidate, I was captivated by the children, saddened by the state of the school environment but excited as to what I could do with it.

The Learning Environment

In my opinion, the presence of the right learning environment plays a critical role in cultivating high standards of teaching and learning and ultimately leads to outstanding outcomes across all aspects. It is key for success. The learning environment is the essential foundation in developing a school to secure outstanding status with Ofsted.

If you do not pay attention to it as a priority in the first instance, you will never maximise opportunities for creative, progressive teaching and learning opportunities for all staff and children in your planning, processes and implementation. Why? In my opinion, if you do not take care with planning the environment,

you will always be on the backfoot. You will find yourself saying, "If only we had done this or that at the start."
The learning environment impacts and determines all outcomes. An unloved, dated and ineffectively resourced environment will potentially lead to teaching and learning outcomes requiring improvement. Staff and children will not be inspired to aim high if the work place is drab, dull, unfit for purpose and has no spirit.

Children and staff learn the most when they have fun with learning and the right modern learning environment is the foundation for this to materialise. We spend so much time trying to improve attendance, punctuality, address staff absence, staff wellbeing plus essentially retaining and recruiting staff.

And so, I advocate, if you invest in the learning environment, then all of the above areas improve; children and staff will perform to the highest level.

Gathering Evidence

From the outset, I captured evidence which demonstrated progress as a leader of change. Before and after photographs were taken of changes implemented at different stages for Ofsted and relevant stakeholders including the community. A similar approach was used to demonstrate the progress made by a child when teaching them a new concept and staff in their journey of Continuous Professional Development (CPD). It is important to keep their first piece of work, the interim piece of work and the final piece of work to illustrate the value added through the teaching process. As for staff, their progress was recorded regarding provision for their CPD. Collective evidence of all aspects of progress is essential.

My First Evaluation of this School's Environment
This school was living in the dark ages, it was stuck in the Victorian era. The learning environment zapped the ethos. It was drab, visionless, cold, spiritless, uninviting and really looked like a sparse convent (as I imagine from the films I have seen).

The staffroom had old, awful chairs, threads lying idle underneath their base, old tea stains and a distinctive stale smell. These chairs were strategically arranged in a huddle round a two-bar electric fire. What was left of the carpet was threadbare. The cooker, (sorry I mean the portable hot plates), surely could not have passed the last electrical test. The odd tables were small, scratched and had cup rim marks engrained deeply into them. There was the odd picture or two, hanging slightly eschewed, unloved and certainly not representative of society's values. And of course, there was the scattered small jars containing old jelly babies and tots. I recall a particular member of staff saying with total endearment, "Oh and the children loved Sister, she gave them sweets out of her special jars." Lovely.

The importance of these small jars reflected what had been important previously. Many rooms were left unused, except to store furniture or outdated resources. Throughout the school, sadly, there was little celebration of work, just the odd written out prayer or two. The walls around the entire school made me feel as if I was in 'Cell Block H', simply awful and I cannot begin to describe the toilets, I just simply cannot go there.

The classrooms were totally disorganised. Every draw overflowed with scraps of paper, pens without lids dried like prunes and the odd crust of last month's sandwiches.

Blackboards had smudges of teaching from years past, still chalked sporadically, unable to be rubbed off. Displays were uninspiring, lifeless, no lessons to be embedded and simply no purpose. The hall, with its stage was nondescript. The walls in the vast hall displayed 'stations of the cross'. These were important, but they were very old and high up so really what was the point, whether an adult or child you could not see the detail. This was a catholic school and the 'Stations of the Cross' had their place for sure, but they were in the wrong position. The detail was lost and so was the significance of their message. The children were in the hall on rotation constantly for PE, assemblies, lunchtimes and extracurricular. The positioning of these pictures was a missed opportunity for teaching and learning. We all know a picture of course can say a thousand words, so why waste such an opportunity?

These pictures needed updating with open access for all, enabling children and adults to really look at them, reflect on the stories they told and associate their meaning with the potential teachings and morals of today.

I believe passionately that all leaders should have an eye for detail. The disregard for it here made me feel melancholic. If it made me feel like that, I questioned what was their true impact on everyone else? So, I concluded it 'simply would not do'.

You may think I am going on a bit here, so I ask you to bear with. The eye for detail on this matter is revisited again later. And you must appreciate by now, in my story, I have no appreciation for those that do not adopt an eye for detail, anything less again 'simply will not do.'

The school kitchen, with the great cook, needed updating. It looked like something you would see in the well-remembered Hilda Ogden's kitchen on Coronation street, just on a larger scale. How the cook had managed to date baffled me. However, she had a work ethic to be admired and she managed. If she had been nurtured and regularly updated on current expectations alongside investing in technology advancements, she could have been more creative with her menus, more cost effective and far more efficient with energy expenditure and resources. I was of the opinion that a new method of working to address this inefficiency was required and this would create avenues to move forward and meet the ever-changing expectations of society.

As to the state of the nursery 'Oh my days', as the youth of today would say. It was desperate, no words really. The nursery in any school is the foundation for children's learning. However, this one was totally uninspiring for anyone let alone a young child who needed to let their imagination blossom. It looked sad. Playgrounds were concrete, rectangular empty spaces. No words.

The front of house was a small window with a rustic sliding panel on the one side. I often opened it in the early days and felt like the actor Jack Nicholson, menacingly peering through the door as in the famous film One Flew Over The Cuckoo's Nest. It was truly, 'a barrier for insanity' for sure. Many staff at the time might agree with that analogy - with regards to me anyway!!

In addition, the front of house had two filing cabinets, a couple of desks and an old, blue swivel chair shoved under the secretary/admin/finance officer buttocks of Mary. Her arm rest was her miniature cabinet, preservation for her energy loss for sure.

My office, mmm, it conveyed all the wrong messages. It had low chairs for visitors and a towering headteacher's chair. Oh dear. The wall paper evidenced the once displayed pictures that were now long gone. Lastly, there was a desk, computer and of course a phone.

Absolutely no investment had taken place in the school environment for many, many years.
The head before me, simply did not have that vision. The state of the learning environment gave me an historical insight to the standards previously accepted. I began to really understand why one local adviser said, "This was a school that requires improvement, or it will go into special measures."

Before I go on any further, it is important to remind you about tasting the 'gravy'. We all choose to taste it in different ways or simply not at all. But gravy is either simply a covering, or it makes a dish delicious so you want more. This school had served the food for a long time with the same old tasteless gravy, a liquid that just covered the food to make it edible. Now, it needed to be made to make the food not only more digestible but licking lips good!

No offence to the cook, she could only do so much without the right ingredients and tools to work with. Believe me she did her best.

As for My Predecessor

Before a leader chooses whether and how they lick the gravy, they have to fundamentally decide what they class as a good tasty gravy in the first place. It is a leader's prerogative and that needs to be acknowledged here. I have no right to judge my predecessor's choice on how she wanted the learning environment to be. The bland gravy was just fine to her, and that needs to be respected, it was not important. I believe she loved the children and they had loved her. I have no doubt she had some special qualities and was still missed by many.

But this gravy was not good enough for me, it had to be more than a covering. It was fundamental to the recipe of the school's future success, the children's growth and was full of enriched opportunities to meet the challenges of an ever-changing society.

First Things First

The first thing I sourced were modern child-friendly posters of the 'Stations of the Cross'. I had them in gold frames and most importantly positioned at eye level for a child in the hall.

Within weeks, the resource room was completed. Every bit of stock was fully audited and placed on the right shelf in the right aisle, subject by subject, year group by year group. Everything was to hand and accompanied with the must-have 'signing in and out' book. Yvonne had this special skill of being able to reprimand staff who had not signed it without them realising.

The centralisation of resources freed up another large room, perfect for an IT suite. The children needed one and they got it. This then required an IT specialist and I knew just the person.

Funny the people you meet as you amble through life, and I had met Chris years before becoming a headteacher. I have always thought staff's wellbeing is imperative for high outputs. Mine for many years always included a massage. On recommendation, I went to see a masseuse called Chris. On my first visit, he opened the door in a sarong. How interesting, I had thought. Without doubt, he was an expert! During my many treatments, I discovered he was also an IT genius. He had been sort out by Richard Branson to work on the new Pendolino trains. He had tested all of the IT infrastructure on the trains from Birmingham to London throughout the night. He was in his own words, a computer geek, and now, I needed HIM.

I advertised, and of course Chris fulfilled the criteria.

IT provision was simply transformed overnight. You need to employ expertise that you simply have not got and as many people will know I was not IT savvy.

Thanks Chris.

Then, I moved on to create a library.

I am extremely fortunate to have very talented parents who love me. They have been always there for me in my trials and tribulations as a head. In the early days, my father went for his interview with the local authority and was accepted to work as a contractor in schools. He was in demand. He was old-school you see, with a work ethic second to none and he whistled, which all the children loved.

Mom and dad came as a team. Mom is an exceptionally creative woman who had the ideas and designs and dad put them into action. They worked tirelessly together at the school to make it happen. Mom's painting was meticulous. She always had that eye for detail, maybe that is where I get it from.

My father, originally an engineer by trade, could always make and transform items from a skip into wonderful resources. They both worked for a pittance, and on reflection, their quotes were far too low. Yes, I feel guilty today when I think of their blood, sweat and tears as they helped me create an environment to be loved by the children for next to nothing. They created a library, whilst other contractors knocked walls down and boarded brick walls. There was no time to waste. It was full steam ahead with a co-ordinated schedule of works managed by myself.

My dad is a wonderful artist and the school became alive with painted stories and children just soaked it all in. As a consequence, the children's love for reading grew and as a result so did their writing, it had more depth. They knew what I wanted to achieve in the library and they got to work. The day we opened it, many visitors came, and stood in wonder and awe. But you must always be prepared for the exception, the 'One!' Sweat, guts and tears created such transformations. The walls were spellbinding. They were covered with fairy tales, fantasies and the wonders of the world. The bookshelves had been transformed from old furniture into book characters. We stood thrilled with this fabulous resource for the children, except the 'One'. This 'One' left us speechless and totally aghast as she coughed and spluttered, "Oh this was our smoking room, where we relaxed and gossiped I loved it. Oh it's sad, I miss it." Not a word about the most fabulous library. Not an ounce of respect for the transformation. In fact, I do not think the 'One' actually saw what was in front of her. She just remembered her ashtrays, dirty coffee cups, bins full of crap and brown walls. The 'One' eventually left, she found an old ashtray to take as her memory.... bye bye!

Lesson

- Sometimes you need to select others to deliver your instruction; it can in some cases be more effective for many reasons.
- When I say it takes time to change a culture of thinking, you must realise there are some people who will never change. They are happy to stand still and be content with 'kippers and curtains'.
- With a little imagination, everything can be recycled, so you can transform things into something wonderful for very little expenditure.

The next major project took place over my first summer break.

The Nursery /Early Years
Early years is the foundation to a child's learning at school. It is so significant for the future of every child's progression. I strongly advocate it always needs investment, time, money and expertise. The learning environment needs to be fit for the curriculum. If you ignore it, you will never get outstanding outcomes and a total false economy!

You do not build a house on weak foundations, so do not invest elsewhere without your early years being an outstanding department.

A few months were spent planning, designing, gathering materials, negotiating deals and implementing a timetable to accommodate all contractors. I ensured I integrated contractors' work schedules to avoid any delays and planned a well-coordinated working site. For this build, my parents slept in the car park in their motorhome.

It was mammoth, involving electricians, plumbers, glazers, landscapers, carpet fitters.
Walls were knocked down, teaching rooms were created in all different sizes and shapes for different activities and everything just flowed cleverly into one another.

Bob the Builder climbing ladders looked real and the unbelievable hand painted story of Noah's Ark swept through the corridors to the main building.

With a day to go until the new academic year, we sat. My parents were beyond exhausted. I was mesmerised and just rambled on about all the learning opportunities. I was overjoyed; it was simply beyond my expectations.

I had arranged for an Early Years' specialist to work with the staff for two years. You must appreciate that changing curriculum delivery and working patterns takes time and I had planned for changing a whole culture of thinking. I organised for the nursery intake to commence at a later date than normal.

This allowed time for some intensive training with our Early Years' expert before the nursery doors opened.

All learning was to be tailored to the learning environment to maximise opportunities for the children's imagination to grow and develop.

I believe, stirring one's imagination opens doors to new possibilities (hopefully you may agree with this yourselves as you reflect with a smile, smirk or something else.)

During the teacher day of this new academic year, staff were milling around looking at the new nursery in amazement, they were impressed. I could not say this with regards to the early years staff. The constant wafts of cabbage floating from their direction gave it away. They appeared to be frozen to the spot at the realisation of what I expected of them. Yes, outstanding standards of teaching and learning.

As I helped my parents take the last of their tools and cleaning materials to their motor home, people just continue to explore. With electric drills, saws and hammers in hand we were suddenly stopped by a member of the Early Years' team. With total and absolute bewilderment, she pointed to some clever seating around a table created like a pond, "Well what on earth are those called?" she looked absolutely mystified.

My mother stood still in her tracks, exasperated by this whilst my father started to whistle and left; he whistled for many reasons.

I looked at her and with a sarcastic edge I replied, "They are pods," as that was the first thing that came to mind.

"What are pods?" she replied looking seriously confused. You must acknowledge here I was someway from my office so I had to be careful. I calmly continued, "As you can see, these pods are attached to the table so they are a form of seating for the children to put their arses on." Although my mother does not like me using such terminology, I think my fruitful description stopped her intervention. It is very rare I sense my mother about to swear at people's incompetence or for anything actually but there is always the exceptional circumstances, isn't that right mother?

"Oh. Really," she answered and then turned to the other staff and shouted, "They are called pods, some form of seating apparently."

Thank the Lord I had booked the Early Years adviser for two years.

The following two years certainly had its challenges, almost to a point where I thought I would need to go into therapy for the sake of my sanity. Fortunately, this was avoided as I have an inner strength in cases of adversity and a vivid imagination.

My vivid imagination became my therapy and so I knew it was time to hit the markets. One early Saturday morning, off I went with mother and accompanied by our loyal flask. This flask had seen many a market with us, actually it was purchased at a market, good price and loyal. So with the flask of coffee plus bacon sandwiches, we were set.

"So Loret, what is our mission today?" I just drove mischievously smiling. Mom got worried and tried again, "What are you up to now?" I made her wait, it was more fun that way. Sauntering through the market, we picked up a variety of bargains for school, including a bulk buy of Zoflora. I did like the children's toilets to smell nice.

As we got to the last aisle, for a moment I felt a slight cloud of despondency wash over me, would my planned purchase not happen? But hey ho, there he was. How could I have thought the market would let me down?

Apologies for doubting Wellsbourne market.

My pace quickened and mom duly followed pulling our trolley. (A trolley is a must for the market, well who wants to be trapping back and forth to the car missing valuable haggling time and it is just knackering, trust me I know from experience.)

Purchase completed, I was thrilled with the quality and the price, seven items in total, safely in the trolley. We heaved the trolley back to the car for bacon sarnies and coffee. Satisfyingly munching away, Mom quizzically stated, "Loret, you don't like them, you never have." I explained the plan and assured her my purchase would serve a purpose and keep me sane for the next two years.

Before she wet herself with laughter, she quickly opened the car door for an emergency wee. Peeing in between passenger and backseat door was something we had refined to a fine art with years of market visits together.

We did laugh and still do on our many market outings.

Back at the ranch, (the school) Yvonne helped me decide. We had a heated debate over my seven items but in the end we finally agreed. We waited for everyone to go home. With the coast clear, Yvonne and I with trowels in hand, made our way to the small flower bank. The flower bank was pretty, the boundary between the nursery and my office. Yvonne and I could easily see it from our windows.

Strategically, they were placed on the flower bank.

The garden gnomes were all named and Yvonne amused herself saying them out loud phonetically. As we admired our handy work, Yvonne in her satirical way said, "Oh Loret, there is something missing." Looking carefully, I was mystified as to what it was. With all seriousness, she looked at them and simply said, "Snow White of course!" Then, she actually fled.

What would I have done without her? She could take the pee out of me and sometimes that is ok. Sometimes!

Each gnome was named after a member of the Early Years team, but only Yvonne, mother and me had the privilege of knowing. The gnomes were a lifesaver over the next two years, I could say anything to them without getting myself into trouble. When one of them fell over, I saw it as a sign that something was brewing. I always picked it up and repositioned it in a safer place. Despite never attending a nursery as a child, I count this as one of my finest, creative and imaginative moments.

The new early years' learning environment was built for progression. This leads to a certain way of working and some staff flourished in it but others did not. So those staff that did not adapt or learn new teaching methods were redeployed to teach elsewhere and these decisions had to be made. What is the point of investing in the learning environment if its purpose is not followed through? You cannot afford to waste money like that. Some staff, who were redeployed, actually thrived elsewhere, others did not and left.

The Rest

The rest of the school was developed to the same high standards.

Every space I maximised to use as a learning space. I wanted small group teaching wherever I could accommodate it. The stage was dismantled and a mobile one purchased. This created space for small group core teaching in the mornings and specialised art/craft teaching in the afternoons. Outside, we built a sport astro turf pitch; the children loved it.

The children chose the 'out of space' themed playground climbing frames. Many of these pieces were also integrated for delivering into the PE curriculum.

At a steady pace, the school became a place the children and many staff wanted to be. Attendance and behaviour was never a problem. Punctuality was not an issue and standards of achievement increased year after year. Children were happy, and most importantly, had respect for the learning environment. They recognised it was theirs and no one was going to spoil it, it instilled a sense of pride within them.

Careful financial planning was essential for the strategic plan's implementation. This was a one form entry school and finances were tight. The plan was achieved by maximising every resource. I effectively researched contractors as I never have a middle person. I managed the projects myself and this saved a huge amount of money. It was very rare I went with local authority contractors or contractors from the diocese. I liked to resource and negotiate with companies without too many overheads and surplus people to pay. It is like managing your own home, just on a larger scale.

Once I found a good contractor, I treated them well and paid them very promptly. Prompt payment is essential if you want to build good business relationships. My selected contractors have stayed with me for a long time and followed me to Dorrington. They do not mess or try to pull the wool over my eyes. They all know I drive a hard bargain and that is respected because the respect is mutual. They have had plenty referrals, which paid dividends for the next competitive tender.

I did not necessarily go for the cheapest. As in all my work, I have no tolerance for people who try to cut corners. From experience, when you end up with cheap and cheerful, it tends to cost more in the end one way or another.

Timing was Key
I rarely had a holiday, my choice! That was the price I paid for putting my heart and soul into it. There was no time to waste as it was essential to get on with rebuilding the learning

environment. If not, the implementation of the right curriculum and teaching methods would be stalled and so time was precious.

There was a logical pathway to its implementation, the pace was relentless but manageable. Taking care with pace is very important as you must always consider those around you. But there was no room for complacency.

Some staff were not on board but I expected that. I was changing a whole mindset and some people just did not like that. As a consequence, I put my energies into those people that relished the change and their positivity carried everyone else along, even when some tried to resist. New staff were employed carefully and stepped on board the plane.

The energy zappers were replaced by the energy energisers!

Slap on the Wrist
Not all went plain sailing and important lessons were learned from mistakes.

As you know by now, the Arthur Daley in me likes to get the deal. A few weeks in, I was driving merrily along towards spaghetti junction when I saw a sign. I screeched and veered quickly to the left, yes left this time. Unit shutters were half way open and displayed quality multipurpose modern chairs. I wanted them as they would be perfect for the staff room and office, well all over the school actually. They were a perfect, lovely lilac colour. Lilac can be calming and the building site at school needed some of that.

There were forty for sale, retail value £125 each, I quickly phoned my first headteacher, Mary. Yes, another Mary. She said she would take fifteen, she liked a deal too. After much argy bargy, we settled on £20 a chair and free delivery. I was beyond thrilled. Mary phoned asking for more, but no, I had the rest and that would be pushing my generosity too far.

Now you must picture the scene, try and recall the scrap lorry that passes your street every so often beeping for your goods. I stood there on the school drive excited for my fantastic bargain delivery. I heard them coming along way off and eventually the horn blasted and my travellers arrived with their scrap lorry. I have bought off travellers many times, they are great for selling artificial grass, especially back at Wellsbourne market. Dorrington, you will find out later, is full of it.

The lorry chugged to the door, the chairs swayed but they were strategically stacked and not one toppled. How on earth they got to me I will never know. They were quickly unloaded, payment was made and as my new season friend handed me the receipt we shook on a great deal for both us. Off they went honking their horn and I stood admiring one hell of a deal.

The chairs were quality and I placed them with so much satisfaction.

A few weeks after delivery, I received a phone call from a lady very high up in the council. She asked if I had purchased forty chairs recently.

"Oh yes," I replied with smugness, thinking she might want my contact.

Not quite. She proceeded to inform me she was in possession of the invoice with its business address at the top. Well, this was normal as then you had to transfer certain invoices to finance.

She proceeded with a clipped tone, "Where did you get them from?"
I confidently told her. Once I confirmed the location, she informed me there was the problem.

Feeling uncomfortable, I enquired, "What do you mean problem?"

"Unfortunately, the invoice has an address on it that belongs to a councillor and he does not sell modern lilac chairs."

Oh s**t! No other words.

She asked for an explanation.

 I said, "Give me five," and she did.

I quickly phoned my contact. Without even a pause for breath I blurted, "Why have you used somebody else's address rather than your outlet?"

They apologised and explained they don't actually have a permanent address, so they just circle an address in the location they are in from the telephone book and put that down.

As I phoned back the lady, I wondered if this was going to be the shortest headship ever. When I think back and recall these early days, I have an element of sympathy for how a certain PM might have felt!

I simply gave her the honest explanation. What followed was one very long silence. Then, she suddenly started to chuckle but with seriousness edged in her tone.

"Now Loretta, I appreciate your honesty but do not ever buy off anyone again without checking it is the proper business address."

I assured her, "I will never ever, ever do this again."

As we were about to terminate the conversation she said, "Well, lesson learned, let us just leave that there, but before I go, I must say you did get a great deal."

I had aged ten years in that half an hour. Relieved, Yvonne got me coffee and cake and I promised myself I would always check the address on the invoices in the future.

Do you know, some of the market traders and travellers have fantastic abodes. I know because I have seen them. I have checked addresses from that day on. You see, we all make mistakes, it is ok once, but not the same mistake twice, this simply would not do!

Lesson

- Investing in the learning environment opens the door of opportunity.
- Make sure it is in alignment with your vision and strategic plan.
- You can easily create more teaching areas with what you already have; you do not always need a new building, just creative thinking.
- Ask yourself what is the purpose of any change you make, be clear what you are designing it for.
- Plan carefully, ask yourself, what do I want the outcome to look like?
- Take time to source contractors.
- Do not always go with the cheapest.
- Ask other people who have done it for ideas or go and visit other school's learning environments that you know are progressive.
- Cut out the middle person if you can, do it yourself and do not waste money.
- Always invest in your Early Years department - it is essential.
- Plan the environment to enable the curriculum you want to deliver.
- Learn from your mistakes, do not repeat.
- Always, always check the address on the invoice.
- Market traders and some travellers really are some of the most decent people I have met in life. Never make the mistake of ever thinking you are better than anyone else. You will always be the fool if you do and you will never get the deal.

Strategic Plan – Teaching and Learning

I have already given you the overview in the summary and the initiatives cannot be exhausted here, there are so many. With all due respect to you, it would be an overload.

Remember, too much gravy can make you uncomfortable or even overwhelm what sits on the plate and again that simply will not do. Furthermore, you have so much more to digest in the Dorrington Academy chapter. That said, I need to add depth to one particular initiative that was crucial in us achieving the outstanding status.

Teaching Assistants

Without doubt, I have the highest regard for teaching assistants and I employed a substantial amount. Very often, teaching assistants have abilities and skills that teachers have not got and these need exploring. No disrespect to any teacher but over the years I have found some teaching assistants can even be better than fully qualified teachers. Often, some have wanted to be teachers, but due to their own circumstance they could not take advantage of opportunities to train as one.

I hired very skilled teaching assistants and intensively developed their skills, knowledge and understandings to teach children. Three followed me from previous schools. One in particular, Issy, she was my teaching assistant when I was an NQT and we are still close today. Issy, had an abundance of skills and qualities that made a difference to children's progress and much more. Another had exceptional skills with children with special needs. Another was just quite exceptional at maths.

At interview, all applicants knew the requirements I expected. These were very different from just being used to photocopy, wash paintbrushes, put up freeze paper and wash the cups.

That limited use of skills, in my opinion, has always been a waste of resourcefulness. Yes, you must be mindful that in the workplace we are all resources.

Once recruited, I bought advisers in to train the teaching assistants. I always had training in-house, as I could have it tailor made to the individual and the school's requirements. They could also be collectively trained and this was more cost effective and certainly good value for money.

The teaching assistants gained such a variety of skills, which included:

- assessment for learning
- modelling concepts
- early years communication techniques
- special needs programmes
- marking against objectives

Plus, a variety of courses to meet their own personal areas of interest and specialisms. The school also sponsored six teaching assistants to attend Worcester University, on day release, to study on a foundation course in teaching. Three went on to the honours teaching degree and some now have leadership positions in education. Many others became higher level teaching assistants.

You must appreciate, without the dedication and skills of these teaching assistants, there is no way we would have received outstanding status. The Ofsted report was testimony and supported my view in its report. The Ofsted framework in 2004 stated if they observed exceptional practice the Chief Inspector could decide to write what they called a 'Cameo', in the report, which was a grade 1 and beyond. The use of teaching assistants to help children achieve the highest standards of achievement because they themselves were of an exceptional standard received such a 'Cameo' and trust me that really was to be celebrated.

The Paradigm Shift Theory
Before I move on, I must explain how I used the paradigm shift theory to achieve the strategic plan.

Imagine you are a pilot of a plane going from Birmingham to Palma. The plane is full. Your vision is to get to Palma and you have your route. Unknown events occur on your journey, maybe bad weather, a thunderstorm, a backup at your destination, traffic control directives or a mechanical fault. As a consequence, you are knocked off course and you just have to find another route/pathway to get back on course to your destination. So, you adjust, and you change the route or pathway accordingly, but your destination is the same, you are still going to Palma.

You may have passengers dangling off the wings, wanting to get off. You may have to land temporarily elsewhere to drop them off.

This is not a threat to getting to Palma. No, you use this as an opportunity. So, as you drop some passengers off, you simply pick up new passengers. You do not waste the opportunity of having a full plane, that would be an opportunity missed, and then you take off again. On some occasions, you may be a little delayed, on others you could actually get there earlier or even on time.

Whatever it is, you get to Palma.
Palma airport -WELCOMES YOU!

You must understand it is rare for a plane to go from one destination to another without being knocked off the pathway. The pilot just adjusts and they are back on track. I was a pilot of a flight taking off from 'requiring improvement' to the destination 'outstanding.' On this flight, I adopted the paradigm theory.

When I was knocked off course for whatever reason, I got myself back on course by sometimes adjusting slightly or taking a different pathway to get back on course.

My vision never changed, we were going to be an outstanding community school.

At times, adjustments accelerated progress. On other occasions, I paused so I could reflect if I was to make implementations which allowed me to take a more appropriate pathway.
I always looked for signposts that could help me achieve my vision more effectively.

Sometimes, challenges and threats presented themselves but I was undeterred.

I used them as opportunities to achieve my vision. One of the diversions certainly led to an opportunity. I received notification from my school improvement adviser that I was to be fast-tracked to become an Ofsted inspector. I qualified in 4 months, it was intensive. Exams were at the Hilton hotel in London, and it was hard, but I passed.

I tended to work with one particular Ofsted team which had two wonderful Welsh inspectors in it. They taught me a lot, from how to have a set friendly smile as I got out of the car at the start of an inspection, to writing concise summaries as we sat writing them in Travelodges throughout the inspection week. They were also firm with me when I was being too soft and telling teachers I would come back later and let them have another go when their lesson was going pear-shaped.

One of the Welsh women was the lead and we always went to her room for downtime at 9.00pm on the dot and she poured us a glass of red; we always needed it.

In her strong Welsh accent, every night she would warn me, "Now no extra chances for them tomorrow or we will be here for two weeks Loretta and that simply won't do!"

They were formidable experts and hilarious.

Thank you to my Welsh ladies

This was a worthwhile diversion on my journey and I was enriched by the experience. Apart from helping me raise achievements in my own school, being an inspector added depth to my understanding and opened doors. I was now in a position where I knew my school was outstanding despite the new Ofsted framework 2004 raising the bar of expectation again. Nevertheless, we still awaited an inspection to confirm or not. Knowing is very different to officially getting the seal of approval.

As we waited for the Ofsted call, there was a twist. An opportunity presented itself.
I had the opportunity to work in education in the international sector for two years and after much soul searching, I decided Ofsted call or not, I would take this opportunity to enhance my leadership and management experience.

So, I resigned!

Sometimes as leaders, you have to take a calculated risk and I did. I would take the position in Norway and fly back to do inspections and private consultancy work for headteachers when I could to keep my hand in.

I wanted a smooth transition for the school. I do believe in moulding leaders within and I had done that with my deputy. She had been on one challenging journey with me and had come a long way. She deserved to take the school onwards and upwards; she had been my right hand.

Thank you, Mary (another Mary). Not that it is stereotypical in the catholic sector.
She was successful in her application to replace me as headteacher.

I was due to leave Easter 2004. As I started to pass over the keys, the call came. When the Ofsted inspection call came, in our minds, we all knew we were outstanding but we had to show the inspection team - the proof is in the pudding!

The Ofsted
The Ofsted inspection spanned over five days and a large team of inspectors came. I must share with you that I always wear something for luck when Ofsted knocks the door but only the select few know what it is and you can rest assured in this inspection my tradition was duly applied.

Actually half-way through this inspection, I recall running into Issy, my loyal teaching assistant. As I gushed into her room excitedly, I enthused, "My lucky ….s I reckon are working their magic Issy."

Upon hearing this, she absolutely lost it. I did not think it was that funny as she had known for years what my traditional item was. I was confused until a shovel of feet prompted me to look behind the door. There he was. The Chief Inspector sitting quietly behind the door writing his notes after just interviewing her.

Back in my office, my head was in my hands. B******s!

Throughout the week, we showed the Ofsted team that working as a community was at the heart of our success. We worked non-stop as we had so much for them to see. Five days of adrenaline rushes galore.

On Friday, it was the final day of the inspection and totally exhausted, I sensed the Chief Inspector wanted to see me conduct an assembly.

It was a Mother's Day assembly and Early Years had the task of leading it. Early Years was now a fabulous, progressive department. The department was the envy of many staff from other schools. We had many visitors come to observe good practice and see the learning environment.

As a leader, you have to step up to the mark. You are the leader and you have to be seen and lead by example. Show people why you are the head. And so, I would lead the assembly.

No matter how many assemblies you do as head, during an Ofsted, one has to showcase the essence of what your school is about.

Early on that Friday, the Head of Early Years came to me and informed me the assembly was about communication. Fair enough I thought, communication being key. As she turned she looked back at me smiling and said, "Oh, by the way, Sue, (one of the teaching assistants) has been teaching in nursery with us as you know…"

"Yes," I answered with a slight wince, as I had a gut feeling what was to follow.

"Yes, we are signing the main messages in assembly and the children are going to teach you how sign so you can do it, 'SNOW WHITE' sorry, I mean Miss Barratt!"

I howled. She had been on one hell of a journey with me and she was now an outstanding leader of Early Years, so I had to give her that one. You see, you cannot just give it, you have to be able to take it too. And I certainly deserved that one!

Assembly was 3.00pm at the end of the day for the inspection.

The hall was heaving, standing room only. It was crammed, I think the whole community came, well slight exaggeration.

The children were great, me on the other hand, well the children collapsed with laughter along with everyone else at my efforts to do sign language. I persisted and got there in the end. The mothers all had bunches of daffodils and were over the moon with them. As the team gathered behind closed doors, I collapsed in my office to Yvonne's special Ofsted cake and a strong black coffee.

The Chief Inspector congratulated me on my assembly and off the record said, "I needed that!"

You see, he wanted to see that I could walk the walk. He knew I was leaving and who was to be my successor.

He returned a few weeks later to present the full report to governors, that is how it was done then. It happened to coincide with one of Yvonne's special buffets to mark my last governors meeting.

"Outstanding!" we celebrated.

The inspector joined us for a beverage and he was as over the moon as we were with the outcome. I will confess I did cry on the way home, it was done! I got to my destination but not in five years, actually ahead of schedule in four years.

Lesson

- Never stop believing in yourself.
- When you want to stop, dig deep and carry on.
- You always need a team. It is impossible to achieve outstanding outcomes on your own.
- Always reflect.
- Have humility.
- Be able to laugh at yourself.
- If you go to an interview and just talk the talk, you will fail. If you actually walk the walk, then you will deliver what you said you would and that is honourable. If you add the jog or run here and there, go beyond sometimes what is just expected, together you will exceed expectations.

Almost at the End

The Local Authority found out about our Ofsted grade very quickly, especially as we were the first school to get outstanding against the new framework and that resulted in a positive outcome for them also. Several days after the Ofsted announcement, we had an unexpected visit from the lead adviser for the authority. She used to be Head of Religious

Education in a secondary school before being lead adviser for the authority so I am led to believe.

She came with a bouquet of flowers and chocolates to congratulate me which was very nice of her. Well, it was a team effort. So as she had a tour of the school by my deputy I put the chocs in the staffroom and told Yvonne not to have the hazelnut caramel before the others had a look in. Yvonne reluctantly accepted and proceeded to stuff herself with a chocolate eclair oozing with cream but gosh she deserved that.
The adviser returned to my office and sat. She appeared slightly perturbed. She congratulated me on the school's success and then she proceeded to say, "But I have noticed you have not got the 'Stations of the Cross!'

Mmm, "I think you will find that we have, they are there. Modern versions at the child's eye level." I replied politely. And then I just gave a look that just said it all.

That was that really.

Some of you may be questioning the depth of my catholicity. Often, I wondered how I actually got the job. As I was a single, unmarried woman, I often thought I was the one who just slipped through the net. It would be only right to inform you that the catholic heads never welcomed me with open arms and it never improved.

It was hurtful, disappointing and it made me question often.

Interestingly, as I went to my last morning briefing for catholic heads, out of courtesy, I informed the Chair of the Catholic Headteachers Partnership before coffee, that I had resigned.

I could not help noticing the whispering in the breeze again, as the news of me resigning gathered momentum and was soon spreading like wildfire, there was a frenzy of looks for sure.

Coffee time came and I sat on my own as usual sipping my coffee. Suddenly, a whiff of Estee Lauder hit me, looking up to my astonishment five ladies joined me. In unison, they sang, "So, we hear you are off to see a Viking then." I took a slow sip, winked at them and left.

A Small Diversion

Whenever I look at the letter I received in Norway some months after I left from the chair, I smile. It was to inform me that the priest had asked him to get in touch to let me know that in the few months after the Ofsted report was published the congregation had gone up 54%.

He was ecstatic and sent thanks. Now, you just want to say to those who question, "Stick that in your pipe and smoke it."

So, to my last day of my first headship.

The send-off from the entire community, including my family and my first team was overwhelming. The children were amazing. It went on all day.
At my final assembly, no one sat, as there was no room.
Towards the end, mothers from the community who I had

helped gain qualifications and diplomas to re-enter the workplace joined the staff. It was led by the teaching assistants and they gathered to give me an extra special send off.

Once assembled, they stood back and Steve, who was now drummer at the 'Jam House', sat proud at the drums. The children loved him, we had some great drummers. Steve, three hits of his sticks and the mothers and staff belted out a song they had written for me.

Finally

Mary, my successor, opened the fire exit and Steve played my special Elvis number and as it built up to its finale he shouted, "Miss Barratt has left the building!" and so I did.
Well not quite, there was Yvonne's buffet and her star turn after the children had gone home. What fun.

Speeches, more speeches and laughter for all sorts of reasons. Remember, you cannot win them all. That would be naive. In a quiet moment, I sneaked off to my office, as there was just something I had to do. My father helped me, I had to replace something.

In my office, soon to be my successor's, I hung a picture. Not quite a replacement of the one at the bottom of the skip, this was better.

I asked Mary, my successor, to come in. As she came in she broke down at the site of the picture. It had taken me a while to find, four years in fact, but I always knew it was out there and I would know it when I saw it.

And I did.

It was the most beautiful picture which was called 'The Mother
of our Children'....
We just stood. Then there was 'The Ceremony of Keys'.

The Interval

Now, get your ice cream. Do not underestimate the significance of taking an interval during your leadership journey. Intervals allow you to reflect upon your chosen signposts to date and allows time for you to contemplate the potential direction for your future. Do not be afraid to put your foot on the brakes and take an interval. This can take courage but intervals that have been strategically planned could give you unseen opportunities to accelerate or open new doors of opportunity on your leadership journey.

The next part of my journey was one of the hardest I have ever made. It was monumental; one that changed my life without a shadow of doubt. As difficult as it was, it altered my path and I am forever grateful.

At last, the grand departure arrived, 29th May 2004. After the closure of appropriate direct debits, came the emotional farewells. The hardest of which was the therapeutic stroke of my rescue dog, Katie. It is funny how dogs do not really need to see the cases, hold-all, toiletries and they must have tweezers at the door to know their owner is up to something.

She let me know without hesitation, a few days before my departure, her disappointment in me. I saw the deepest sadness in her eyes; it devoured and filtered into my soul and I hurt. Despite talking to her of my love for her and stroking her ear, she still looked at me with confusion at such abandonment. I was consumed with guilt. I recalled a book I had read of a family who pursued their dreams of living abroad and the grieving dog who followed them across terrains all over the world to find them. I shared this book with my mother who agreed with me, viewing the owners as selfish for having no regard for leaving this dog, a living creature who depended on them. I reflected on my interpretation as I continued to pack the last few things. It is so easy to judge others by our own standards of what is acceptable and unacceptable, especially when the chances are, we will not have to make such choices in our own life journey.

Much to my mother's disappointment and heartache, I was leaving her and many others. I now found myself being guilty of having to make similar decisions as those of the family in the book. I had read and judged so harshly.

And so, I reassured Katie I would be back. You see, she was not just a dog, she was like a human being with feelings. I laugh at the memory of my student days when we debated animal life over human life and vice versa. It was an absolute no-brainier for me in those days: humans over animals every time. Today, it is more complicated, not so cut and dry.

These days, rather than jumping straight in, I have my pros and cons list to justify the actions I take and the views I have. So human life over animal life. I ask myself, well it depends on who the human being is. Choices are not always so cut and dry as we think.

So, I am ready and I have one last coffee and a cigarette. I knew I must give up but I convinced myself I would be mad to tackle it at that stage of life. I convinced myself, as I sat, that the signpost was right for me now. The timing was right.

Yes, I accepted the voice of the cynics, who had scepticism over this choice. They may have had their own hidden agendas, they may have been envious due to their own dreams not being fulfilled, they may have wondered why they could not be brave enough to make such decisions to pursue their own dreams or they fundamentally may have not wanted you to go because they would just miss you as they love you.

Saying all of this, there were many positives to my choice to leave my headship. As after its success, the time was right. They encouraged it and supported it. I assured them I would be back soon.

Of course, as I made my way to the airport, knowing I would be back, I recognised that when I returned back to my home, things would not be the same. I did not think it would be healthy to think otherwise. What would the journey I was about to embark on be for if nothing changed? I did not want to take this journey to come back to exactly where I left off. Yes, sure I thought, it would probably, pretty much all look the same, but this signpost in my journey gave me a sense that I would have changed.

What is the point of you taking a journey if you are not going to grow through the experience in some way? So, as I approached the airport, I understood the risk I was taking. I was leaving stability and success behind but I hoped to become richer for the experience. If I chose not to go, would I look back later in life and regret what it could have led to?
If I had any hesitation, then I would think it was not the right 'timing' for me.

Yes, I thought it was ok to think I was crazy, have feelings of trepidation and knowing there would be rollercoasters. But hesitation - NO.

My mindset was open. The thought of not got going was intrinsically linked with the word regret. There are many roller coasters in life: you can ride them but remember, you can get off.

Some cynics may read this and shout, "Yeah love, you will probably end up penniless, without a job, a year or two older and depressed, oh and your dog has p****d all over your silk rug in a display of disgust for your desertion." Of course, I had considered all of these possibilities, well the dog bit at least. But like my career to date, I believe if you go into anything with the right attitude, you will always move forward. And for the record, rugs can always be cleaned.

Joking apart, I encourage you to recognise that signposts come in all guises, one signpost can simply take you to another. You may take a wrong turn on your way; sometimes left; sometimes right. It might be just a diversion for the better.

So as my friends followed me with the trolleys laden with my baggage to the airport entrance, I thought, who knew what or where this journey would take me. I had understood the signposts, recognising it was a scary direction but it felt liberating at the same time.
My loyal friends were with me at the airport. I was flying with a small private airline owned by ex British airways staff who were brave to set up their own airline.

Very impressive, cheaply priced tickets but first-class style. I mean, what airline offers you real wine glasses, stainless steel cutlery, Crunchies and wine to take with you for free when you get off. Absolutely marvellous!

Anyway, I am not here to market the airline and future ideas for other redundant airline workers. I was concerned about my baggage.

My ticket allowed me 20 kilos. I anticipated prior to this departure day my choice to take more - a woman's prerogative.

I phoned the airline to inform them in advance that I would be exceeding the baggage allowance by approximately 25 kilos. Esther from customer services assured me this was no problem as long as I paid £4.00 per kilo. Relieved at there not being a problem, I confirmed this would be absolutely fine. Actually, if Esther and I had chatted a bit longer, we might have become seasonal friends.

At this point, I had no time to waste as I had more packing to do. I weighed as I packed. The weight increased at a steady pace. On some occasions, it actually went down. On reflection, maybe I was holding the bags too much in order not to break the scales. I was on course for the agreed weight until I sat on my toilet when it suddenly occurred to me not only was I packing for between seasons, I needed to pack for my guaranteed times of constipation - a must.

If there was one thing on this journey I could be sure of, it was what I call 'the trial pregnancies', from previous bouts of constipation on my travels, I experience most of the symptoms of 'the immaculate conception'.

I was guaranteed an overnight bulge, back ache, and a craving for chocolate. This was followed by the growing depressing thought of trying to fit in my new 'Miss Sixty' jeans, even if they were my TK Maxx bargain. A bargain for sure, but actually, getting into them whilst feeling nine months pregnant squashes the thrill of such a trendy jeans bargain.

So, M&S comfort jeans are a must; what would we do without these elasticated waists?

I ask you, why is it that when we step off a plane in foreign lands our stomachs inflate to sumo wrestler size before we have got to customs? Despite the good old laxatives amongst other things, there is never any movement until thirty seconds after we return home.

Off the toilet, I phoned my friend Esther again, lovely girl, who confirmed 30 kilos extra would be fine. So, I merrily packed my maternal wear with three dozen packets of laxatives. Instant gratification - I was now prepared for any occasion for an extra cost of £4.00 x 35 = £140. There was simply no option. I never wanted a Nokia 6200 with video anyway; somethings just have to be sacrificed in life at times.

Feeling confident, I approached the Duo Airlines desk smiling sweetly at the check in girl who had already clocked my three trolleys and the strain on my friend's face. I thought, do I mention Esther? Only if there is a problem. I just hoped she was not temporary, seasonal or that Esther had recently been promoted over this sweet girl perched on her pedestal. She was in control of what felt like my destiny. I just hoped she was a sympathetic constipation sufferer. My doubts regarding this quickly dissipated as she stood ready for action. "How many bags?" I mean, as if she could not see.

You must always try and look confident even if you do not have a clue what the hell you are doing, I replied with six, in at least three languages, and explained how Esther said she had noted it on my booking. I sounded guilty of a crime; pathetic.

Her eyebrows raised as she looked. Her eyebrows, I might add, had obviously been plucked in her premenstrual stage. The silence between us was deafening and oh so long. It actually became painful.

Suddenly, she broke it in a monotone voice, "Put each bag on the scales ONE at a time and we shall see."

I successfully, with grace, obliged. Why I thought I could actually defy the scales by pretending these cases were not bloody heavy escapes me. The silence resumed for an eternity. She turned to me. My facial expression distorted slightly but those eyebrows were something Dennis Healy would have envied.

My fondness for Ester was further cemented when Miss Eyebrow confirmed, "Yes I see Esther has mentioned 55 kilos extra." Miss Eyebrow Check-In Girl 2004 informed me that I had in fact 82 kilos extra. Thinking on my feet, which every leader has to do at times, I went into actress mode. I explained in a quiver that one of the cases was full of teddies as I was leaving my mother to go and live in Norway and needed so many comforts at this emotional time in my life. She understood immediately. Cheryl and I became instant reason friends.

As she laughed at my pathetic attempt at begging for mercy, she not only allowed me to take all of my baggage, but only charged me for an extra 10 kilos. God, I thought she was fabulous. She was obviously a fellow constipation sufferer and what fabulous eyebrows they were. They simply framed her face. Esther was eclipsed from my memory. Cheryl was new favourite, how fickle is that?

Running to the toilet, I crouched. Yes, ladies must always crouch. Relieved I had got over the first hurdle, I shared final farewells with my loyal lifelong friends Pat, her partner Tim and of course my trusted friend Keith.

Of course, Pat gave some photographs. She drew my attention to one. The day my friend helped me shift forty tonnes of Cotswold stone for the garden in my first house. She reminded me of the girl staring over the fence counting each wheel barrow. Pat, forever sharp, put her in her place at number thirty-six.

I recalled how Pat collapsed; I thought she was having a heart attack. Job done and it looked great, but my back garden became the most popular litter tray, no barbecues for sure.

Anyway, as we sat reminiscing, she handed me the photograph, she had taken of me that day. Why do mates always keep the negatives? I know I had ripped this one up; I looked like I had been dragged through a hedge backwards many times.

Another photo was a reminder of a particular fancy dress party. Pat always fancied herself as Dolly Parton and I, well I was Julie Andrews of course. Pat, I remember looked like a blonde bombshell and as I looked at the photo, I did look pretty good in my habit with no back, stockings and suspenders.

I recalled a great party: oh yes, the bathtub. Wow, it was filled with bottles of champagne to celebrate forty years.

Who says the best place to be is the kitchen at a party? Pat and I liked the bathroom very much that night. In fact, too much, judging by our fingerprints in the Camembert the next day and to my dismay also one of Pat's false fingernails. Such memories.

Always remember the camera is an amazing gadget, and I do love gadgets, but stay focused.
Photographs come with a health warning. There is always a negative or potentially it can be found in the cloud. So, beware.

Of course, Pat, having a fetish for cards, had hers all ready. Over the years, like I have mentioned earlier, Pat had a passion for cards. I reckon she always needed card therapy. I had received every poetic verse on friendship ever but I loved her, always will and needed her with me that day; my lifelong friend.

Keith, well, we stood to say goodbye and I thanked him for moving into my abode temporarily to look after my dog, Katie.

I have always described him as the David Niven of this world, a true gent, who did and still does conduct business on a handshake and he always walks on the outside of you on the pavement so the car would hit him first.

Simply, I saw the signpost many years ago regarding the importance of his friendship and still do to this day. He is a lifelong friend, warts and all.

Talking of warts, here is another health warning. Do not ever allow anyone to try to remove your warts unless trained medically. My mother many years ago attempted to remove mine with red cotton in the hope that it would wither and die overnight with no trace.

Oh yes, to my mother's satisfaction, it had withered but I was left with a bright red birthmark of a different kind. Scarred for life, but hey, what would you do without your mother. Now, I am sure you realise just how much my parents mean to me so you may be wondering why they were not at the airport to bid me farewell.

For those of you that are close to your parents, this will need little explanation. My mother just held on to the fact that Norway was introducing no smoking in bars, so she held on to the thought of her daughter having a new found opportunity to give up that terrible habit. Ex-smokers are always the most critical; I wonder why? In addition, we had an agreement. I was simply going on an adventure and I would be back. So, in mother's words, "Let us not make a drama out of it." As I faced security, I was grateful for our pact.

Going through security, I was frisked in Diana Ross style. I was greeted by an overzealous security officer. I stood unaware that Bertha, in her robust way, was feeling my crutch as I drifted in and out of thought. I was worrying about whether I had shown my loyal friends, who had just said farewell, as much friendship as they had shown me over the years.

I was quickly brought back to the present by a whisper in my ear, "You can put your legs together now madam." Dazed, I acknowledged the woman who had groped my inner sanctum and been paid for it.

That gives a new dimension of thought when you say at an interview, yes I would like to start at the bottom and work my way up. Well Bertha had a natural gift; one, two, three, four, oops five with acceptable pressure and precision.

What can I say ladies, if you ever need those pads for our laughter spoils, wear them at airports just in case you meet a Bertha.

I met Melanie the flight attendant as I boarded the plane. I was trying to look intelligent and portray someone who had a very important job to go to. I casually carried my laptop bag on my shoulder. Heaven forbid she could sense that the enormity of what I was about to do was dawning on me and I was now becoming a potential flight risk. I was now getting scared.

An actual signpost highlighted, "Melanie is here to serve you today; anything you need ask Melanie who will endeavour to accommodate."

Me: Can I have a cappuccino?
Melanie: Can't do that.
Me: A double espresso?
Melanie: Can't do that.

Me: Any duty free?

Melanie: Can't do that - sold out.

My mind drifted back to Bertha; I wonder what her signpost should have read "Bertha is here at your cervix today, if you have any complaints about her technique please contact the handling department to straighten things out."

Back to reality.

Me: Red wine please, Melanie.

Melanie: Yep can do that.

Thank god, for small mercies. I sipped and thought, oh was this a sign of things to come? I closed my eyes. Arriving at the airport, sadly there was no Love Actually scene, no duty free but there was the small blessing of my emergency packet of Marlboros.

Fortunately, I had made many season friends over the years as I love travelling. Many were here in Oslo and they had arranged accommodation for me and a 'welcome to Norway party' in a very famous and brilliant Elvis bar. This bar became my new-found friend over the next two years, well most of it. They were all so kind to me and I made many more friends but the journey ahead was tough. Actually, much more challenging than I had imagined.

The Job

The job finished before it started. The Education Department for Leadership & Management had to make redundancies. After my introductory meeting I was informed of this unfortunate state of affairs. They apologetically thanked me for all of my ideas and awkwardly explained we must look after our own first. It was a matter of fact. There was simply no room at the inn no matter what my successes in the UK had been. They were totally irrelevant here.

I was living in Oslo's answer to Notting Hill and most bars were outside. Norwegians love being outside: it's part of their cultural way of life. So, after receiving this bad news, I sat in one of the aforementioned bars contemplating my next move.

I purchased a bike; bad choice as I had not anticipated the hills in Oslo and this bike was so heavy, even with an empty basket. To make matters worse, there was a driver's strike. As a consequence, there was no food on the shelves. The lift in the apartment block was broken and of course, I lived on the top floor. Apart from all of these minor hiccups, I was living the dream. Drinking an extortionately expensive thimble of red wine, I briefly considered the scenario, "How much would a return ticket to Birmingham set me back?"

However, I went with my gut. I made the decision not to run back to safety, but to stay. I just had that feeling it was the right thing to do and sometimes you have to go with your gut. Friends rallied round and helped me stay positive.

It is funny, when you visit a place for a vacation how different it is compared to living there. Norway is unbelievably expensive (now do not forget this was 2004). My extensive shopping list was as follows:

- Bread cost approximately £10 and
- Cheese, if you could get it, £6 for something that made Edam look mature.

- Red wine by the glass...I would prefer not to divulge.

One friend used her contacts to get me a bank account as you cannot get one without a job. I queued for two days. Yes, two days at immigration to get the visa as you had to apply in person. As I had money in the bank and was self-sufficient, I was issued with one.

I soon learned, to get a job in Norway as a foreigner you had to demonstrate you were learning Norwegian. So, I enrolled at the local university.

Sometimes you need a bit of luck in life and it came my way. I visited the International School about thirty minutes from Oslo. I met one of the heads there. There were two heads, one primary, one secondary and an overall director.

Everybody in management in Norway at this time, had to do compulsory teaching of at least 30%. He wanted me to teach year 1 and utilise my experience as a headteacher to improve their practice in many areas.

Before I could commence my appointment, I had to have an interview with the Director, Barbara. I dressed smartly for the interview, which was good for me, as in Norway dress is very casual. After a while, I understood why, the weather!

As the door swung open, a magpie flew in, oh god a sign I thought and I saluted. I do not bother these days.

Oh the 'shabby huts'. What a nightmare I thought. As I waited for the interview, I thought how I have always found Barbara quite a strong name. As I walked in, judging by the luxury of her office versus the state of the school, I quickly got her measure.

It did not go well. Embarrassingly, I witnessed power struggles on the panel. Barbara was obviously threatened by what I had to offer; it was exceptionally uncomfortable. They wanted to observe me for a day doing various tasks: teaching and exploring my knowledge of leadership and management. I duly did this a few days later. The train journey back to Oslo after this particular day was agonisingly testing. I had been led to believe it was a formality and they would snatch my hand off. However, Barbara took great pleasure in sending me off with a, "We will let you know later this week." I could not believe I was putting myself through this; what was the reason? I was ready to pack my bags. This was all a waste of time. The UK education system appeared so far ahead. Maybe my leadership and management style would just not fit.

Heavy hearted, I strolled to university for yet another agonising Norwegian lesson. Thinking of my extra three vowels and how the grammar was on another level, my mobile rang. It was 'Babs', "We would like to offer you the position." I manoeuvred myself through all the cyclists, to a quiet spot and simply declined her offer. She gasped. Babs was obviously not used to anyone declining a position. She obviously gathered herself and asked, "Why?" I explained that although I appreciated the offer I had given it much thought and believed I was not right for the position. I was bold and informed her that I knew myself well enough to recognise I would want to introduce change. Something which I did not think she would appreciate. Nevertheless I thanked her for her time.

You could just tell Babs was stunned; we wished each other well
and terminated the call.
Sitting in the park bar that afternoon, Friday 2 pm, it was busy.
All my friends had gathered, Friday really is no work day in Oslo,
everyone finishes really early afternoon and all dress down,
even further than normal and it works.
When my friends realised I had turned down a very well-paid
job as a foreigner in Norway, there was a collective sense of
shock around the table.

They all thought I had totally lost the plot. I tried to explain how
I felt and they got it, but they knew how difficult the job market
was and they did not want me to go home. Norwegians are very
direct with their speech and not exactly known for empathy.
They really just say things straightforwardly, no flowering it up:
it's just the way they are. So, when I turned around and said, "I
wonder as I sit here, feeling a nobody, will they forget all I have
done in education back home?" I was greeted with Norwegian
bluntness.

One of my friends, larger than life, not to be messed with but
astute and kind, took a gulp from her lager and said, "Now you
listen, let me just say this...Does a bear shit in the woods?"

I had no time to think, I cried with laughter and emotion at the
whole situation I had found myself in. It was my round and you
must never forget your round in Norway 'that simply will not
do!'

Standing at the outside bar, the music played and the Friday
night atmosphere began to build. As I waited patiently to be
served, my mobile rang once more and I was asked to

reconsider. I started the following Monday. It was one of my best decisions. By the time I left two years later, I had the utmost respect for Barbara and she for me.

This school had both primary and secondary under one roof. A community of children living and learning in a different country. Most staff had moved to Norway for love as their partners had moved there because of their work in oil and engineering. There were many expats, they are very important in Norway.

All expats had so much in common. We were away from home and everyone needed that school community to cope and find our place. Barbara managed us all and that deserves respect. She was fluent in Norwegian which definitely deserves respect; it is a hard language to learn but it is useful. When you learn Norwegian, you can pretty much understand Swedish and Danish too.

Learning the language, I found challenging but I managed to get to a working level which stood me in good stead. In-fact, no miming was required here.

I met some great characters at university and we all agreed how hard it was because the Norwegians have such a great command of English. You see, they have to learn English at a very young age. When you consider the size of its population, you can fully appreciate why. Norway is small but not to be underestimated. By insisting their population are bilingual, they are rich and powerfully independent.

Over the two years, I realised how much I loved teaching again. I had much to learn about teaching in the international sector and there were some tricky moments. Although, of course, all the principles of teaching and leadership and management are the same irrespective of the country, there must be an appreciation for difference and certain nuances relevant to the country.

Never underestimate a child no matter what country you teach in.

One particular day, I was animated in class and I said the word, 'poor'. A rather intelligent boy said, "What is a 'poo..A?"

The teaching assistant and I laughed knowingly; teaching in an international school requires you to speak clearly and get rid of dialects.

I caused an uproar one day. Only one I hear you say, well no there were quite a few moments. I really did not give much thought to Norwegians being into healthy eating until my reward system came to light. I had a usual fast-paced numerical competition in class and there were rewards for success – sweets! Remember, everyone likes a reward for success. This particular day, I gave out sweets. Not quite out of a jar like Sister back in England, but sweets nonetheless.

Oh, the complaints poured in.

I reflected on the train journey back to Oslo one night and thought, what a load of hypocrites. Every lunch box had a state of the art compartment for everything: fruit, different fruit, cheese, more fruit, two minute 1cm x 1cm cubes of brownie. I would not mind, but many parents worked at the school and they would give Yvonne a run for her money. Whenever it stopped snowing, they would bake the finest cakes ever and trays and trays of brownies for the staffroom. But I took heed, no sweet rewards from there on in.

My difficulties were not limited to the classroom. One particular train journey at the end of the day was particularly traumatic. There were horrendous snow blizzards which resulted in us having to jump off the train in the middle of nowhere with a long wait to be rescued. I really thought that I was in a remake of Dr Zhivago, my favourite film of all time, with the beautiful Omar Shariff and Julie Christi. Another very tricky moment was when the secondary teachers plotted quite savagely to get rid of me. Someone had found out, actually, an ex-head from England like me, that I was doing the strategic planning behind the scenes for the secondary head. Wow, another infamous five tried to see me off.

You see I had an arrangement with the powers that be, to keep a low profile with this aspect of my work. Some of the secondary staff were difficult to manage and the secondary head wanted to keep some credibility. If people knew I was writing his leadership and management plans, it would only undermine his efforts. I absolutely honoured this secrecy.

Unfortunately, the only reason I was found out was because the secondary head had mistakenly trusted the wrong person on his staff who told all. Even the primary head did not know this part of my work. The plotters' mistake was to concoct a scenario that suggested I was undermining the director, Barbara, and so they decided just off the record to tip off the primary head to this load of nonsense. Sadly, the day he challenged me was the day the penny dropped for him, that he had sadly fallen for the charms of the famous five.

He was informed by Barbara herself, that it was actually her who had directed me in the first place to help the secondary head and that would always stay the arrangement. My position went to a higher level of respect that day.

As for the famous five, well they treated everyone pretty much the same - energy zappers.

One in particular, thought she ruled the roost just because she had been there the longest. Shortly after the failed sting, she accosted me in the staffroom, spouting off a load of nonsense. I shut her down by suggesting to her that she obviously, when moving to Norway, had literally brought all her baggage with her and so I offered her a brownie. No more trouble.

I did quite a bit of leadership training and as I made my way to the conference room I was astonished to hear my own voice advising a group of teachers about assessment for learning. I had not even made it to the room. Turns out another trainer was using the assessment for learning video I had made all those years ago, gosh I looked younger then.

June is a very important month in Norway, the country virtually closes down. Most people go on holiday and pay no tax that month, they even have a rebate. Sadly, people do not realise it is their money anyway, as they have been paying for June all year round through Norway's high taxation system. Nevertheless, June was a bumper month for spending, holidays and happy days, plus often no sleep as it does not go dark in

Norway during this time. Everyone is out socialising in very civilised park bars with no comprehension of time. Yes, I was guilty of one day going to work with no sleep, just lost track of time on a lovely warm night. Interestingly, leaders can often talk the talk but cannot walk the walk with regards to work life balance. I found that Norwegians really understood how to walk the walk regarding work life balance. I acknowledged the benefit of the Norwegian approach. I have incorporated this in to my leadership style and encourage others to do so.

One day, at the start of the summer, there is a holiday bonanza in Norway for one day only. It is like buying a lottery ticket for ridiculously cheap holidays. You only know the destination, not the grade of the hotel or even if you are sharing a room with a total stranger. I was lucky and got two tickets to Sicily. My friend warned me on the plane for the first time that it could be dire or it might not have a toilet.

"What?" I screamed, "No toilet." Well, you know what that means for me, another new country. I suddenly became scared of the prospect of two possible weeks with constipation, laxatives and no toilet with strangers. I need not have worried. We ended up in one of the best hotels, a view over the bay to die for and a toilet.

Thank you, Lord,

Although there were many good times working in Norway, overall everyday was an effort. I sat waiting for the train staring at the same Benetton advert for two years. An ad which I never really understood as Benetton sell clothes yet the advert simply displayed a mass of naked people. Actually, upon reflection, I think the advert was highly effective as I can remember it clearly today nineteen years on. Mind you, I never did actually buy anything from Benetton.

As I sat there wondering how those naked models possibly intended to survive in -16 degree temperatures, I started to question what on earth I was doing there more days than not. I missed home, family and English culture.

We all know the saying, 'you do not really appreciate how important something or someone has been to you until it or they have gone.' We are all creatures of habit, people get use to routine, where they live, its culture and generally people do not like change. Very often people are happy with this as they have never known any different.

Norwegians absolutely love their country and very rarely leave. They have a good life and Norway has one the best health care systems in the world. You must remember it is also a very wealthy country that sits nicely under the radar. Norwegian consumers are influential too. Clothing manufacturers trial their latest lines in Norway and neighbouring Iceland. If they do not take off there, then apparently the line is not distributed to other countries. Just thought I would share that snippet of information with you.

For me, no, it was a definite. I missed England, its culture and above all my family. I also missed the theatre and the beauty of our landscape. Yes, Norway's fjords are beautiful, but in my opinion, when you think of the landscapes in Scotland, Wales and England, ours are hard to beat.

On a positive note, Norwegians embraced the community spirit. My workplace certainly did. This experience furthered my belief that all leaders should try to ensure community is at the heart of their organisation, where everyone thrives and is valued and cared for.

Before I took leave from training leaders at this international school, I led my last two days on how to accurately moderate work practices. This training was the culmination of all the training I had done there. On the last day, a concerned colleague came to me as the day finished. I was struggling a bit from fatigue and she said, "You know Loretta, you are looking a bit orange."

She was right, but I had given up smoking and had become addicted to satsumas and carrots. Yes, I had become very healthy.

As I finished, there was a community send off. Barbara gave a moving speech, amongst others: the Norwegians are into their speeches. In England, we pleasingly do not put the same emphasis on speech making. I once attended a ceremony where there was a two-hour speech for a dog's birthday. It was 'ruff'. My speech was brief but heartfelt. I think they all knew how grateful I was for their friendship and community spirit and I told them I would be back soon after a little interval. Barbara and I had a chat and we both knew I would not renew my contract. We had total respect for each other. We said our goodbyes until our paths crossed again.

Although it was one of the hardest experiences in my life, without any doubt, I was richer for it. My educational experience in leadership and management and of course my understanding of teaching and learning had been extended by working in the international sector.

In my opinion, it is important to remember you always have to love what you are doing - in my case it was teaching - if you are truly going to be an outstanding leader of your establishment.

No, absolutely no regrets, onwards and upwards. I read the right signposts.

During my time in Norway, I had kept my hand in the UK's education sector. I regularly flew back to England doing leadership consultancy work for headteachers. I never advertised, they just contacted me and I hope I helped them in some way.

As I finished my contract, to my delight my parents flew over for a visit. I had done my best to afford some decent food. I was so happy and so relieved to see them. We went for a long walk and snow literally came over our knees. It was lovely and fresh, we breathed in the air, it was good.

The next day, I met my lovely Irish gynaecologist whose daughter I had taught at the international school. She was over from Ireland leading training for gynaecologists at the top hospital in Norway. She became a much-needed 'reason' friend for sure.

At 10.00am
The following day, dad was still trying to find a shop that sold bread under £10.00. He came back after an hour ecstatic, no

bread, but he had found a small corner shop, yes, corner shops exist in Norway too. This particular one, according to my father, was run by a Chinese lady selling the best apple strudel ever, I could not believe it. After two years of starvation, this gem was literally just around the corner. And how much did my father willingly pay for this gastronomic delight? Wait for it - a measly £2.00. The cheapest thing on Norwegian soil. Dad whistled triumphantly.

11.30am
I was induced. Yes, I was about to give birth.

Four Days of Hell
Mom and dad were with me all the way. You see in Norway, the Norwegians like all births to be natural, no classes on how to avoid pain, they believe just let nature take its course. I had an answer for them but we will just leave it as - really!?

Third day in and my mother and myself lost it. I was standing, hanging over the bed when the midwife came in and looked at a monitor. She proceeded to put her arms around me and said, "Oh you are doing so well...yes, really well." I just looked at her IN DISBELIEF. My head spun like the girl in the exorcist and then with a terrifying calmness replied, "I think you are mistaken, it is the lady in the next bed that is doing well, you will find I am not strapped to any machine! I am simply in agony hanging over this end of this bed." Realising her mistake, she sprinted out to avoid any daggers that may have come her way.

I looked at my mother. We absolutely lost it. In our delirious state, we just cried with laughter and desperation. Eventually, I composed myself and turned to mom and just said, "Oh mom, it is time to come home."

Day Four
Another day, the door sprung open, yet another change of the midwives; oh, you simply could not write it. Guess who came in and said, "Right enough, let's get this baby out." The 'Oh you are doing so well' midwife, who had previously believed me to be possessed by some kind of demon entity, had returned.

A Beautiful Baby Girl
Mother stayed the required six weeks before I could get a passport issued for my daughter, receiving birth certificates and health checks all take this amount of time.

Mom and myself will never forget trying to get a passport photo of my newly born baby five days after birth; a comedy sketch for sure.

Going to the British Embassy to get my passports was a very nervous one. Would my daughter's photograph pass the test?

Passports were finally in hand. The difficulty of obtaining her passport was in complete contrast to the ease of fulfilling a very important Norwegian tradition. It is the custom in Norway to give a baby a football kit. Yes, they do baby size football kits, irrespective of gender. Whatever football kit you are gifted is the football team your child must support. My friend turned up with a Manchester United one thankfully only a day after birth. I proudly put it on and my daughter proceeded to do what I still cannot believe to this day. She virtually exploded and the poo went right up to her chin – everywhere! Unbelievable.

One week before I came home, it was Easter and we went to mass. I was grateful and needed to just sit. You see my faith is important but I give to it and take from it what feels right for me. I will not pretend to be any different. My faith will always mean something and as the saying goes, 'Once a Catholic always a Catholic,' a great play by the way.

As my mother and I sat, we noticed the woman next to us constantly swigging from a bottle. We were horrified and just could not believe it. She had not a care in the world, just swigged away and listened.

Remember, not everything is what it seems. As the mass proceeded, she got up, not a swagger in sight and approached the priest who was standing at the altar. We just held our breath in anticipation. 'What on earth is she doing?' we thought. Seconds later, tears strolled down our cheeks; we were hysterical. It only turned out to be a bottle of olive oil. Apparently, another tradition in Norway is that if you get your olive oil blessed on Easter Sunday, you are, apparently, guaranteed good health. She was sober as a judge. She got back and offered me a swig. Well, you will appreciate I could not resort to my, 'I do not have hot drinks' tactic so I had no excuse. Accepting the bottle, hoping the blessing had eradicated her germs, I simply drank for good health whilst noticing my mother had already made a hasty exit.

Mom had to fly home without us, it was time. Dad and Mom needed to be reunited. I had one more document to collect before I could return home. No way could I have got through those first six weeks without mom, too many stories to tell here but treasured memories for sure.

My mother had never flown on her own before. Dad had gone back earlier as he was working in a school. Yes, another project, he was known as the whistler whatever school he went to. Mom was scared. At the airport, I was allowed to go near the gate, a woman took pity and allowed me through; we were very grateful. We cried with mixed emotions. Love for something or someone can give you the courage to do brave things. Mom made it home.

Goodbyes done, my luggage was packed and I was heading home at last. Arriving home, I had the most joyful welcome from my dog, 'Katie' and she welcomed my daughter. I was 'home' and thankfully my silk rugs remarkably still looked silk – just a different colour.

Although this part of my journey had challenged me every day for many different reasons, it had been worth every second. All the experiences, all the people, new understandings and knowledge had further equipped me on how to lick the gravy.

But most of all, I had a gift; my absolutely beautiful precious daughter.
Thank you to all you Norwegians.

Lesson
- Sometimes you have to just follow your gut instinct.
- Sometimes to achieve great things you may have to be a bit selfish.

- Do not be too quick to judge others, you may be oh so wrong.
- Not everything is what it seems.
- At the first obstacle, do not give up.
- Do not be too proud; something good might pass you by.
- Sometimes you have to go back a little or take a diversion to then move forward. You will have accumulated more experience, knowledge and understanding which leads to greater achievements.
- Always be open to learn and experience new things; you will be stronger for it and who knows what opportunities are around the corner.
- Love for a job, person, or thing can make you brave.
- You need friends whether for a reason, season or lifetime.
- Do not fall out with your parents. They are not friends but more they are your mom and dad; always there.
- Norway is always worth a visit but take plenty of spending money.

Second Serving

How the Headship Came About
Approaching the end of my maternity sabbatical and before my brain cells totally dissipated in to mush, it was time to return to the workplace.

What to do?
As I had enjoyed helping leaders in different settings, I became an associate adviser for the local authority. Despite my Laurel and Hardy presentation that was linked to an aspect of beleaguering leaders not going down a storm, I was successfully taken on the local authority books!

When I had a meeting about possible ways this could work, the adviser, the same one who had congratulated me as the first head to get outstanding against new Ofsted framework in 2004 with flowers and chocolates, gave a condition.

I was informed that under no circumstances would I be allowed to enter or work as a consultant in any catholic schools as I would not be welcome.

Now, I ask you, was that because she also had coffee with 'infamous five women' from years gone by? Or was it because I was an unmarried mother with a child? Or simply because people with her ear in the catholic system simply didn't like me? All of these reasons came via the grapevine drums and whispers in the breeze to my ear ….mmm! I simply thought, fair enough. Whatever the reason, who was I to even attempt to raise an eyebrow to this. It was understood!

It would be accurate to say this adviser never really warmed to me. I would go as far to say according to others, she did not like me much. One of her close advisers actually took time out to inform me she told many I was 'cold'.

I always find it disappointing when people can make that perception of anyone after a visit with flowers and chocolate. Was it all simply down to her not liking my modern version of the 'stations of the cross'?

Some people never want to get to know you unless it serves a purpose. I was an asset just to do a job, no more, no less. Again, that is fair enough and quite frankly it was totally accepted.

I do believe it was a group of experienced male leadership advisers who had worked with me before, who insisted I would be the best person to quote, 'sort out Dorrington'. The adviser upon hearing this advice was not overly enthused for sure and that was from my own observations with her, which I doubt she would argue with.

You must remember, sometimes no matter how respectful and polite you are to someone, if they still do not like you, do not waste time trying to change their mind, you are far too busy and it will be a total waste of energy. That is life I am afraid, so best to just keep dignity. Be respectful but acknowledge you will not be sending each other a Christmas card as that would be false and simply will not do.
Interestingly, I did respect her for her work for Ofsted. She knew it inside out and worked hard to pass her knowledge to many heads and that is to be respected.

Just a thought, before I move on. I recall coming across a statistic that highlighted how if you are successful, 95% either do not like it or do not care and only 5% will be pleased for you - at a push.

Sad really, but that seems to be prevalent across society. If only that could be reversed, then maybe the country would be far more progressive than it currently is.

I am sure columnist Amanda Platell for the Daily Mail could add her perceptions on this.

Coffee and Amanda Platell has always been my Saturday morning treat during my headships, she just says it as it is. Refreshing I always think!

Eventually, this adviser approached me to become the strategic adviser for Dorrington School in October 2007.

Lesson

- Accept you will not be liked by everyone. People will always have different perceptions of you but that can be as much to do with themselves as it is you.
- You simply cannot get bogged down in this. You cannot win them all. If you want to be popular with everyone, do not aim to be successful in leadership and management, you will find it too hard.
- Despite what is thrown your way, always stay respectful. It costs nothing and it is important.
- Never go into leadership and management to make

friends; it is simply an added bonus if you do.

- You have so many difficult decisions to make on your journey. Accept you will upset people on the way. Some people just might not like you, irrespective of how you look, what you wear, how kind and warm you are, they simply do not like you, end of.
- Whispers in the breeze will be part of everyday work as a leader, accept it.
- Respect people's different ways of life. We have to acknowledge difference, that is the way of the world.
- Ensure you surround yourself with as many positive people as you can. For as many who do not like you for whatever reason, there will be many that do love and respect you for just being you.
- Believe in yourself and like yourself. Just do your job to the best of your ability.
- Stay professional at all times, even when you want to give someone a piece of your mind. You can always get frustrations out of your system in your office but never lower yourself outside of it.
- Have respect for yourself at all times.
- Be happy for another person's success; it might help you experience some for yourself.

I remember when I was head at my first school during 2000 - 2004, Dorrington School had a good reputation. I even recall the well-established headteacher's farewell retirement at a local consortium meeting.

And with this retirement, came a change of leadership and management which required sustaining what was working well and implementing change for future progressive growth. As to what happened during this time of change, is not for me to surmise or speculate. But in 2007, the local authority shared their evaluation that Dorrington School was about to go into special measures.

Unfortunately, it had gone through a turbulent time and issues with leadership and management had resulted in staff taking union action. The depth of its troubles had resulted in an emergency one-day closure, pupils left in droves to the equivalence of two-year groups, there was under performance in all aspects of teaching and learning and an extremely despondent workforce. There had been a mass of resignations resulting in thirteen supply staff being employed on a daily basis. Standards of achievement were very low from the day to day organisation to teaching and learning. There was an exceptionally unhappy community and the school was approximately £100,000 in deficit!

Such was the state of Dorrington School, it had attracted media interest and action was needed quickly. Trade unions were instructing all staff about the working conditions at the school.

The local authority had looked at various options, including utilising the experience of a national headteacher, but it was soon to be realised that the enormity of rescuing the school would need a long-term, committed and substantive headteacher, which understandably proved difficult to find.

Ofsted had suspended its inspection. A later inspection had instead been agreed to allow some form of stability in the school community.

The local authority had put the existing deputy head into an acting head role and they wanted me to work behind the scenes as a strategic leadership and management consultant. I agreed to go and have a look. Essentially it was a visit to assess if I could potentially make a positive difference in the capacity that was required. My visit did not go well. The acting head did not feel any help was necessary and who was I to argue.

Later that evening, after my visit, I was contacted by the local authority to see if I would undertake the role.

"Absolutely no way," was my answer.

I was still quite mortified from the visit, with the sheer desperate state of the school in every aspect. I had empathy with the staff to a degree. Quite frankly, I could not see how I could support the journey of improvement when really it was not wanted by its current acting head. Furthermore, this impression was exacerbated by the diabolical courtesy shown during my visit.

After much persuasion, I was given time again to rethink. A glass of wine was needed as I contemplated if I could really help, as honestly, I was not sure. Further conversations over several telephone calls took place and I eventually agreed to contract myself to strategically assist for three months. This was stipulated with an important 'get out' clause if I felt it was too unproductive for everyone.

Lesson

- Changes in leadership and management brings challenges.
- It is not always easy, for a variety of reasons, to take over a school or any establishment.
- A leader has to work with the existing community carefully when taking over a school to bring them on board.
- With any change, difficult decisions may be required.
- If new leadership and management is not effective, there will be a downward spiral effect.
- Experienced leadership and management is key when governors are making such important decisions. Inexperience is not advisable.
- There can never be complacency as a leader at any time. There is no room for basking in the glory of any success. You must always, not only endeavour to just sustain but continually be energised to move forward and grow in an ever-changing society.

November 2007

First day as strategic consultant.

Before my arrival, no one told me it was a voluntary one-way system on Dorrington Road at the beginning and end of the school day. Hence, my car and myself were nearly wrapped around a tree by 8.45 am on that first day.

After unwrapping myself and being somewhat bedraggled, I eventually made my way to the school office to find myself at the centre of another Jack Nicholson scene from that famous film 'One Flew Over the Cuckoo's Nest'. This time, I was not playing the role of Jack. I was on the other side of the door, on the receiving end of, "You are not wanted!" Totally stunned at my reception, I was frozen to the spot. It was obvious to me that the front of house staff were certainly p****d off that day and there is no other polite way of putting it.

The front of house staff were clearly in the, 'I am in no mood for this job'. They had zero tolerance for who I was and why I was there and in no uncertain terms told me to, "Sling my hook and take my bag with me."

So, I sat as instructed and waited and waited with my very important briefcase. After 30 minutes or so, I eventually tried a second take of knocking on the office window and saying, "Darling I'm home."

With reluctance, I was finally escorted to my wonderful welcome meeting with the chair, acting head and of course the adviser. Arriving originally on time, I now looked as if I was 45 minutes late. No one was happy, especially me.

After frosty stares of disapproval, I was half-heartedly encouraged to sit on the reception-child seat in this dull and desperate headteacher's office. I constantly had to strain my neck like a kid looking for the sweetie jar simply just to remind my welcoming committee I was actually there.

Did I say to you, I had a 'get out' clause in my contract?

After unsuccessfully taking any sweets, I was tempted to tell them all where to put this job but something nagging inside forced me to stay and listen a tad longer. Mmm, I listened and had no doubt that if I stayed, there would be stormy seas!

As I listened, I thought how sometimes people believe they can read the theory books of leadership and management and all will be well but that is an absolute load of garbage and extremely naive.

I believe you have to have a balance of experience and practical and theoretical knowledge to actually know what you are talking about with regards to leading, managing and respecting people. And by midday, I had literally seen no evidence of this.

You must appreciate at this stage, I was supposed to be behind the scenes supporting the existing leadership and management team.

This arrangement would have been fine if the acting head was receptive to why I was there and open to advice. But this proved to be disastrous, as the acting head went to great lengths to ensure I fully understood no help with anything was required. At the same time, I sensed everyone else involved with this arrangement was really hoping for another immaculate conception, which frankly was not on the cards.

One exception, and there is always one optimistic event in the day for anyone if you look, I eventually stumbled on a toilet.

I had not been informed where the ladies' toilets were, never mind fire exits, what were they? With plaited legs, I found myself shovelling into what I thought was the toilet, but no, it actually was an outlet branch for 'the Bank of England'.

I stared at the wads of notes in all denominations! I kept staring and staring, then shaking with panic as I had forgotten to put my Tena Ladies on. Staring in shock, I wondered what the hell was going on! These notes were piled high, flicking in the breeze through the cracked brickwork. What a masterpiece, quite beautiful, it was a work of art to be admired. Obviously, these wads had taken a rather long time to create.

My bladder seemed to have corrected itself, except for maybe a little dribble as I ran to find the acting head. "Where is the safe?" I gasped.

"What do you mean a safe?" she nonchalantly replied.
Oh dear, this was worrying, I thought.
With renewed vigour, I did not ask but instructed her to order a safe immediately. As she disappeared casually into her own private toilet, it was quickly apparent she would not do anything I proposed. I had given my word to the adviser that I would try my best and I really do believe that is what she wanted me to do. So undeterred, I opened door after door until a kind lunchtime supervisor took pity on me (I believe another Tena Lady customer). She directed me to the toilet and as I crouched (sitting, simply would not do) a flood of fear came over me as I realised I had only peeled off the first layer of the onion. Without doubt, this school was in a terrible, desperate mess! Beyond the pale.

Relieved from my excessive load, my shuffling immediately ceased and I honourably stayed the rest of the day, the day after and the day after that. Three weeks later, give and take, I was acting head. This was not in the original plan as you all know.

First Mission

The safe was ordered and in situ - an old fashioned dial one. I am sure this safe was actually at the Great Exhibition in Crystal Palace in 1851. I had seen many of these safes in many a movie, guaranteed not to get in quickly and I can to this day confirm it is virtually impossible to get in at all!

All these years on, the safe stands imposing and unbreakable, coding takes on a whole different dimension with 'BOND'.

Action was required at a pace with full audits and surveys throughout the community.
All staff were interviewed to find out their opinion. They were asked what they liked about the school, what could be improved and what was it they personally wanted for themselves to develop at the school.

There were plenty of pupil conversations, observations and surveys. They wanted a computer suite first.

I met with parents during the days and evenings over a week. I ensured I reached out to everyone, this was essential.

The Governing Body, all 22+ had an audit of their skills set. This resulted in re-evaluation and the formulation of new committees. Extra meetings of the governors were implemented, allowing me to set the overall vision and strategic plans. I hit the short-term ones with immediate effect, due to the absolute urgency.

We established we would attempt to move forward with a collective vision to be an outstanding inclusive community school.

Change
Without doubt, the pupils, staff and parents were upset, angry and very disillusioned.
As the new acting head, I had to take care not to breathe in the negativity.

Stakeholders rightly insisted they would reserve judgements until they saw the fruits of what I was promising and that was totally fair.

One of my first fundamental priorities was negotiating with trade unions to get staff to work in accordance with contracts, no more working to rule and a positive pathway forward. Union representatives came from London and from local areas to represent the staff and necessary policy and agreements were put in place.

I decided with staff union reps to meet on a regular basis. Breakthroughs were made and we moved forward. This was a union honeymoon period for sure, as you will see from later events.

Lesson

- Be grateful for small wins.
- You must always have a collective vision that everybody owns, otherwise it will not be understood or fulfilled.
- Before negotiations, always know your line and what you ultimately need. Then you can make 'free passes' and win for all, but you have achieved your main agenda to move forward.
- Unions have a job to do and they will never go away totally empty-handed and, generally speaking, that is fair.

Next steps

A string of adverts went out for teachers, teaching assistants and front of house staff.

To this day, I am grateful to Reverend Clifford. 'Reverend' as I affectionately called him, was a governor with exceptional intelligence, empathy and humour, which over the next few months I welcomed.

Thank you, 'Reverend'.

Together, we interviewed for days on end. He kept going and going, interviewing with me. He devoured cream cake after cream cake. Basically, he could have had as many cream cakes as he wanted as I needed his shrewd perceptions and we worked very well together. There was no way I was having thirteen supply staff at a ridiculous daily rate cost a day for longer than I needed to. Supply staff was a major factor in the school accumulating a £100,000 deficit and this was exacerbated by tumbling numbers of pupils on roll plus so many staff off with stress. And of course, we needed recruitment for the front of house. As you know by now how I feel about the important role of front of house staff. Plus, I also needed an IT geek!

Interestingly, I learned during this time that Reverend had designed a major breakthrough for Dulux paint which made the brand very successful. Never mind ever judging a book by its cover, never judge a certain collar by its cover. He stayed with me for many years and was totally invaluable.

One particular day whilst interviewing, I had to travel further afield to pick up the cakes as Reverend fancied an apple turnover.

As I blustered in, he looked at me with such disappointment and said, "No apple turnovers?" I could not speak and simply handed them over.

Whilst I got my breath, Reverend took a bite of the usual cream edging with the corner of his mouth. I felt rather flushed. As I eventually shoved the turnover in my mouth he asked me what on earth was wrong, asking quizzically, "Is your apple turnover sour?"

In between choking and spitting it out on my favourite silk scarf, I conveyed to him that God had shown a sign and I had seen some form of vision. I told him I had seen an enormous billboard whilst driving. Intrigued, he asked what was on the billboard. "You are not going to believe it," I replied and explained it was an advert for an education consultant and it was only our previous departed acting head of a few days. He immediately started to choke and spit blobs of cream on his signature dog collar!

Apple turnovers were an absolute no no for the future.

Collectively, we made some useful appointments, including some from my past experience, people who I knew could benefit the school and move it forwards. The phone rang many times as the drums beat loudly in the area informing all where I was now in situ. IT geek Chris, Steve the drummer (now top billing at the Jam House in Birmingham), plus teaching assistants and of course, the help from my original family/friends' team (Pritt Stick culture had seemed to follow us), they all phoned.

Do not be under any illusion, this work was at a pace and for me and there was an increasing cost in baby sitters' fees, as I worked many occasions past midnight. Much work had to be done at weekends and when the children had gone home to adhere to health and safety, which as we all know, must always come first.

All hands to the deck resulted in a tremendous amount of change taking place very quickly.
A press release celebrating our new ICT suite stated, 'the underperforming school making great strides for its community.' This, alongside word of mouth, resulted in children starting to come back for places at the school.

Ofsted soon knocked the door as previously agreed. HMI came in and we had done enough in those few months not to go into 'special measures'. We celebrated with the local authority; 'satisfactory with elements of good.' The picture looked bright. Many letters of congratulations followed.

And now, the governing body had time to reconvene to advertise for a substantive head and I was going back to being a self-employed strategic consultant for leadership and management.

With the advert placed nationally, I was approached to apply for the position many times and every time the answer was no. You see, I had already done my headship and I wanted to carry on with strategic consultant work.

It was only when I walked around the school one day laughing with the children, I saw they looked happy. It dawned on me, that maybe I owed them more.

Days passed with many hours of reflection. I had so many plans for the school and constantly the same question came to the forefront of my mind, was it right to waste them? I found myself in a dilemma as to what to do and looked for the signpost. Eventually it came. As I stood on the school gate one particular evening, a prominent man in the community spoke to me and asked what were my next plans for the school and I said, "Well, the new head will decide."

This prominent man of political significance in the community looked hurt and betrayed. He turned to me and stated, "You stood and promised this community that you would put us on the pathway to make this an outstanding inclusive community school, you cannot leave us now." As he spoke, a crowd gathered around us. Moms looked at me with disappointment and I stood flushed with embarrassment. You must understand this was not a threatening discussion, this was simply a good community, but a disappointed community, suddenly in me!

Later that very evening, I spoke with friends and family. As my head slumbered on the pillow, I knew I had a job to complete. I owed it to the children, community and myself to apply. I had finally deciphered the signpost.

And so, below is my application for the substantive headteacher position at Dorrington for April 2008.

The application lists actions and outcomes of my work from November 2007 to February 2008.

- Implementation school evaluation process/draft school evaluation form/strategy in place.
- Clear leadership/management schedule in place to raise standards.
- Audit of policy and practice involving all stakeholders/report to GB.
- Following analysis of data using Raise on line/Family Fisher - implemented SIP/action plans to address underachievement.
- Introducing robust pupil progress tracking system/redeployed teaching assistants to enhance intervention work. New school timetables to maximise teaching and learning.
- Introduced new marking/targeting policy, which impacts on teaching and learning.
- Implemented new monitoring/evaluation system of teaching and learning.

- Utilised networks and external support to increase professional knowledge/expertise at all levels.
- Introduced support programmes for underperforming staff.
- Intensive professional development/new/long/med/short term planning.
- Defused union action/enabled withdrawal of trade union action.
- Analysed financial expenditure/rectified overspend/inappropriate expenditure.
- Implemented a 3-year budget forecast, strategies to compensate for decreases in pupils on roll - ensured high accountability.
- Improved admin/finance systems to maximise effectiveness/efficiency of resources.
- Implemented new staffing structure/new job descriptions for all staff.
- Implemented performance management / reviewers training cycle.
- Implemented new behaviour policy based on positive strategies.
- Employed part time learning mentor to help pupils with behavioural issues.
- Negotiated with pupil support, to train teaching assistants in behaviour strategies/counselling techniques.
- Re-introduced school council/peer mediation/new extracurricular activities.
- Arranged for new house system/good work assemblies/training for pupils to lead assemblies/pupils to have a voice/initiative to improve punctuality.
- Implemented new type of residential, which enables all children in designated classes to attend.
- Improved communication with parents through my acting headteacher's updates/new style weekly

newsletter/coffee meetings with governors/leadership.

- Designed and developed new foyer/reception/admin and leadership areas.
- Upgraded electrics in school to enable ICTsuite for school community.

- Placed bids and secured £16000 funding for sport development/£10000 awards grant for leadership training for pupils/expertise to support PE curriculum/extra activities/equipment.

OUTCOMES TO DATE

- Foundation for school improvement in place.
- Reduced level of unsatisfactory teaching from 70% to 25%.
- Staff stability/intensive professional development which is improving teaching and learning.
- Assessment for learning is beginning to support personalisation.
- Marking policy is helping pupils take ownership of learning and targets.
- Additional resources are supporting effective teaching and learning.
- Procedures in place to have high quality staff by September.
- Stemmed the flow of pupils leaving/attracting new and old back.
- Improved accountability/maximised efficiency/effectiveness of resources.
- A friendly welcoming ethos.
- New partnerships, which raise standards in aspects of school life e.g. behaviour/sport.
- Improved communication for all stakeholders.
- Equal opportunities/community cohesion/improved inclusivity.

- Motivated staff/improved professional standards.
- Increased profile of school/high volume of applicants for leadership posts/new pupils to school.

The advert attracted much interest, especially because of the scale of salary due to the school's exceptional challenges.

I spent hours, days and weeks preparing for the interview. You may think, why? Surely the job would be mine.

Well, actually no. It is important to understand that anyone applying for a post when you are already at the establishment has to be go the extra mile. It is often harder, as the panel already know you and not the other candidates. There is always the possibility the panel might be impressed by a candidate who is a high flyer promising the world. Remembering lessons from my earlier career, I knew that you are only ever as good as your last sale and I really had to sell myself now if I was to be appointed.

I wanted to be the substantive head of Dorrington and I made sure my presentation conveyed to the panel Dorrington's first chapter and the potential chapters to follow.

I based my interview around a 3D spiral cone cut in circular levels. A solid foundation, peaking at the top with a thread of string running from the bottom to the top. It represented how I perceived school improvement at Dorrington. Essentially, the cone had a strong base, each circular level spiralled onwards and upwards. At each level, I illustrated how we would sustain and grow all aspects in a constant cycle. Emphasising where we would analyse and implement actions whilst constantly monitoring, reviewing and evaluating. The spiral indicated we would always be moving upwards until we reached our vision.

My presentation focused on applying macro and micro processes of actions at every level of the spiral. I described each level under the headings of teaching and learning, the learning environment and leadership and management. Fundamentally, the thread throughout the cone, from top to bottom that would drive the processes represented the pupils of the school.

My accompanying slides reflected the main points and were put to music at the end of the presentation. This allowed the panel time to visually look at pictures of the past, present and mock ups of the future and importantly allowing the panel time to reflect before questions. It was a montage of music, a snippet of Elvis 'Caught in a Trap', and 'Suspicious Minds,' Queen, 'We will Rock you,' Tina Turner, 'Simply the Best' and finishing with Diana Ross, 'Ain't no Mountain High Enough!'

Appointed April 2008

And so, the journey continued. Strategic planning was key to the school's success and this process was long term with development plans within it, both short and medium. The plan to get outstanding took until November 2019. We were the first to get outstanding against the new framework and still as I write today we are one of the very few to have achieved this outstanding status. Throughout the journey, Ofsted expectations continually changed.

Many practitioners thought the latest Ofsted framework was elevating expected standards of achievement far too high. In my opinion, far too much time can be spent on exploring why it is just too high, rather than just getting on with it and trying. And as the bar of expectations continues to rise, we rise with it.

Leaders have their own reasons and ways for dealing with expectations constantly being raised by the government. In my opinion, we are constantly dealing with adversities in this world alongside technological advances from countries such as Russia and China, which pose challenges and competitive threats to our future generations.

Therefore, I advocate we need to reflect on our positions as leaders. Surely, we need to believe we can prepare our children for the next generation and the demands it brings. The minute we stop aspiring as leaders to do our best, maybe is the time we need to decide what we are doing with the gravy and why. It is a choice for sure, but is it a right? Some leaders may argue they do not want to get outstanding status because there is only one way to go after that and that is 'down.'

I totally disagree. Surely, it is about constantly improving on previous best, endeavouring to obtain, retain and grow even further.

I ask you, why are billions spent on trying to get into space, year in year out across the world? Why are we trying inventive ways to sustain our environment? My answer is to obtain further heights of achievement and discovery to improve, ultimately our future way of life. We ask our pupils and staff to try to exceed expectations. Therefore, surely we should, as leaders, ask the same from ourselves.

Unknowns and circumstance can knock any leader off their outstanding perch. If that happens, we need to pick ourselves up, brush ourselves down and strive forward to achieve outstanding status again. All we can do is try our best with the hand we are dealt, wherever the journey ends. We may get exasperated at another increase in level of expectation or another disappointment, but it is how we deal with it, that determines the type of leaders we are.

The choice and answer are always yours and that is to be respected. So, I have been asked by people from all walks of life many times, 'how as a leader did I create Dorrington Academy, an inclusive community, to be outstanding?' Well, it simply took time, with many lessons along the way and so you will be taken on its journey. A journey that could not afford to leave our community short changed.

Refining the Recipe

The Strategic Plan

The collective choice for Dorrington was to achieve our vision, even when the going got tough and it certainly has been tough no disputing that but we got there and this is how we did it.

As substantive head the journey from April 2008 took on a new level, both on a macro and micro level, until present day.

The strategic plan had intertwined actions under three headings: learning environment and teaching and learning underpinned by effective leadership and management.

Every stage of improving the learning environment led to further advances in teaching and learning opportunities and development. Throughout, we continually introduced and embedded practices. We constantly reflected, adjusted policy and practices to accommodate new government directives and our own progressive developments, whilst always being mindful to embrace our forever changing demographic picture in our efforts to be an outstanding inclusive community.

Adopting 'the paradigm theory' once again, was central to progression.

Most significantly, we introduced a 'Respect Agenda,' for all stakeholders within and outside our community. Those that obstructed progress were not encouraged to stay as part of our community, we recognised their happiness lay elsewhere.

Our plans involved integrating creative and logical thinking with calculated risks. Each stage was based on a rolling five-year cycle that was continually reviewed and revised where necessary.

You cannot be under any illusion that the honeymoon period continued after my appointment. The long journey of implementing change was now just beginning.

If you recall my example of the paradigm shift, the plane I am now piloting was a long distance haul with stopovers on the way. Like marriage today, the honeymoon is often lovely, the marriage has good times, bad times, laughter, tears, disagreements, agreements, change, adaptations, celebrations and challenges.

By adopting our motto, 'Together we are Stronger', we kept working at the school's marriage as a team at every level and we continue to do so.

We introduced staffing structures A and B, which allowed for flexibility as the school developed. We adopted each one over the years depending on the school's needs at the time.

Everyone was encouraged to work collaboratively, to share the workload, to learn from each other and be progressive in thought processes and ways of working effectively. All planning, preparation and assessment was organised in year group teams to facilitate planning together and working effectively to obtain work/life balance. Maximising opportunities to excel and learn together to raise standards of achievement for all became fundamental to progress.

All staff with different levels of experience were put in subject teams and teams for departments, initiatives, projects and community events. All school improvement and aspects from day to day organisation to teaching and learning were conducted through collaborative teamwork.

Lesson

- Collaborative teamwork equals progress.
- No one has all the answers, leaders included. When you work collaboratively at every level, you learn how to implement effective working towards a goal through listening to different perspectives.
- Often, we may have not thought of a perspective someone puts on the table and that perspective could make all the difference to your success as a leader, so listen.
- Everyone in an establishment needs to learn and if we are true leaders, we are also pupils.
- We need to stay open to learning from others then, in my opinion, we can realise the goals more effectively.
- Teamwork, if effectively implemented, can make you a successful leader.
- All staff need continuous professional development to improve practice. But it needs to be in alignment with your steps of development, so ensure it is focused and the impact is measurable.

The Learning Environment
Staff, in teams, enabled the flood gates to open.

Planning the huge revamp of the whole learning environment has taken up to the present day and potentially there is some sky left, for a couple more creative ideas in the future, but that is for my successor to decide.

The school was designed to be a hospital in the war and it was well beyond its sell by date. Every aspect of the school needed an overhaul. During this overhaul, you must know they never called me 'Florence,' other names for sure, but not 'Florence.' However, I would like to think that I have been the lady with the lamp, shining a bright light for its future.

I wanted the environment to be a place where everything needed to be bright, clean, orderly, creative, progressive, future proof and with a buzzing working atmosphere. Ultimately, an environment which opened the door to wonderful opportunities and possibilities for 'ALL' involved with Dorrington's community.

This was essential if we were to maximise every learning opportunity to develop the whole child and staff.

A very significant part of the plan was to create every possible room to facilitate small group teaching. I am a firm believer that small group teaching enables teaching to pupil's ability and accelerated personalised progression. I advocate, why stick to teaching thirty pupils with the constant headache of true differentiation for that number of pupils? I had previously recognised whole class teaching with such large numbers can only achieve a certain degree of success, even for our most outstanding teachers. Whereas teaching in small groups, especially for the core subjects, enables a more productive workforce and happy pupils. It facilitates pupils to have the confidence to ask when they do not understand concepts and enables them to have more opportunities to be given different approaches to try so they do understand. Ultimately, this enables more progress and both staff and pupils can celebrate accelerated success.

With this in mind, it was essential to create as many teaching spaces as possible. A plan led to another plan, which led to a further plan. Overtime, we knocked through rooms, partitioned rooms and extended the building in every place possible both inside and outside to create teaching spaces. To do this effectively, with quality and creativity, a logical stage by stage approach was implemented, ensuring at each stage it was affordable and appropriate. Once each stage was completed, teaching and learning initiatives could be implemented as appropriate and embedded overtime, which then led to more recruitment and further redeployment of resources and opportunities.

And so, the next stage would begin.

All stages were manageable and appropriately paced to be in alignment with the strategic overall plan. The logical plan was created by ensuring we had no waste, rigour with resources, competitive negotiated contracts with expert contractors, bidding for grants, redeployed staff and recruitment for building the schools future with NQTs (now ECTs), alongside up-skilling teachers and developing teaching assistants into higher level teaching assistants wherever possible.

The Dreaded Huts

Getting rid of the classroom huts was an early key part to the plan; they were an embarrassment and not fit for purpose for our pupils and staff. As a priority to get these replaced, we devised a bid for a capital grant for a new build and was successful.

The plan was to knock down all huts and have a new build extension on to the existing site. We celebrated when we received the letter which granted us the opportunity to achieve this. What followed was a year of rigorous planning and we were ready to go. Expecting bulldozers to arrive on site imminently, we instead had the arrival of a representative from the council saying due to unforeseen circumstances the grant had to be withdrawn. As far as I was concerned, 'That simply would not do'.

I wanted a face to face with the council to discuss. I am sure the representative, who pulled the short straw to face the music, will never forget the room full of people wanting answers. It took two visits to the toilet before she braced herself to enter the forum. We were respectful but we were not for moving.

After the meeting, I put pen to paper. According to the council, I wrote one of the best letters they had ever received arguing our case and for such a dreadful decision to be overturned. It took me a week to write and I certainly needed a proofreader as my terminology slipped into the fruitful kind and was corrected many times.

Whilst waiting for an acknowledgement, we marched!

Yes, ninety of the staff marched in solidarity down Dorrington Road to the Church Hall where councillors sat for their monthly meet. They were not ready for the invasion at their monthly committee meeting for sure.

Placards down and I was allowed to present my case to councillors, I did not sit for a long time. That night I will never forget, 'Together we were Stronger'. Whatever the staff and community thought of me, was put aside that night, we were together in solidarity for our pupils and I felt proud!

A month later, the grant was re-issued, the build was back on!

Lesson

- Planning must be manageable.
- Careful meticulous planning to ensure value for money at every stage.
- Do not run before you can walk.
- Alignment in policy and practice is key.
- Do not give up the fight at the first hurdle, stay respectful and march on until every avenue is exhausted.

Alongside this new build, we undertook construction for the whole upper and downstairs floors.

I managed all the projects to cut out wasting money on unnecessary middle people and I really enjoyed this part of my work. A special hard hat designed by front of house staff with diamantes was presented to me and I was ready for action. Contractors old and new, including my father, set to the task.

I have been very fortunate to develop a relationship with contractors over the years who get my way of working: no nonsense, please do not try it on. I do my research and I always know when contractors are trying to pull a fast one by cutting a corner and I show them the door.

Many have stayed with me for the entirety and have never got complacent with their quotes or work. This has been based on mutual respect.

To highlight two:

One in particular, is a man called Neil, from Davroy contractors.

Never once has he let me down. He sees a job through from start to finish and has always appreciated my expectations. Never once has he cut a corner. In fact, many times he has gone beyond the call of duty to help us with so many things. He has taught me so much and I could not have created this wonderful learning environment without him.

His contractors could always work around others very effectively. It all worked. One Saturday, he even came with a backup team to help me deal with contractors who had given me a lake rather than a sports pitch. A disaster that eventually was put right and I was still in one piece, just.

Thank you, Neil.

Another contractor, who came on board later in the day, is Ian, from Milliken builders. Interestingly, as we were chatting one day, discussing the new purpose-built hot yoga room, we discovered a past connection, the Bull Ring.

It only turned out he worked for 'Harris,' the renowned market trader selling the best cheese and eggs in the Bull Ring market.

He claims 'of course, he must have flirted with me over the 'mature cheese' all those years ago. I am afraid that tactic did not work, he still had to always 'sharpen his pencil', so we got the' best value for money'.

Remember, it is a very, very small world!

Thank you, Ian.

Health and safety always came first when doing any building work. Asbestos checks were the first thing to be undertaken before we started any building work. We will revisit this later.

Not everyone on the staff was on board, renovation and rebuilding was inconvenient for some, energy zappers for sure. I remember the day before the building materials and contractors arrived for the upstairs renovation. A disgruntled member of staff plodded down the stairs holding her head, she shouted, "The contractors have started and a nail has just fallen on my head."

"Really," I replied, followed by, "Try again tomorrow."
She went for an interview at another school the following week and while doing her lesson observation, apparently a clock fell on her head. Needless to say, she was on borrowed time and did not last.

Lesson

- Health and safety are always your number one priority.
- Always do full risk assessments and plan to walk the build every half hour to check against them.
- No cutting corners.
- Get asbestos checks.
- Keep staff and community fully informed of plans, it is common courtesy and avoids complaints.
- Select your contractors carefully, the cheapest is not always the best.
- Works need to stand the test of time and be done by professionals who actually do what you want.
- Have the confidence to suggest ways to improve plans to save money and again maximise opportunities.
- Take the advice from contractors, they may suggest something which you may never have thought of and it could turn out better.
- A health warning - remember, it is a small world we live in, so be mindful.

The Odd Occasion

Sometimes you have to source a contractor to do a job that you did not foresee in your planning with urgency or out of hours. This job is often crucial for development and needs to be addressed quickly in an effort not to halt progress. This takes real negotiation and I had to accept on the odd occasion when this happened, I was going to have to pay a bit over the odds to address the situation.

I recall one occasion when a very well-established scrap metal company had to do some pipe work on a weekend that was essential for our schedule of works. Twenty plus men arrived on site at 5.30am on a Saturday morning, no exaggeration. The job, I envisaged, would take two days, so you can imagine my delight as I watched the burly men leave by 2pm on that Saturday afternoon. Job done, £1000 more than I wanted to pay but wow marvellous work, worth every penny and we were still on track.

Downside, I did get complaints from neighbours regarding the 5.30 am start on that Saturday and, let us just say, a few choice words they heard from this workforce, well a lot actually.

In this situation, it was fundamental to quickly apologise for the inconvenience. I rescued it with chocolates, all friends again, well except for the one lady over the road who has been an acquaintance now, for gosh how many years! She also got four new slabs for her drive that she claimed had been damaged by their truck. Mmm funny that, I clocked their state on my first day as I made my efforts to drive to the school. But you must weigh up the pros and cons and choose your battles carefully, so new slabs and she was happy for the time being.

This was a mammoth project, outside demolition and new build started with the entire community cheering when the first outside hut was removed. Whilst that went on, we started the whole renovation of inside the existing building, firstly upstairs and then downstairs classrooms using the same method and same contractors. A total modernisation with every single available cupboard knocked through to make a teaching space, followed by the rest. We knocked through stockrooms to create teaching rooms, classrooms were partitioned to make another, new windows were installed, new ceilings and boarded walls, old floor taken up and new floors down, plastering, painting, dad's creative workstations, cloakrooms, shelving, sink unit areas, painting, new lighting, Wi-Fi cabling, interactive white boards and so on.

All corridors were no longer called corridors; they were teaching spaces.

All resource rooms were strategically placed but relevant to the key stage teaching areas to enable efficiency and effectiveness and we utilised all dead-end spaces.

Early years was totally redesigned to have three classes knocked into one with only slight partitioning in areas to allow for free flow, communication, numeracy and creative curricular work with the most amazing full stage in the middle.

Yes, once again, the stage was designed, built and creatively painted by my wonderful parents, this was a wow factor and still is for our pupils, role play galore!

All this took place seven days a week and while the school was still open during the school week. I have always planned how I can safely have projects done whilst school is open for business and with careful planning you can achieve anything with a professional team. This way of working has saved hundreds of thousands of pounds over the years, enabling us to afford and have the environment we wanted. You see, all contractors are usually booked by schools for the holidays and contractors know this is their lucrative time. You can never negotiate a good deal for school holidays, contractors will hike up the prices and to be fair so would I if I was them. Contractors respected my Arthur Daley gene and of course when they could do my work in school time for us they could ensure other business elsewhere in holiday periods. Consequently, they had more and more business and I had great prices, so, win, win for everyone. If I had the slightest sniff of anyone getting greedy or cutting corners, they were finished at Dorrington, fortunately, that happened only twice.

Lesson

- Try and plan to have work done by contractors at their less busy times of the year; it will be cheaper by a substantial amount.
- Meticulous planning and constant monitoring of progress alongside effective communication is vital with any build.
- Sometimes you have to bite the bullet and get a job done, even if it costs a bit more, this is usually governed by health and safety factors.
- Never cut corners.
- If you cause inconvenience to others, apologise for actions and try not to repeat.

Everything was strategically going to plan, the community were excited, well most. As the saying goes, it is great when you have a plan until you are punched in the face. Not literally a sock in the face but my plan was hindered when a member of staff decided to flex her muscles in the most unnecessary way.

Her unhappiness with plans for her redeployment may have played a key part in what happened next but who knows for sure. Not wanting change became masked behind her accusations of many things, including neglect of asbestos, which was exceptionally disappointing as great care had been taken with health and safety, especially asbestos checks with the council. The contractors and leadership had read every report regarding asbestos produced by the council for the school and much care had been taken with such a serious matter. Despite all health and safety being adhered to, the member of staff wanted to open a hornets' nest as she was obviously aggrieved.

And so, with the support of several trade unions, they soon endeavoured to remove me and other leaders from the school. It was an awful time but one you learn from.

Up until this time, many staff had decided to leave for various reasons, some due to capability issues and the change underway.

And so, for sure, my honeymoon period with trade unions was long gone.

Like I have mentioned previously, trade unions have their job to do and so did I.

There had been mutual respect of sorts to this date but over the next two years that evaporated. I remember one encounter involving a union rep, who had waited for his day with me, from the days of my first headship and his day finally came.

As I observed his entrance, I could not help noticing he was excited with anticipation of getting things well and truly off his chest and he certainly did.

Sitting opposite me, smugly across the table he posed a question far too early to be of any help to his member, "So where are your high boots then and your w**p?" he chortled.

Flabbergasted, I calmly asked him to leave and he did. The poor member of staff was equally stunned as me. As for the HR rep, I never bothered to use her again.

There are limits to what I will put up with, no matter what tactics people play.

Yes, I have had over my life, what I call many a 'f**k it boots' moment, as I am sure many of us have. I ask you how many times have you walked past a shoe shop, stopped in your tracks, looked at those boots and said 'I must have those, but I cannot afford them, I shouldn't' and then after minutes of deliberation and drooling, you say 'f**k it' I am having them anyway.' They are purchased and without further ado they are in the bag.

So, boots yes, I have purchased many a pair, but never a w**p, simply not my style, that you must appreciate 'just simply would not do.' Standards must be maintained. Boots are lovely and yes, I have a variety for many landscapes, weather and occasions.

During another meeting with the trade unions, a union rep howled with laughter with his member, who I had never met before because she had been off with stress from the days of my predecessor. The member seemed more concerned with throwing insults. She threw a cracker as she sat down, "How strange, you are definitely not as attractive as some suggest," she sneered. This was probably her only accurate point from that meeting.

There is a professional way to deal with trade unions and I made it a priority to source all my own HR and solicitors. Most have now been with me for years, they have been essential and worth every penny. Sometimes you have to pay for the best, it pays in the long run, both in time, money and outcomes. The height of professionalism is important in this domain and expertise is vital.

Importantly, you also need the right governors with the right skill sets on the right committees. This is so totally fundamental to the overall leadership and management of any school, especially for discipline and capability cases involving trade unions. Most importantly, if you recall I have an eye for detail and detail is key when dealing with any disciplinary or capability procedure. I train all my leadership to have a book with them at all times and note conversations including actions with time and date for any school matter, this is essential, no 'ifs or buts.' They have all learned over time how they could not do without them. No matter how good your memory is, you simply have got to be accurate and, with the best will in the world, you will not remember everything as you are so busy. I guarantee it is the detail you have forgotten that you will always need, so the rule of thumb is record everything down as it is all in the detail. This eye for detail was exceptionally important as the school faced a huge tribunal, followed by another back to back.

Without doubt, it was gruelling. You learn a lot about people, yourself, systems and technicalities. If the people involved with them are honest, they would admit it is not pleasant for anyone, except maybe for the person off the streets, who sits in the tribunal room to kill an hour or two, or to simply keep out of the cold.

Overall, I think it is sad for all involved, except for legal teams and unions who do it day in and day out. For them, it is simply an aspect of their job. All I will say, staff came out of the woodwork that had left unhappy and still some within. It was unpleasant, exceptionally hard work, but with a team committed to the process, you go through the procedure and come out the other end.

Whatever the final outcomes are, tribunals are not something you should ever wish to have to go through, but when you have a job to do you have no choice but to simply do your job.

It is expected and that may involve a tribunal or two. If you do, take on board what a barrister told me one day, "Tell the truth and the doors keep opening, don't and they will firmly shut." This piece of advice I have never forgotten. Furthermore, it is important to take care of your health and those supporting you. Tribunals take their toll on many people including family, I imagine irrespective of whatever side of the court you are on.

I needed my inner strength at this time. It does get personal for heads or any leader at tribunals, you have to expect that, but you do learn from every experience and you do move on.

Thank you to all the legal teams.

Lesson

As a leader, if you find yourself in a tribunal follow **advice**, procedure and be supported. Pick yourself up and move on.

- Never ever conduct meetings on your own, always, always have somebody with you and take minutes and get them signed by all parties. This is time consuming but exceptionally important and imperative to success.
- Follow advice.
- Have an Eye for Detail.
- Have a daily book to record instructions, actions and conversations with the time and date.

- Follow procedures.
- Build up your own legal team from the beginning of your headship for day to day advice and much more. You will always need them, even if it is checking what looks like a simple document or procedure, just check before you do.
- If you are never sure of what to do in any aspect of your work, simply do not do anything before you seek advice first.
- If you are asked something by pupils, staff, parents or members of the wider community and you are not sure how to answer, just inform them that you will have to come back to them on that. Then find out and take advice.
- During a tribunal process, you should hold on to many things, especially the decisions you make. Your actions are always ultimately for the good of the pupils and the future of the school/academy.
- Even though one party wins at tribunal, I am not sure anyone does really, but you must do your job, you are accountable to governors and the school/academy you lead.

Moving on from this, I was tired, but my vigour was soon renewed.

The contractors had all loyally carried on with their work, probably even better than before, as I think the beat of the drum had informed them of the challenges we had been facing. Always remember contractors can be very astute, never to be underestimated and very caring when you have a working relationship built on respect.

And so, tribunals over, the classrooms were finished and the new build was also completed at virtually the same time.

During this demanding time, we also put an application forward to be one of the first schools to become a standalone academy, one of Mr Gove's initiatives. We were a leadership and management team always 'thinking outside the box', and an academy standalone status would potentially enable us to think out of the box on a larger scale, enabling more creative opportunities to give our community the best in all dimensions. And it certainly did.

The day I received the keys to the new building and it was signed off was also the day we were no longer under the powers of the Local Authority.

We were awarded a standalone academy status and it felt great.

I did however, receive a phone call from the council saying, "Maybe I would lie low for a while if I was you," he was referring to us having a new build and then becoming an academy away from their grips of power. I took heed of this for about a week, as there was too much to do. But at the end of the day, we were now an academy and we served a community that would still benefit the council in the long run. It is a pity they have never felt the same.

Becoming a standalone academy involved a lot of administration. Without doubt, I could not have done this without my PA/senior office manager at the time. Although we parted ways without further Christmas cards, I will always be grateful for her invaluable contribution to that process, it was a real team effort.

We just knew to achieve our vision it was the right move for us and we were very grateful to the council for our build. Timing was important for the academy's success and now we needed to just embed practices and breathe before we embarked on the next stages of development.

We also took time to celebrate our journey so far as a whole community. The new autonomy that comes with being a stand-alone academy, the opportunities to think out of the box and be even more creative in all aspects of running and progressing a school excited us all, well nearly all.

All progress was advancing, we were making a difference and busy revisiting our strategic plan to develop our next progressive stages of development.

All good, I thought, proud of how far we had come together and then the most awful
bombshell was dropped at my door.

Somebody I trusted, did the unthinkable and as a consequence the SATs papers were annulled. This type of behaviour has happened at other schools and is simply awful.

It was an unbelievable shock. We had one of the most highly-performing Year 6 ever and they had no results to show for their hard work and achievements. Yes, we had robust teacher assessments but it was not the same.
I was almost broken and I definitely needed family, friends, governors and staff to help me through this awful, awful time. If you google me, I have no doubts you will see a couple of articles that are negative. Again, that is life, news is news and often in society the focus is on the bad news. You have to accept that. Even though many newspapers are tomorrows 'fish and chip paper,' for those that it affects, it hurts.'

My inner strength and support were required here, all the hard-progressive work over many years felt snatched away by someone overnight, it can happen.

My focus was to deal with it head on for our pupils, staff, parents, governors and community. So rather than hide away, I immediately invited the community in to see the governors and me. Oh, and the press came too – uninvited.

I remember sitting at the front of the hall, aware it was full of angry parents wanting answers. Asking the chair to sit, I felt it was only right to stand and take it on the chin, I was the headteacher and the community wanted answers.

Legally, I could not answer some explicit questions as it was inappropriate. But I stood firm and reassured the community we would continue with our journey. Bruised and battered for sure, but I believed we could learn from this terrible time and work harder and be stronger than ever for all in the community.

I believe we can often learn more from challenging times compared to when things run smoothly.

It took time to rebuild the trust and move forward again but as a community we did it. Do not underestimate that you can be scarred by such terrible things as this because you do not ever quite trust the same and that is accepted. Please do not be mistaken, the pain went so deep.

We recovered slowly. Yes, the wheel paused, with such a major mechanical breakdown it needed time to repair and as a community we all had a part to play in repairing it, that was respected and we did it.

We all picked ourselves up, brushed ourselves down and put the shoulder to the wheel. Everyone was even more determined than ever to move onwards and upwards to our vision. So, the plane took off again.

Back on course to our chosen destination, passports were checked, yes the right passengers were on board, with a few new ones and I took my usual pilot seat and we were off. Maybe a bit later than scheduled due to the thunderstorm but back on course nevertheless. Too many passengers were enjoying the trip and they were looking forward to their journey, they had earned it and sunning themselves in a bright, warm destination appealed even more.

Lesson

- You cannot always prepare for the unknown event no matter how rigorous you are with procedures and policy.
- It is how you pick yourself up and deal with it which determines future successes.
- Allow yourself time to grieve when unknown events occur that affect you. You are human and support is vital.
- Be optimistic that there are many, many good people in this world.
- Be prepared for the journalist who will always get that story. Take legal advice at all times, the less said the better, as often everything you say is open to interpretation and the truth often is distorted to sell the story. As we all know, this is not helpful, so, the less you say the better.
- Legal advice is a must.

The Journey Continued

For the next stage to work effectively, the day to day structure was organised similar to that of a secondary school. For this to be successful, the investment in staff has been very significant. Running the academy like a secondary school with approximately 700 pupils and employing 100 staff required the recruitment of even more staff with varying skills, knowledge and abilities.

Pupils have a form teacher and then a variety of teachers throughout the day teaching to ability and specialisms. Pupils are used to having different teachers from reception, so transition between year groups is always smooth. The pupils are simply used to movement around the schools and no set teacher, it works extremely well.

This expansion allowed for more developments in the learning environment and even more smaller group teaching areas and specialist teaching for the entire curriculum. We developed the outside learning area; it is a marvellous development, exciting and the children have always loved it.

This learning area had a massive impact on all core subjects, as well as cross curricular learning and the development of the whole child. Key to its success has been down to having the right staff teaching in it and they are teaching assistants who have become higher learning teaching assistants. They have had extensive professional development and are extremely highly skilled.

These fabulous staff, Clare and Helen, were trained, skilled and qualified to teach in the outside forest school.

They go out in all weathers, no moans, well maybe the odd one. I simply do not know how they do it in some conditions. The bottom line is they both have a great work ethic and know the children love it and without fail they want that to always be respected.

Both were involved in its development. We had everything from pizza cooking domes, to pit fires, to ponds, to tree houses, different terrains and plantations and a science room. It also facilitates the most amazing Christmas grotto each year. The pupils queue in anticipation every year, parents wonder what the theme will be and all are struck with wonder and awe. This has been extended over the years and another outside classroom has been constructed.

The latest addition is a new 'Alan Titchmarsh kitchen' so pupils can cook the produce they grow. The outside learning environment has been built to accommodate all curriculum teaching initiatives and they are endless.

The sports pitch was completed, this was challenging, especially as the school playgrounds had a steep gradient but with careful planning it was achieved. The academy truly celebrates the importance of sport provision for our pupils.

This led to the recruitment of a secondary PE specialist, and partnerships with another plus an extremely important man. He is heavily involved in sport for the community; opening doors for all children, especially those who have needed the outlet sport gives them. In addition, he is eyes and ears in the community and has always kept me informed of matters that may result in more initiatives for our pupils.

Outside partnerships and expertise have been vital to our progression, we have nurtured partnerships over the years and these sporting ones have proved totally invaluable. Again, we would never have reached outstanding without them.

We now have children as sport leaders, who train other children not only in our school but other schools. The initiative has been so successful over the years it has been acknowledged with many awards. Investment in sports leaders has been a key factor in increasing the love of sport amongst our pupils. Pupils, who have needed an outlet, have had tailor made sport activities to target a variety of needs, which consequently has enabled them to build confidence and to demonstrate this within the classroom when learning core subjects, resulting in more overall progress for them. Participation in sport whatever their ability has helped all pupils believe and have confidence in themselves and apply it to many other things. Such initiatives have been crucial to the development of the whole child and when they leave the academy gates they are ready to move on and have confidence in how unique and special they are.

In addition to sport, we really believe in the creative arts.

To facilitate both over the years we built a new dining hall and sports hall to accommodate all the activities on offer. We modernised the existing hall to have a state-of-the-art sport facility, with full indoor sports pitch, sprung floor and the most amazing climbing wall. The climbing wall was built by a company who had worked for Bear Grylls, it is absolutely incredible. Staff were trained to teach the children climbing activities, twelve in total, including me. When I recall my training, I was partnered with Glen. All 6ft 4 of him, really! I survived, so did he, and we all had much laughter and slight discomfort as we trained.

The construction of a new dining hall was an achievement.
When I had arrived initially at the school, the kitchen consisted
of three hot ovens, a curtain and a sink.

In the early days, we built a small kitchen and now that the
main site teaching facilities construction was completed, it was
the right time to build a purpose-built dining hall, with a proper
kitchen.

The new dining hall was designed for multipurpose use, for both
the children and wider community. The kitchen staff have been
loved over the years and are very much part of our community.
The build of the dining hall was challenging for many reasons,
but we had expertise regarding architects and engineers and
this paid dividends when the contractor kept disappearing to
Benidorm.

We got there in the end, a wonderful resource and timetabled
for so many things. So, we now had two halls, facilitating sport,
the arts and community events. Teaching assistants, higher
teaching assistants (HLTAs), teachers and senior leadership took
up the challenge of training to specialise in trampolining, rock
climbing, well-being and sports leaders training. These required
commitment from all involved.

The trampolining involved one HLTA going off to various parts of
the country followed by exams and assessments and now the
trampolining coaching is absolutely brilliant, the pupils love it.

Many years ago, staff, children and parents were timetabled to
go to a yoga studio in the local area, for their health and
wellbeing. Everyone loved it. So, when the owner said she was

closing, we built our own studio on the academy premises which was opened seven days a week and run by the same yoga teacher.

It was loved by all of the community. So, when the yoga teacher moved on, we invested in training one of our own staff and so the yoga room is still a height of activity, as popular as ever. Staff dedication has enabled for this community yoga room to continue, it is respected and loved by so many in our academy's community.

As part of our strategic plan, we continually train staff. All newly qualified teachers (ECTs) readily take on the spirit we require when it comes to embracing continuous professional development. They are encouraged to take on additional training and this ensures continuity for the future.

Key partnerships with experts have helped us implement an outstanding sport and wellbeing curriculum. Their passion has never faltered for our sport provision without their commitment and expertise learning opportunities could not have been maximised.

The outstanding outcomes of these initiatives has enabled us to open the doors to other schools who do not have such facilities. Interestingly, despite contacting numerous schools, emphasising how we will accommodate their pupils and our staff would teach without any charge to them, sadly there has been little uptake. However, those that have love it. I recall one boy, from a school who had severe hearing and visual impairments, on the climbing wall, then on the huge trampoline and upside down in the hammocks in the yoga room. It came to the end of the afternoon session and he simply said "This has been the best day of my life." This visiting school, I know were so grateful and it really felt good to help, we were also grateful.

Thank you, Glen, the kitchen staff and all the staff involved in all these developments and initiatives. But special thanks to Jo, a member of the Dorrington family for years, an expert in PE and an instrumental governor of our academy. She committed herself to the academy's vision. She unselfishly trained so many of our pupils as playleaders, as well as staff, to have confidence in teaching PE. Her expertise was invaluable to us all. Sadly, Jo recently passed away, far too young to leave us and we already miss her. Thank you, Jo.

Lesson

- Have the courage to grasp new opportunities to enable thinking out of the box and train staff.
- Develop higher level teaching assistants.
- Encourage partnerships with specialists, they have skills maybe you will never have.
- Sport and outside teaching positively impacts on a child's learning and overall achievements.
- Arrange timetables for such activities to start before school, your punctuality issues, if any, become less of a problem. Children want to be in and having their turn, they love it.
- Do not ask anyone to do things you are not prepared to try yourself, lead by example.
- Always take time to value 'ALL STAFF,' irrespective of their position.
- Everyone has a fundamental part in the wheel that determines whether the wheel turns at all and how it does.

- If the wheel becomes dysfunctional, a spiral downwards defect will occur. There have been times at Dorrington when the wheel needed a spray of oil or a small mechanical hiccup needed fixing but the wheel was constantly maintained and upgraded when necessary. So, always keep it moving at the appropriate pace and direction, never backwards, only forwards.
- Keep developing the environment to open further learning opportunities.

Technology Hub

We constantly continued to achieve our vision and so we built a new technology hub with multi-purpose use for the present and future.

This facilitated even more opportunities for further small group teaching and that was very much in mind with the design. Constant assessment and tracking enabled us to pick pupils who needed help with different concepts in all subjects and the hub teaching space provided this.

Without doubt, our ever-growing teaching spaces and staff drove personalisation in pupils' learning as a consequence, these increased standards of achievement. Teaching has been tailor made for the uniqueness of the child. Technology is key now to our future initiatives. So, we have invested greatly in it.

The hub has its own suite, specialised VR room, radio station and one of our most recent developments is a state-of-the-art library, with an accomplished librarian. The whole hub is geared to support the curriculum.

Most importantly, it is fundamental to our latest huge commitment to independent learning to support our 'Know More, Remember More' agenda. This agenda involves every child having a personalised learning file for all subjects, allowing them to recall, test and expand their knowledge, all within 'The Hub'.

This work is exciting and ongoing and will always be.

Further developments will be mentioned in the 'next steps' chapter.

Staff training underpins any initiative's success. As already mentioned, we have invested in a tremendous amount of continuous professional development (CPD) starting with early years, as this is such a significant time in a child's learning and then so forth.

All CPD is in alignment with all initiatives, in a very well-planned, systematic way. We have always continued to train within the premises, buying in expertise, ensuring all training is tailor made and specific to our environment, staff and pupils.

All teaching assistants are continually trained alongside teachers in all aspects of teaching and learning. We constantly assess and tap into learning new skills on a wider scale in the third objective in all staff's performance management.

In addition to what I have mentioned already, twelve staff were coached to become counsellors, one TA is now fully qualified to teach aerial yoga in our purpose-built yoga room. Three TAs have been sponsored by the academy and are now successful teachers and our deputies are fully qualified 'Team Teach' instructors, which makes training for all staff in safe pupil handling far more cost effective.

We have trained many learning mentors and five teachers have been to university to become qualified SENDCOs. We have had a worry clinic for the pupils for years and they use it if they have a worry or just need someone to talk to.

This department is integral to the academy meeting every child's needs, irrespective of what, who, how many. What the pupils need, we endeavour to deliver.

We constantly fund training in such a variety of things to widen the opportunities to develop the whole child.

ECTs, we have recruited probably about 60, who were intensively trained. Some immediately go into management and have leadership training, others specialise in areas particular to their interests and others have extra training to become outstanding teachers.

All middle leaders have achieved National Leadership Qualifications and are heads of departments. Senior leaders have all completed the National Professional Qualification for Headship and are set to advance in their careers when it suits them. Office staff are included, they are training at university to be counsellors and bursars. I have spent six years training to be a clinical aromatherapist and reiki practitioner and I am heavily involved in wellbeing at the school.

All training is geared to the children, if your staff are highly skilled, supported and happy, there is a good chance the children will be and they are. All staff are supported to realise their talents and that is a passion of mine, always has been, always will be.

Lesson

- Think outside the box.
- Constantly search and invest in the talent within your own staff, it always surprises.
- Embrace the personalisation of pupils and staff.
- Have a systematic, aligned process of working.
- Invest in technology for the future.
- Think strategically about leadership succession in all departments, every member of staff is a leader in some capacity.
- Plan for pupil's independent learning, it will be key to future ways of learning.

The Curriculum

The curriculum is constantly revised and adapted as the learning environment continues to develop. One particular year, we revisited the curriculum provision again. The senior management led by myself spent twelve months totally overhauling every aspect of it. It was time to have a curriculum that was designed to fully enable our vision. The entire curriculum for each year group is built around a book, different for each half term and for each year group. It was a colossal undertaking. Many hours, days and months was spent developing it.

We had many exhausting professional discussions, especially over the choice of books. Compromise took on a whole new meaning, as we all had favoured books. Everything is now planned cross curricular from the one book. It has been an essential key to achieving higher standards and it works. We update it regularly, especially when we audit pupils' progress and assess any new curriculum requirements. We were actually filmed through the process and its outcomes.

Lesson

- Sometimes a fair amount of time needs to be dedicated to a major initiative that is central to success.
- When the going gets tough and you have to revisit an idea that is just not quite right, keep going.
- You have to compromise at times for the right outcome.
- Constantly review and update when necessary but do not reinvent the wheel if something is working.

The Shows
Over the years, creative arts have been integral in our curriculum, they are extremely important in the academy. We invest time and money in it. It is one of our outstanding developments and believe me, the entire community loves it.

We have done many shows and each build on the previous best. They get bigger and better.

We started off by having a show once a year but due to the investment now required we do them every two years. When one show finishes, people want to reserve their tickets for the next one. The children without fail check for the audition dates. I lead the shows and it is great for me. As heads we are so busy, but this gives me an opportunity to enjoy working with pupils, it is crucial to know your pupils and for them to know you.

Over the years, I have had the opportunity to be trained by one of the best choreographers in my opinion, Audrey Styler.

Audrey was part of the 'Betty Fox Dancing Teenagers' many years ago.

She has done fabulous choreography work all over including TV, for example 'Let's Celebrate' and 'Songs of Sunday'. Audrey is respected and admired by her peers and fellow professionals. I have been extremely lucky over my entire teaching career to have had training and guidance from her. She has certainly put me through my paces over the years. In my early teaching career, I was a total novice at putting on a show with pupils, Audrey taught me, helped me choreograph shows and gave me great ideas.

Anything less than fantastic for Audrey, 'Would simply not do!' Many times, through some of her demanding routines, I have wanted to throw the towel in but Audrey has a way to motivate you to keep going and the odd tap of her walking stick helped too.

Without doubt, Audrey gave me the confidence to put on shows over the years and, like I have already mentioned, it pays to learn from an expert if you can find them. She has also offered words of wisdom. I might not have taken them all on board but she was an expert for sure and now I may say an invaluable friend. I was so lucky I found Audrey; the wise, experienced expert.

Thank you Aud.

Without doubt, the shows have taken on new heights of expectations. We are lucky to have two members of staff, exceptionally talented at writing our scripts for these shows plus the annual staff panto, obviously with inputs from me of course. Yes, I am probably a pain but I always interfere on this.

Sorry, Dave and Helen.

Once the script is completed, the auditions start, we now have approximately 145 pupils from Key Stage 2 regularly in the shows.

All pupils across the whole academy are involved in 'Showtime' even if it is not the performance itself. We link the show to all aspects of the curriculum and a display for the show is something to be celebrated by the whole community. This is a whole academy team effort; all staff are involved and many parents, plus contractors of course!

Staff give up so much time before the school day, lunchtimes and after school helping pupils with their lines both singing and acting parts. Contractors build the sets and many make costumes galore. Parents are wonderful help too. Very often the parents, who are normally maybe a bit too reserved to come in, come to help.

The shows certainly break down any remaining barriers in our whole community, everybody just loves them. I have another team who helps me put the show together.

Make no mistakes, we go through different pain barriers, there are many interesting discussions, disagreements but absolutely plenty of laughter.

I always hit the Bull Ring with my team and they expect us; 'Is it showtime again?' they chant, as we order everything from fabric, to Peaky Blinders caps, to beds.

We have great prop companies and people over the years have built helicopters, elephants, you name it, we have probably either made it ourselves or others have. As an added bonus, many donate for free, especially if we promote their company in some way. Remember Arthur Daley can always do that! After every show, all props are recycled to support the curriculum in some way. The boys love sitting in the helicopter to read. We hire the same sound company every time, they are brilliant. They are always booked up for festivals such as Glastonbury, so we always, as one show ends, book them for two years time. The sound team moves into the academy two weeks prior to the show and stays until we clear up.

Their expertise is unbelievable. They put up with me and I must confess I am probably very challenging. I probably go over the top, just a little, aiming for perfection at all costs. But if you are going to do something, then I believe in going the extra mile to do it right. I blame Audrey.

My team is required to be in the show in some capacity, plus a few others. Now you must remember, heads must lead by example, so yes, I have a role too, mmm I hear you say. One memorable time was when the team did a 'celebrity take' in part of a show.

The team did a video for this aspect of the show. We had ordered favoured famous celebrity cardboard cutouts from the 'Rock' to 'Marilyn Monroe' to of course the king himself, 'Elvis'. Armed with our cardboard cutouts, we clambered on to an open top lorry for our arrival. Yes, you have probably guessed that a contractor helped us for free and let us just say the pupils appreciated the sketch and we had a good laugh too. It was very interesting what I found out about my team during that show. I believe leaders must always look for the opportunity of a nugget and these shows give amazing insights to staff's hidden talents and so potentially more skills are continually uncovered.

Feedback from the parents is always encouraging, many often say, 'It is our own night at the West End with our children in it.'

Pupils simply grow through the shows. Some, who have had main parts, have had severe learning difficulties and taking part simply changes them in the most wonderful ways forever. Hard work, sweat and late nights are worth it just for that alone!

We strive to develop the whole child and the shows are an integral part of this vision. They bring the community together and so long may they continue.

Lessons

- Enjoy working with the children when you can as a head.
- Have shows, the learning opportunities are endless.
- Source your experts.
- Try and ask for things for free, you may be surprised.
- Get the whole community involved.
- Have fun and celebrate how great being a head can be.

Health and Wellbeing

This has always been important at the academy. Apart from the well-being curriculum filtering through the curriculum, we have rooms specifically for wellbeing courses and lessons for all. When the caretaker took retirement and moved out of his house, we redesigned the house and gardens and totally modernised it for multi-purpose use. The pupils named it 'The Manor',

It is used for all our 'passport to life curriculum' for the pupils. They learn so many skills in the house including cookery classes and gardening. We have community activities, training, interviews and a wellbeing room. Our recent initiative in the house is the creation of 'Dorrington's bookshop'. The book shop is similar to St. Giles Bookshop. We open several times a week for parents to have coffee, buy books and catch up. If the parents return a book, they get 50 pence off their next book, all books are under £2.00.

One of the main activities held in the house is our wellbeing special weeks for staff and children. Once a term we hold these, and it is appreciated. I am a firm believer that if staff are looked after, they are happy and as I have said previously, if staff are happy, then there is a good chance pupils will be too.

We deliver numerous courses for parents, especially concerning healthy eating. As part of our wellbeing programme, we hold a 'Fun and Fit Week' every year for the community. In addition, we hire Alexander Stadium once a year for our sports day, the parents are in training most of the year for their races and they are so fast. It is always a special day.

Covid

During Covid, everyone in the country was affected regarding their health and wellbeing. We tried our best to look after staff during this time. Everyone played their part helping not only key worker children but all our children in the academy.

One effort we made was buying test kits in the early days for staff to help ascertain if they had Covid. These were appropriately approved. Sometimes when you are thinking you are helping, you can guarantee maybe not everyone wants it.

One member of staff accepted the help, but then chose to contact her unions about it. Before I knew it, the unions knocked at the door again, they did not like what we were doing. They wrote an article about it for their members. All I will say was this article proved to be totally unjustified and the events it portrayed were inaccurate. The Public Health Department contacted me for an explanation and they were more than happy with our procedures. In fact, rumour has it we may have been instrumental in encouraging the roll out of test kits to schools later in the year.

Someone else reported we washed the entire academy daily with vinegar. A health and safety executive came out; we were awarded 5 stars, no issues anywhere.

Despite this, staff were very grateful for how their well-being was cared for and thanked leadership, including Governors, for its support during the dreadful time of Covid.

Staff worked so hard with virtual learning every day and a rota for key worker children.
My management and I worked everyday at the academy, we had to lead by example, especially at this anxious time for so many.

We were a community working together and as a head it made me proud, 'together we were stronger.'

The children returning to the academy after Covid were offered the opportunity to take part in our catch-up programmes.

One specific initiative was aimed for all children but with special regard for children who had become what we term 'the invisible child'. The child just hovering underneath the radar that you really have to look for and we were very mindful how we could potentially have many as a consequence of Covid.

I was so concerned by this prospect that I found myself, early hours, one morning in a yard even Selwyn Froggatt would have been proud of. My deputies and myself travelled up north to meet Mike. I had discovered Mike sold most things, including tanks to Zimbabwe. What interested me was his American yellow bluebird bus. I had also investigated a company further north who converted a bus for a charity into the highest spec sensory bus. And so, the idea was set in motion. This was an exciting development.

Mike sold me the bus for an exceptionally cheap price. Ultimately, the bus would be stationary at a spot I had allocated by the special needs department. However, before it could be parked for good, it had to have several trips up and down the M6.

First trip, we stripped out all the seats. Second trip, we insulated the windows. Third trip, up to Warrington to be fitted out with the most amazing equipment. Final trip, back to us.

Mike, free of charge, did every trip, what a great man. I believe each trip needed an MOT for the journey! A team of experts made everything work on site. The technology and equipment are so fantastic and it is linked to all aspects of the curriculum.

All I can say is WOW, the children wait with excitement for their turn, it is fully timetabled.

Impact - the 'invisible children' aren't invisible anymore.

Lesson

- Wellbeing is essential for all.
- Look after your staff.
- If you are going through a challenging time, keep going.
- Never worry about action but only about inaction.
- Always adhere to health and safety.
- The way to restart after a crisis, is to quit talking and begin doing.
- Always look carefully for anyone just hiding under the general radar, they might be good at it. So, it is important to look out carefully for everyone and their welfare.

Community Events

They are important at the academy.

Over the years, we have done cultural evenings, sports events, focus weeks, fusion days and endless fairs. One event I will never forget was our Fusion week.

This was a celebration of diversity, different cultures and total fusion across the curriculum. We hired a country and western band. Canopies up with sand bags strategically keeping them in place and stalls were all set with absolutely everything the children had made to sell over the previous three months. The truck arrived with bales and bales of hay. The band arrived and set up outside. They were playing away, keeping all the staff happy, whilst we put the finishing touches to our food market.

We were all set to go and suddenly the weather changed, almost instantly, it was like a tornado. The canopies went up and I ended up headfirst in a bale of hay.

Talk about teamwork. It was not funny really but I think the staff were entertained by my new scarecrow look and together we somehow transferred everything into the hall except the band. Hilarious, the band just played and played and everybody just danced and danced. Everyone just had a great time.

One member of staff danced to exhaustion, so much so she tore her tendon and had to have three weeks off! Obviously, she keeps asking when can we have another one! We never used the canopies outside again for such a big event.

Parental Involvement
We have built up over the years parental involvement as barriers have been broken down.
We have done many courses for them. The parent's homework classes have a good impact. This involves year group leads teaching parents the concepts needed to help them assist the children at home. We have weeks assigned where parents are timetabled to spend a full day looking through their children's books and working with their year group teachers to understand their child's work, marking and assessments. This is informal and relaxed with refreshments and cakes on the go throughout the day. Leadership including governors are there throughout the whole week. Parents really enjoy the opportunity for quality time understanding their child's progress and how it all works.

They are fully informed through this initiative of their child's next steps in learning. In addition, parents are involved with strategic planning by attending evenings where they have worked with leadership in the hall looking at what is working, what are the next steps and importantly what they want as the next steps too.

We have many initiatives and part of our endeavours to be more accessible and effective with parents has come about with the massive overhaul of our front of house. Communication and ease of access has been key. We have built a new reception, parent meeting room and invested in completely new software for everything to be done online, from payments, to information updates, to registering for clubs, trips and much more. All software and data has been aligned and now our efficiency and effectiveness of resources is maximised.

This has been exceptionally effective and our front of house is welcoming through the new phone system and of course those that still want a face to face service. This overhaul has taken a good year.

The parents enjoy many community events but I do not think they would forgive me if the Christmas market did not take place.

People come from all over for the Christmas markets; they have a reputation for being special. We plan for them from September but collect things throughout the year. Yes, I hit the markets in September, the traders expect me. Mom does not bother with a trolley, we have a truck strategically parked so we can get the toys, games and anything we think the community will want in it without too much trouble. The toy juggernaut is always crowded.

Over the years, we have got it sussed. We go very, very early and do our negotiations before really the market officially opens. The tombola is something to make the eyes water; the queues are endless for the two nights, we do auctions, have preloved stalls, games, Father Christmas' grotto and food. And of course, the fun fair. ECTs are always our elves and that is compulsory. The children vote each year for the raffle prizes they want and the event is always a success. None of our community events are for profit. We always just aim to break even. These are simply community events to have fun together and they are loved. So many community events, too many to mention.

When you open up your doors to the wider community, security goes to another level. Risk assessments are a must have to ensure the day to day safety for pupils and community. At any events we put on, safety is always a number one priority. As a consequence of so many events throughout the year, we have continually upgraded security and safety systems. I believe we were one of the first schools to introduce lockdown systems, about 10 years ago.

Initially, some heads were slightly perturbed when I introduced this. However, security for the children and staff is essential. I have great electricians who carried out the work. All areas have a blue light and one key. If the light flashes, staff simply lock the doors, several centralised activating buttons enable this with one push of a button. All rooms have a phone to communicate with 'front of house,' this ease of communication improves efficiency. I certainly sleep easier knowing this is in place. I do believe other establishments have now followed suit. Health and safety is always a first priority. The importance of this has been a constant thread throughout our journey. It is always under review. We have recently added to health and safety measures by having our own 'Team Teach' team. In addition, we ensure a minimum of twelve staff are fully trained in first aid.

Lesson

- With careful planning and team work you can really put on an event well.
- Community is key for breaking down barriers.
- Be careful with canopies outside, the weather might suddenly turn quickly.
- Sometimes the traditional games are the ones most loved.
- Source the bargains.
- Everyone wants a bargain and the occasional win on the tombola.
- Have fun with your community, celebrate them.
- Value your parents.
- Use every opportunity to break down barriers, the progress for pupils will accelerate.
- Do not shy away from letting parents be involved in strategic planning, they will own it with you if they are involved.
- Let parents work with pupils in school as much as practically possible.
- Have fun with your parents. Make them feel they are really part of the community.
- You will never please all parents and that is simply accepted.
- Security is of paramount importance.
- Budget for security.

- Installing security systems is not complicated, unless you make it so.
- As head you are accountable for the community's safety in school, ultimately the buck stops with you.

The Governing Body

Over the years, I have built up teams and surrounded myself with people who have a positive outlook and can make a positive contribution.

This applies very much also to the governing body. We have moved from twenty-two plus when I first arrived, all have been valued for their input and time over the years. As an academy, we now have twelve, all with special skills and experience to fulfil our needs and accountability. It is always important to include governors in as many initiatives as you can.

It is common practice at the academy for governors to be in the academy on a regularly basis. The chair always spends at least a day with staff and the children each half term and follows up with a report. The Chair of Finance and Staffing is in at least every two weeks. The governors are part of the fabric of the academy. I believe it is important to build a relationship with governors that is not only productive from the business aspect of academy life but from a social perspective too.

Our governors are supportive, critical friends but more than that, they are like family to Dorrington. We laugh with each other and at each other, we know each other that well. Importantly, there is trust, even when we disagree, we conclude that we are all content in the end. We have had many challenges through our journey to become outstanding, but for sure many laughs. I recall one evening when a governor came in to one of the meetings, normally a very calm person. This one particular evening he came in all of a fluster, flushed and annoyed. He proceeded to tell us at the ripe old age of seventy-six he had just got a speeding fine, 37 mph in a 30 zone. He went on and on and on, wondering if he would be allowed on one of these driving courses to avoid penalty points on his licence. We all knew he was a careful driver, some of us had experienced his snail pace driving many a time, so we were all amused. Whilst he panted and puffed, another governor stated that she had been on one of these courses. I will never forget how she seriously sat there recalling this course. She said "Honestly, it was a total waste of time, I really don't know why I was there, I mean I said to them it was not my fault someone ended up on my bonnet in Harborne High Street, I certainly have no idea how she got there."

Well, let me just say we all lost it, except the governor agonising over his possible penalty points.

We eventually composed ourselves and carried on with the meeting, all conscious of this governor still upset about his speeding ticket. Then suddenly in the middle of my deputy's presentation, he blurted out, "Isn't it great you can get strawberries all year round." We really did lose it then, totally hilarious.

They are committed, no way could the academy have progressed the way it has without their trust in me and my trust in them. Thank you, governors.

Lesson

- Ensure you have the right skill set of governors on your governing body.
- Beware of governors who have their own agendas, say goodbye to those.
- Involve your governors as much as you can in school life.
- Nurture, train them, keep them updated.
- Respect them, do not waste their skills, expertise and knowledge.
- Have a laugh with them, it definitely helps.

Experts and Partnerships

I have talked many times about experts and those that have had a positive connection to the academy. One person I have not mentioned yet, is Brian, my trusted adviser from the day I became headteacher at Dorrington. He had history with the school before I became head as the adviser. So initially, I think we would both acknowledge the early days were tentative on both parts.

Over the years, the respect for each other has grown to a point where again he is like family. He is exceptionally skilled, qualified and experienced, having in days gone by, been a headteacher, Ofsted inspector and the lead adviser in leadership and management for the authority. Furthermore, he is highly respected by his fellow colleagues and heads. He has challenged me throughout, raised the odd eyebrow and howled with laughter at some of my thinking out of the box ideas, but he has without doubt supported me every step of the way.

It did secretly amuse me recently when he looked as if he had just got off The Big Dipper at Blackpool, after I made him go through the human body on one of our VR headsets.

We share a similar sense of humour and never take offence when our sarcasm pushes the line. Like I said, we now know each other very well and he will be supporting the panel for the appointment of my successor. He knows the academy and understands our next steps to progress even further.

He has been an essential cog in our wheel. I have needed him for sure. We have a mutual respect for each other and I will be forever grateful for his advice, humour and letting me bend his ear too many times to mention. He has not simply just been there, he has encouraged the journey to happen.

Thank you, Brian.

Lesson

- It is important to find the right adviser for you.
- It is important you share similar outlooks, otherwise it will be an unproductive partnership and what is the point of that, a total waste of time.
- Accept advice, listen to it, hear it, but remember you do not necessarily have to always act on it. You are the head and you will decide what is the way forward as at the end of the day, that's your job. Importantly, different perspectives help you make informed choices, so listen, hear it, discuss it and then you decide.
- Your adviser is your adviser so nurture the relationship and make sure you have a few laughs along the way.

Apart from advisers, it is good to build a relationship with at least one other head. I do not really do a lot of networking but it has its place. I have met many heads and I have enjoyed their company but few I have chosen to work with collaboratively, probably in the main because I have been so busy.

We work with a variety of schools for monitoring purposes and that is very important to ensure effective moderation. Working with the consortium is also important. For six years, we did a tremendous amount of work as we were the secretary school for the consortium.

I think my team building ideas pushed them a bit too far so they got tired of us and had a change. But now we are back again, helping to move the consortium forward and so now one of my deputies is the chair of the consortium. I suggested the appointment of having a deputy as chair for future leadership progression and it is working very well. We always need to be open to new ways of working.

One head that I have always respected is Gill Turner. We became heads at a similar time. Our pathways did not cross much in the early days but through consortium we have gotten to know each other and this has enabled us to work in partnership for different types of work, in particular moderation between the two academies.

We have different styles in many ways but the same principles and philosophy regarding headship and what it actually means. We share the strong belief that headship is a privilege, one of the best jobs and the importance of every child actually really matters to us both. Gill is also head of a standalone academy. We attract different types of staff to our academies, which always makes me smile. What works for one, does not necessarily work for the other. It is important to work out as a head what suits your establishment.

But both of us value our staff very much and respect them.

Moving away from the staff to the learning environment, again these are very different and both work effectively. To give you an example, when Gill told me she was having alpacas, I laughed my head off and thought she had lost the plot. How wrong was I, they are loved dearly and not just by Gill.

We celebrate our differences, challenges and successes. Without doubt, over the years it has been good to discuss, update, share experiences and support each other over a coffee and the odd glass.

As we have become friends over the years, we can also trade a few more insights and laugh plenty too. A friendship and professional expert to be valued for sure.

Thank you, Gill.

Lesson

It is important to find the right fellow head who you can trust and respect. Someone who understands what comes with the territory of being a headteacher irrespective of differences.

Collaboration

A thread that has permeated throughout this book is the importance of how I have invited passengers to board the plane who make a positive contribution to the journey. Managing people is one of the most challenging aspects of leadership. Collaboration and teamwork is key to success on every level, in all aspects, every step of the way.

Over the years, I have introduced initiatives to embed collaboration at Dorrington. As part of this, I initially introduced the Christmas challenge for staff. Six weeks before the annual Christmas feast on the last day of term, I set the whole staff 'the challenge'.

The challenge involved learning a new skill collaboratively, in teams, over a six-week period.
The staff would present the final outcome in front of the whole staff and judging panel at the end of the year feast. Staff would be asked to pick names out of a hat to establish the makeup of the team. Then, I would announce the task.

This daunted the staff at times but they were amazing. Staff always had amazing fun whilst working collaboratively to learn the new skill and ultimately win the competition and of course the ultimate prize! There have been some absolutely fantastic outcomes and the fun in learning a new skill has simply amazed me every time.

The competitiveness and the secrecy of the teams during those six weeks is quite something to observe. It is taken very seriously; each team wants to win.

The judging panel was always made up of myself, two other members of staff unable to participate and an invited judge with experience in the skill staff had to conquer.

You may think I got off quite lightly, but no!

Some of the tasks over the years have included: baking the wedding cake for a member of staff getting married the day after we broke up for the Christmas break, The X factor, Cirque du Soleil and Strictly Come Dancing.

I will never forget the 'wedding cake' task. The teams not only had to make the cake but produce a video of how they did it together.

The results were simply overwhelming, we were all close to tears when the final cakes were produced simply, utterly breath-taking. The person getting married was overcome with emotion. The next day was a challenge in itself when we had to take all six wedding cakes to Stratford upon Avon for his wedding, in the minibus, in the snow! Now that was a challenge, but worth every wobble of the tiers!

Cirque Du Soleil left me speechless, it was unbelievable. I will never forget when a member of staff, after a whole routine, appeared out of a suitcase ready for the catwalk, just all brilliant.

Strictly come dancing was done slightly differently and staff until this day say it was the best. We decided that particular year to extend the challenge, the whole staff had to learn a whole school dance, videoed for the whole community to see. In addition, they were partnered to perform a dance together in front of all and a special judging panel.

Now, I needed someone special to help with this.

So, I made the call to Audrey. Fortunately, she was free from engagements and agreed to choreograph the whole school dance in six weeks. Every Monday, Audrey would arrive, believe me no one was ever late for her class in the hall.

They really did give blood, sweat and tears. Staff had made every member of staff an amazing costume. When it came to the filming, I can honestly say, the look of pride on all the staff faces at what they had accomplished was simply priceless. Gosh they were proud of themselves and the community just loved it.

On the last day, Audrey arrived with another special choreographer to join the panel to judge the paired dances. What a night, we had our own comperes, Tess and Bruce in those days. Everybody dressed for the occasion.

Just to remind you, I advocate heads must lead by example. So, whilst staff learned their new skill I would spend weeks making an appropriate video to the theme of the task with fellow judges Dave and Dawn. No one, even invited celebrity judges, were privy to this top-secret video. The video launched every finale of the task and staff wondered each year if we would better the previous years, but of course!

Every time we made our video, we had so much fun and many people were so accommodating, letting us use their facilities for filming. We had the Snowdome for free for the Cirque Du Soleil sketch based on the film 'Frozen'. After filming, I must say we collapsed with exhaustion. It was not easy dragging Dave out of the snow fully clothed as Elsa in his wheelchair. We laughed so much and so did the staff.

The Strictly Come Dancing one I must admit was our favourite. We went backstage at the Birmingham Hippodrome and then up very high scaffolding back in the hall. We covered many dances in many costumes. These included us as three John Travoltas, another was based from a scene from a very famous movie in which we did keep our hats on plus much more. This video went down as one of the best. Strictly night, well what a night, true collaboration from everyone and the staff were never the same after that, they were better, and better together.

Teambuilding
Striving to always be progressive, we expanded this form of collaborative working to team building days and weekends. I will always encourage any leader of any establishment to organise these, they are invaluable for enhancing work ethic and a happy collective body of staff.

At Dorrington, every teambuilding activity involves challenge, competition and pushing oneself to have the courage to try new things. Activities differ for every team building trip. I cook throughout except for one night when we have a catered meal for our theme night. I always visit in advance the destination of any team building event to ensure everything is well organised. As I have illustrated to you many times, preparation is key for optimum outcomes.

Our first weekend teambuilding, we hired a large house. It was a competition, simplified to ladies vs gentlemen. The themed evening was 'wigs'. After a full-on day of activities, the atmosphere in the house went to new levels as staff changed for the evening. Much hilarity, as people had made such an effort.

Taking a few extra moments to gather myself after an exhausting day, I finally made my entrance. You see on these weekends, a leader has to join in to embrace the whole concept of teamwork, but of course, I was still very much the pilot.

As I came down the stairs, a male NQTs stood in shock, I am not sure he ever recovered.
I do recall him saying, "She could be a stunt woman for Joan Collins in the film The Stud." If only, but it did make me smile. Marvellous wig though. Everybody simply looked fabulous and we all laughed many times at the memories of our first weekend away together.

Our second venture was a step up, a bargain, two fabulous properties in West Bay. A company had just started this venture and we were their guinea pigs.

The theme for the whole weekend was 'Kings and Queens' and for the Saturday evening, the theme was 'black and white'. I had organised for the only kiosk at West Bay with a licence to host us for the Friday evening. Thirty ladies went as 'Elvis' and fifteen gentlemen went as Her Majesty. The ladies won for sure.

All in costume, we hit West Bay. The owners of the kiosk did the best fish and chips and we all had the most wonderful night with the community. In fact, many of the community followed our competitive activities throughout the weekend and cheered us on.

When we had two speed boats racing each other across the seas, it was the moment I really thought the end is near. I have never in all my life been so scared. I made the mistake of looking over to assess where the other boat was only to witness them actually off the water flying in the air. Well I thought, if they were in the air, then so were we. My bruises, from hanging on for dear life, remained for many months. The black and white theme for the Saturday, well let me just say everyone was easy on the eye. It was just a wonderful weekend. Again, new friends and a happy staff. Being such a large academy, some staff rarely work with each other or know each other and these weekends rectify that, new friendships and respect for each other is a major outcome.

Staff decided on the next weekend, a castle in Scotland.

Wow, you may think, trust me, my Arthur Daley gene never fails much research and the cheapest yet. The theme was 'The Highland Games.'

We travelled by coach overnight and 'my bucket seats' on the way back. No, I was not the pilot this time, thankfully. It will live in all our memories, so many laughs and tears.

I will never forget the night we dressed in costume and the piper piped us in for the traditional haggis. We all glazed over, very emotional. Later, we learned Ceilidh dancing together and simply bonded as a staff.

The staff did laugh as my bucket seat on the way home put me next to the local postman. Let us just say this was a push down the runway aircraft, it did amuse the staff for sure. We reminisce often but each team building weekend made a difference, we really came together more as a staff the collaboration and teamwork simply went to a new level.

We have over recent years just focused on one day events. We all found our team building day at Snowdon, a seat of your pants job. Yes, we all had to do the longest zip wire in Snowdon; yes, the one where you lie down.

At 7.00am, we arrived. I will always remember a scream from a certain member of staff as she looked up and shouted, "They have fallen off." We quickly reminded her, they were only testing the zip wire and actually no one was ever on it.

Now this was a challenge for everyone: staff were pensive and quiet, but we did it. Sitting outside having our lunch, a member of staff said, "I never ever thought I could do it and I just feel yeah, I did!" The main purpose of this activity was to instil in staff the 'I CAN', attitude. It is amazing what we can all do, even when it is out of our comfort zone and this simply was for everyone. Again success.

Teambuilding days have also involved water rafting, all none swimmers took part at the Olympic water rafting centre in London. The second day was in Stratford, the staff were in teams of seven and all had tasks to do. Much to their disgust they had to get back to Birmingham with only £10.00 per team to meet governors for a meal that evening.

The photographic evidence was very entertaining. They arrived to the meal with sunburned red faces, due to it being one of the hottest days in the year. They have not really forgiven me for not having a coach to pick them up. Incidentally, they were very creative on their return journey.

Our latest teambuilding day involved all staff climbing the O2, let us just say I am still recovering.

Lesson

- Never underestimate your staff, they can surprise themselves and you.
- Team building is essential for progressive collaborative working.
- I always say when food is the prize at the end of the day, people make most things happen and they do.
- Team building is essential if a head wants to maximise staffs' potential and working together to make a difference for the children. It also has the added benefit that staff grow in confidence, overcoming their own barriers and belief in themselves. They are stronger for it and will have a go at things in the workplace more readily, they just give it a go with positivity.
- Prepare these team building events well, always do your risk assessments.
- Mix up the teams so staff have the chance to work with staff they have not much contact with within the workplace.
- Negotiate your deals, explain to businesses what you are doing and why. It is amazing how much they will help and the price you can arrange it for.
- As a leader, have fun with your staff, yes, always be a step removed but you can still have fun joining in and being very much part of the team.

- Sometimes in activities, it is positive as a leader to show vulnerability, you are human after all and staff respect you more for facing challenges too.

As we Waited for Ofsted

Over the years, Ofsted came a couple more times and each time the academy was good with many outstanding elements including leadership and management. We were building each year and Ofsted would always encourage our next moves.

One of them acknowledged we were close to outstanding but more development in outside learning for early years would be key. We knew this already but everything had to be done at the right pace and the right time. So outstanding would take a little longer, we recognised, acknowledged and respected it.

And so, after each inspection the academy continued to grow in all respects. We continually embedded practices and creatively thought out of the box for our next steps. Everyone at the academy is always having training to extend opportunities for the community. For example, deputies are now trained plasterers to help pupils learn lifelong skills, we have more mentors and more specialised staff. I finished my training to be a clinical aromatherapist and staff have loved the use of essential oils during wellbeing week. The outside early years department was fully developed.

With the latest new Ofsted framework, the bar was raised again but that was just fine. As a community we felt we were ready, irrespective of its new criteria for outstanding.

Eventually, they came and informed us they would be back within twelve months as we potentially could be outstanding. We prepared and waited. In November 2019, the phone call came and we went through two extremely busy days, no stone was left unturned, not one pebble.

Of course, I wore my lucky p****, I wished my previous assistant head was there but she had retired. She always wore her tatty, old, red shoes for luck, irrespective of her outfit or season. When I phoned her the night before Ofsted was due, she offered to send them by courier but it would not have been the same.

We were ready, although lucky quirks had to be done. We knew we deserved outstanding but knowing and getting it are very different things, as many a leader appreciates. When the HMI announced 'Outstanding,' I sat and felt so overwhelmed. It had been such hard work for many years but worth it.
The inspection team were thrilled for us, they had certainly put us through our paces.
I climbed the huge trampoline to tell the staff, not a pretty sight but who cares. We had achieved the great heights of our vision together and it felt GREAT!

Lesson

- Nothing is impossible if you are determined together.
- See Ofsted as a positive, it helps you to improve practice.
- You will always get the odd inspector who is not your cup of tea but if prepared you can easily deal with this if it occurs.

- We all are accountable and the minute we think we are not, things slip for sure.
- Reflection and constantly adopting the strategic planning process is essential.

Front of House

After the Ofsted, there has been no room for complacency, business as usual, onwards and upwards. You can guarantee change continues and adapting to it is necessary as you will see in the 'Next Steps' chapter.

If you recall, in my psychometric test all those years ago, it stated I would always need a good PA. They were right. Jan, who was my PA for many years, she retired last year.

People often think your deputy is your right hand, but in my case they will not mind me saying they are my left. My PA is my right! Well, they do know from my competitive squash days, I learned to be ambidextrous, so, I am sure they will accept the hand I give them. Jan was my right hand, she has been there through all the trials and tribulations. She encouraged my trailblazing moments and was a pillar of support.

Thank you, Jan.

We now have a new way of working in the front of house. My finance officer Julia has grown in confidence and experience and does an amazing job. Dawn, our new member of staff, keeps us all on our toes and Julie, my PA, now knows the smile I have when I bustle in with another idea and deals with it calmly. They all know the signs and they brace themselves but I will never change and actually they would not want me to - I think!

When people retire or leave for whatever reason people can make the mistake of trying to follow in someone's footsteps but that is a mistake. I believe people should just be themselves.

Importantly, my front of house is my team. A crucial team who I can trust with confidence and you need this team, as it can be a very lonely job being a head. A front of house team like mine keeps you going with a laugh or two along the way. Thank you, Julie, Julia and Dawn.

Lesson

- Know your limitations, acknowledge them and cater for them.
- An effective, accessible front of house for staff, pupils, parents and the wider community is essential. First impressions count and are vital alongside a caring ear when anyone needs it.

Gravy Masterclass

So, to the Next Steps

We have had an extended day for some years now, so, we plan to extend this to two or three.

This is in addition to the vast array of extracurricular activities which take place before school, lunchtimes and after the school day.

We are in a society that is seeing a change in workforce, recruitment and retention. This is a problem now and anticipated long-term for this profession. The possibilities of this eventuality has made me strategically think as a head to plan, implement and develop strategies to see this threat become an opportunity for the profession and our future generations. I believe virtual learning is part of the answer.

With this in mind, we are developing purely virtual teaching spaces. We will be experimenting by teaching virtually two/three times per week then one face to face. Research has shown not only China but America are already doing this successfully. Presently, teachers are recording lessons in all aspects of learning for this. Plans are drawn up, the curriculum and associated assessment methods of outcomes are evolving.

We initially aim to experiment with small groups during the extended day period and go from there. Obviously, the book only enables a brief outline. With our 'Know More, Remember More' agenda, this way of working will be an extension of our systems and practices already in place. It will promote the extension of the independent learner through a mix and match teaching process and potentially long-term be an avenue to cope with the lack of people coming into the profession.

Our recently recruited librarian is in full swing, gosh she is good. We have so many exciting initiatives to encourage reading, communication and support the 'Know More, Remember More' agenda plus 'Dorrington Parents' Bookshop' in the Manor. The art and plastering room are completed and my two deputies are now fully trained plasterers and their overalls await. They are learning bricklaying next, well, I am sure I have told them that.

We are recruiting apprentices and advertising for retired people to re-enter the workplace and come to our academy part time to help with the wider curriculum, such as artists, potters and elocution practitioners. The list is open and endless.

One of the most successful recent initiatives was having a mobile pool. We built the infrastructure for it which included showers and a solid flat base with drainage. The company providing the pool also fully staffed it with lifeguards and instructors. We had the pool during the autumn term and all pupils from all key stages had weekly lessons. We even opened it for parents who wanted to learn to swim. Without doubt, this has been a major success. The percentage of pupils learning to swim was phenomenal. As a consequence, we are now having the mobile pool all year round.

Our most exciting venture will be the launch of Dorrington Consultancy, a new arm of the Academy. We have decided to take the policy and practices of Dorrington with its outstanding status into the local, national and international community.

The vision is to provide opportunities through the consultancy for practitioners to access digital online resources and training plus visits.

Dorrington's consultancy will sell everything we do in packages under three main areas:

- teaching and learning
- developing and maximising your learning environment
- leadership and management

Packages will be the A, B, C step by step guide to everything we do within those areas.

In addition to the packages and visits, the consultancy will offer an annual subscription for those who want to access our monthly blogs on:

- teaching and learning
- leadership and management and issues
- the political landscape local, national and global that may have an impact on our educational landscapes

Everyday practice will be continuously revisited as part of the academy's cycle of planning, development, review and evaluation.

Dorrington will continue to embed what works well and amend as necessary any policy/practice that can be improved. There will be no room for complacency.

All adaptations or new ways of working will be added to the consultancy arm of the academy regularly.

My Next Destination

I will be retiring as headteacher of Dorrington Academy in August 2024, to pursue my next journey in the arena of leadership and management as a consultant. This consultancy will be for business and education leaders in establishments locally, nationally and internationally. My purpose will be to advise and assist you as leaders, helping to maximise your opportunities for success.

So, having given you an insight to Dorrington's and my own exciting next steps, I will move you swiftly to your final serving.

All Aboard The Gravy Train

Every country, every person, every living thing and every material has a history.

Every second, every minute, every hour, every day, every year becomes history.

You cannot change history, but of course, it is always open to interpretation.

Holidays become history. When we go on holiday, often we have good memories and not so good memories. They have an impact. Generally, we want another holiday. We might go to the same place or we may make a change to the destination, to the mode of transport, the length of time, the hotel, the food, the clothes and even the company we take with us.

Some of us will be satisfied with the mix of the some good and not so good. Some of us will think no we want a better holiday and will take the risk of trying something new and different. Of course, we could just stay at home and be happy with that and that is just fine.

We are unique individuals. As leaders, we serve: the one, the few and the many.

We should be mindful of the cause, effect and potential interpretations of our choices as individuals.

As leaders, one size does not fit all. Some of you may be content being the leader of yourself, others the leaders of the few or many. One thing we know for sure, the choices you make will always have an impact.

If you are a leader of others, remember your choices will affect far more people so choose wisely.

Remember as you travel on your leadership journey, there will be many signposts along the way. Some may encourage you to stay on track, others may suggest a diversion or change of direction and some you may misinterpret. The key to success as a leader is the ability to be honest and acknowledge when you have misread the signposts. Then, you must have the confidence to take another direction to improve yourself as a leader.

So, in an ever-changing society, I remind you that we must be mindful of what we do today as choices will make history tomorrow. The choices we make will have some form of impact on someone, something or yourself. Whatever we choose, we write our own history.

I encourage you to periodically reread the lessons previously overlooked or parked as you never know when one will resonate with the situations you will find yourself in. You never know when one of these lessons may point you in the right direction.

As your journey progresses, it is worth remembering there is always a price to pay for success.

Unfortunately, it is a trait of this country that when you are successful, people always want to knock you down. As a leader of any establishment, this invariably could happen to you on more than one occasion as it has to me.

What truly guiles me is when people want to bring you down when you have been successful or just because they simply do not like you. These people tend to inappropriately misuse important mechanisms for the wrong reasons and very often do it anonymously just to bring you down or mar your success. I am of the school of thought that if you are unhappy with something, then stand up, say so and put your name to it! To try and bring people down unjustly for a selfish, individual or political agenda can be deemed as malicious, cowardly and so wrong! But nevertheless, it happens. Do not be naive if you encounter people wanting to bring you down unfairly, it can be challenging. You may have to swallow adverse publicity and suffer individual and family stress. And if this happens, remind yourself of the saying 'that people who live in glass houses shouldn't throw stones.'

The main point to remember is it is essential that as a leader you always follow correct procedures in everything you do. Always follow your convictions with integrity and confidence, whilst also acknowledging outside influences, whether individual or political can be beyond your control. If you are a leader with professional integrity with belief you will always have the strength to face challenges of adversity, whenever they may come and whatever the outcome. When the going gets tough, remember why you are a leader and remember there will always be people who may recall themselves chanting an old playground saying 'cowardly, cowardly custard,' and like I have said previously, it is very rare you can change a leopard's spots. Remember you are your own judge and believe in yourself.

My overriding advice is to never become arrogant or complacent. If you make the mistake of believing you can succeed on your own, I guarantee, 'you certainly will end up pissing on your chips.' They will not stay crisp; they will become soggy, tasteless; just a mouthful of starch; no amount of gravy will rescue them.

One thing I do know for sure, the beauty of all our journeys is that they are never predetermined. Your destination is unknown. The sheer thought of trying to lick that gorgeous gravy off the plate is exciting in itself. Please do not make it frustrating, be kind to yourself. Whatever signposts come your way, they are just there as a guide. You can choose to read them, ignore them or follow them. You can fantasise over them or take the direction offered. Whatever you choose to do, the timing of your choice is essential.

Ultimately, I wish you well. Enjoy the journey, do not let time simply pass you by. Believe in yourself, trust yourself and most importantly, be true to yourself. By the time you sit down to a celebratory dinner, you will be a connoisseur so savour the gravy and congratulate yourself on what a success it is.

My Recipe for Success as a Leader:

- Value the uniqueness of the individual and those you lead.
- Strategically plan, implement, develop, review and evaluate.
- Work collaboratively at every opportunity.
- Create teams that have an accumulation of diverse skills.
- Having respect for difference, respect is so important.
- Never be too proud to seek advice or help. Then, thank them for it, you may need them again.
- Sort out the experts who can really help.
- Always plan for leadership succession.

- Take time to enjoy working with the trustees of the board.
- Network with those you value only, the rest are a waste of your time.
- Remember you are ultimately accountable.
- Be open to taking ideas from others, it is very rare an idea is original.
- Absolutely no waste is allowed in any organisation. Remember, not too many Pritt Sticks, value for money always and the pennies make the pounds.
- Know when to park or drive.
- Value your good contractors and staff.
- Drive the extra mile to get the deal and always negotiate.
- Acknowledge when you have made a mistake. I make them everyday, the best lessons can come from mistakes.
- Be careful with the use of social media. Really think about how you manage accounts such as Facebook, Twitter and Instagram. As a leader, I do not use them.
- Be careful if you congratulate staff for their work in their Christmas/festive cards. At a later date, the messages could be used against you. Especially in disciplinary or misconduct processes as many people keep them.
- If the drums beat and gossip interferes with the running of your establishment, firstly, source the 'wooden spoon'. Talk to them carefully and fully take back control using policy and practice. When settled, remove the wooden spoon if necessary.
- Remember a 'leopard never changes its spots'. Please take note, they never do, irrespective of how many

times they try to convince you they will or have. It simply does not happen.

- Always make notes, especially for speeches, the best can forget, even Churchill.
- Take an interest in all members of the community. Notice the small things that mean a lot to someone. If you remember them and ask them about it, it makes such a difference. It matters.
- Everyone is on their own journey and that needs to be respected.
- Do not waste your time trying to be liked as a leader. You are not there with the sole purpose of making friends, respected yes, that is a different matter altogether.
- If you fall, just pick yourself up again, brush yourself down and continue journeying more wisely; onwards and upwards.
- Try and think out of the box.
- The eye is in the detail.
- If you are not sure what to do in any situation, please do not do anything immediately. Take the time to analyse, investigate issues and potential actions from different perspectives. This will give you confidence with your informed decisions and actions.

Appendices

It is important that all leaders are open to evaluation of their own standards of achievement.

I advocate that every leader should regularly have evaluations, not only externally, but very importantly by the staff you manage.

This enables you to address as a leader, perceptions of yourself as a leader. Significantly, you can reflect and adjust if necessary or not if all is well.

I asked a cross section of staff to evaluate me as a leader for this book.

1

How did you come to work at Dorrington for LB:

I was working for a heating contractor that had previously done some work at Dorrington Academy and had built up a good relationship with the ladies in the office there.

I had a few days annual leave and was browsing the online jobs and funnily enough there it was an advert for an administrative position here at Dorrington. I was like right, 'I am applying', and the next day I got a call from Loretta to say she would like me to come and have a look around the school and have a chat.

I was SO excited by the call I almost talked Loretta's ear off as I wanted to come so badly but was waiting for the plumber to come to my house as my boiler wasn't working, Loretta told me to take a breath and get here when I can.

Later that morning, I got to Dorrington and was met by Loretta, she was larger than life and so warm and comforting, with an air of strength about her.

She wanted me to look around the school and get a feel for if this is somewhere I could see myself, as she said this is one of the most important things. If you can't see yourself here, then it's not for you.

Sean, one of the deputies took me around the school asking me questions while I was trying to take in the huge buildings with all the fabulous artwork displayed around the school. With welcoming faces from the staff and the excited children walking past into their lessons.

Once back from the tour, I was taken back into Loretta's office and the first thing she said was "well what do you think?"

I was just amazed by the whole experience, I think my reply was "wow, I can't get over how huge the place is."

I'd like to say I remember the whole interview but it was like a complete whirlwind. Loretta could see how nervous I was, I don't know how she did it but she made me feel so comfortable. I don't think I have ever had an interview like it, just amazing from start to finish!

I remember being asked to sit on the sofa outside her office and after about 10 minutes being asked to come back in, to Loretta saying well we'd like to offer you the position. I felt like my jaw hit the ground and bounced back up, I was like "wow thank you!"

She asked me how quick I could start and just over a week later I was here as part of the staff at Dorrington.

Three areas LB has helped me:

Loretta has been one of the only people I have ever met that has helped me find my confidence. She has a way about her that makes you feel comfortable and confident to laugh and not always take yourself so seriously which I often do.

Loretta asked me if I would like to do a course for Business Managers for Schools, I was extremely nervous and unsure, but Loretta told me I would do great at it, and she would help and support me as she wants me to be a key part of the school, not just now but for the future.

Every time I have thought I can't do something, she has told me I can and pushed me to do so, even when it's out of my comfort zone.

During the summer last year, we had a training day at the London Olympic whitewater rafting. I was so scared I wouldn't fit in the wetsuit and it was too heavy for the boat. I said I would just sit on the side and take pictures of everyone else.

But no, Loretta was straight on the phone and spoke with the company to make sure it would all be ok for me to take part. The next thing I knew I was told not to worry "it's all sorted, you're doing it".

I have got to say if it wasn't for Loretta pushing me and telling me it would all be ok, I would have just walked away and not done it. To say that is still one of the most funniest days I've had here at Dorrington does not do the day justice.

Since Loretta made me a part of Dorrington Academy, I feel I have grown with confidence and felt a sense of worth again. To be encouraged to do things I have never ever even dreamt of doing, whether it be whitewater rafting or doing a course to become a business manager.

To say I'm honoured is an understatement, I feel very privileged to be part of Loretta's team.

Wanting an extra drink – ONE WORD – FRIDAYS!

Friday is always the day to brace yourself, as soon as Loretta comes out of her office and goes "I have a brilliant plan, grab pen and piece of paper!"

Always on a Friday is when Loretta has come up with her next brilliant plan or idea, you know to brace yourself and get your thinking cap on.

Loretta says get on the phone and see if we can get this, or get a coach for 650 people as we are taking the whole school to Blackpool in June!

There have been a few Fridays when I have gone home feeling like "what just happened?", never in a bad way but it always makes me laugh. I love the ideas and plans that she comes with and how she always looks at how to include the community.

Many times I have sat there in awe of the way Loretta effortlessly comes up with these ideas, and every eventuality. The way her brain works sometimes it's a bit scary as this will happen then weeks later it does.

I was asked to put one thing I would remember about Loretta, well that would be near impossible as the wealth of knowledge and self-worth she has given me will never be forgotten.

2

Looking for a position as a new teacher felt incredibly daunting and after visits to primary schools, I just could not seem to find 'the one'. That is until I came across a school on twitter whereby the head teacher had been photographed taking part in a Key Stage 1 Easter Hat Parade... Loretta. I thought to myself, 'that is someone I would like to work for.' As soon as I saw the post, I searched for jobs and there was one, I knew I had to look around. I looked around and it felt like I had been there for years. It felt like a place I would love to work: the gym for staff, the astro turf for the children to have P.E lessons on and the overall feel of the school. During my time at Dorrington so far, I have learnt a great deal from Loretta. The first of these things that come to mind is that as a senior leader, there are times that you need to rely on your colleagues for guidance and support.

So, having strong professional relationships with all, is vital to success. This has led to me gaining a deeper understanding of the strengths of the staff that I lead and how to best use their strengths to develop their teaching and in turn, the learning of the children. Secondly, Loretta has taught me many lessons on dealing with disagreements in school whether that be with staff or parents/carers. The main lessons that Loretta has taught me from events happening are that I must always keep a note of everything that happens and the art of choosing when to react. Before this lesson, I would have reacted as soon as anything happened, however now, I understand that in thinking about what I want to do, how I will say it and where will it happen that I am placing myself in a much better position to handle disagreements.

Although I have learnt many things from Loretta, including how to run an effective outstanding school, I think the final lesson and perhaps the most important one to me is that of respect and understanding and in Loretta's words- "if you are not prepared to do it yourself, then don't expect your staff to." When working for Loretta, I have seen first-hand the positive effect that leading by example can have for staff morale. For example, during the first Christmas market that I took part in, Loretta was working the tombola stall all night, every evening. Loretta leads by an outstanding example and because of that the staff and pupils around her strive to be outstanding too.

I will remember Loretta as being the first person to say that I could be an outstanding teacher and leader. She saw this side of me in my first interview and I have believed it ever since then. Every day since, she has given me sometimes small and sometimes huge nuggets of know-how to be what Loretta always saw, that I could become. I will always be forever grateful to her belief and knowledge.

3

How I came to work at Dorrington

For a long time, I was going to be a dentist. Everything was geared towards it. Subjects selected, on track with required grades, parents happily roll on 2 weeks work experience in Year 11. The dentist could only offer 1 week, so the second week was filled at the primary school where my mother taught.

This was a tale of two weeks, one bored rigid looking at teeth, the second teaching children to use paint on a 'state of the art' computer that took up half a table – from this point on I decided teaching was for me.

Fast forward to teacher training, 4 years with a QTS and a separate biology degree (as a back-up). Time to get a job, no pool this year so start checking the adverts of which there are not many. Nevertheless, I secured an interview, long story short, not successful. It had gone to the student already there – annoying.

I have continued to help out at my mother's school over the years, one of the teachers tells me her husband is a governor at a school, a new Headteacher is in post and she is looking for NQTs. Application submitted.

I head off to a residential area with a group of Year 4 children for the weekend. Friday afternoon my phone goes. This is my first conversation with Loretta. She proceeds to tell me she has my application and the Reverend Clifford has passed on that his wife speaks very highly of me. Can I come for an interview next week? I explain I am on a residential back on Monday night, try to buy myself a bit of preparation time so we agree later in the week, Thursday. About 5 minutes later the phone rang again, the interview was now Tuesday morning. Looking back this was my first lesson from Loretta, get things done ASAP.

I don't remember much about the interview but it was successful! I loved the school, the improvement project and the opportunities that working at Dorrington would bring. Time to celebrate. To top off a good day I then get a call from the first school I applied to. Another position is available, would I like the job? No thanks!

Three things Loretta has helped me with

Loretta has helped me in many ways, it seems a bit of an injustice to narrow it down. There are many practical skills needed to be a leader, examples of which Loretta has spoken about already during this book. It is a Headteacher's job to train leaders and develop skill sets. Many Headteachers do this by simply sending staff on courses. What I feel sets Loretta apart, and what she helped me the most with, is the care for people along the journey.

So, the three things:

1. **Confidence** – Loretta has always shown confidence in me. Even when things might not have gone to plan she has never tried to knock my confidence. As I reflect throughout my career, I can see how she has identified a lack of confidence and tried to build it, either with a supportive chat, a helpful insight or a strong word. There are many examples, too many to list but the perhaps the best is that I can still vividly remember her taking the time when I was an NQT to pop into my classroom at 5pm on a Friday evening to check in before the weekend, it is amazing how far the words 'you're doing well' can go to an NQT at that time on Friday – it gave me the confidence to come back on Monday.

2. **It is ok to have integrity** – Integrity is a big thing for me. Loretta has supported me immensely with this, especially as my Christmas card list has shortened. The first instance was when I lost a good friend over performance management. We had worked together since NQTs, his partner then came to the school. I was

her reviewer, I saw her lesson and it was inadequate, despite it being a supportive process it caused tension, he sided with her and I was finished in their eyes. Out of the friendship group. I discussed the situation with Loretta, my reviewer. It was hurtful how they acted but I could deal with that. It was at that point she said 'always remember, you are here to do a job and not make friends. If everybody loves you then you probably are not doing your job properly'

On the flip side to this there are times when having integrity can be beneficial. As an NQT there was a contractor who worked in the school and was installing different things. I would see him around and about and having been brought up to always be polite to people (not that I always get this right), I would say hello. We eventually built up to mostly moaning how badly Birmingham City were doing. Others wouldn't necessarily talk to him. I didn't think much of it at the time, the school was mainly a female staff so I just assumed they had limited conversational skills. One morning as I walked in Loretta commented that her Dad had said how shocking the Blues were at the weekend. A little confused, the penny then dropped who her dad was! Lessons learnt – always try to be nice to people, you never know when it might be your boss's dad.

3. **Plastering** – What a skill! Loretta challenged me to learn how to plaster in order to teach the children. Outside the box thinking whilst also stretching me. A week in Coventry on an intensive training course taught me so much more than just plastering, the inner workings of the Coventry narcotics industry to name but one. I met a variety of people with brilliant skills that could be

utilised. I was amazed by how many of them thought what I was doing was brilliant, how it would have kept them in school. It was hard work but made fun by those characters on the course!

Three times LB has made me need an extra drink

I do like a glass of wine. Having been on the journey of improvement at Dorrington at different levels throughout, there are occasions where I may have had to pour an extra glass but they are probably the things I have learnt the most from.

1. Miss J – That parent. Loud. Abrasive. Difficult. Naughty child. Then the child makes a serious accusation about a member of staff of something that is not true. 'You phone her John and tell her he is excluded for the week'. Great. Not a pleasant phone call but actually what did I learn here. Be prepared. I had all the facts and knew it was the right decision. In fairness, Loretta and I had also role-played the call and how it might go. Now, I do not worry about having to make a difficult call but if I had not been made I never would have and would be a lot less prepared for leadership.

2. Chair of Consortium – A new Chair was needed, established Headteachers were not offering their services – workload issues. Loretta then announces, why don't we have a Deputy Head as Chair? Nods of agreement. Good – I nominate John, anyone seconded that? Everyone else – yes! So now I am Chair of the local Consortium. Great. Actually, having had the role for a year now being forced outside my comfort zone has been so beneficial. I have built relationships and hopefully some respect from people who before would

have seen me as just Loretta's Deputy. In hindsight, I understand this was a selfless move by Loretta, one she had no need to take but did for me.

3. Upgrading the office – Many glasses here. The best until last. The long serving office manager and two administration assistants are leaving. We are replacing them with new computer systems for finance and pupil management. Loretta tells me I will be leading the change-over. Great. Hindsight (what a wonderful thing), what area did I have no real understanding about with the school and now, two years on, what do I understand so much better. I learned so much from the process of change. The new learning, how technology can make us more efficient and how some are opposed to / scared of that. I will never forget the sleepless night worrying if the registers will work on the 1st September, thank god they did!

The key to all of these examples and why they have been successful is because although I may have been at the front, at every turn Loretta was there to support, guide and challenge! A valuable lesson for anyone looking to develop staff.

Memorable moment

It is very simple. The 7th November 2019. Ofsted – Outstanding. First in the country against the new framework.

One thing I will remember Loretta for

How she treats people. It is a lesson for anyone. She has helped me with things that go way beyond her remit as a Headteacher and made things happen for me and in turn my family. I will always be grateful for this.

4

How did you come to work at Dorrington?

Having had time off to care for my family, I wanted to get back into the world of work. A meeting had been arranged with Loretta to discuss working in a voluntary capacity at Dorrington Academy. After meeting with Loretta in May 2017 and because I had my PGGE, she asked if I would be interested in taking on the role of teacher of small groups within Year 6. Nervous but excited for the challenge, I accepted the position and have been with Dorrington Academy ever since. For this, I will always be grateful to Loretta as she believed that I would fit in with the Dorrington team and was willing to open doors for me.

Three Areas LB has helped you

Example

Following on from how I came to work at Dorrington Academy, I was placed in Year 6 working with small groups of children to support them and help them to further develop. Having been out of education for a number of years, this was daunting and challenging but encouraged me to restart my career journey. This new journey allowed me to work on a part-time basis and allowed me to gradually build on my previous skills.

Lesson Learned

Loretta allowed me the opportunity to gain inner confidence in myself, to flourish within the field of education again and to work closely with many different people. This taught me to seize every opportunity, explore it because it may be the best decision you make.

Example – Due to retirement, the position of Office Manager became available within Dorrington Academy. Loretta is a great believer in enhancing the 'whole person' and utilising all their skills, where possible. I had previously worked in HR and was responsible for managing the HR Administration Team. After many discussions, Loretta encouraged me to put forward an application for the role and made me realise that I had many skills necessary for the job. Following my interview, I was successful and offered the position of Office Manager.

Lesson Learned – Loretta's view is to consider the skills of the 'whole person' as their strength and develop them further. She taught me to have self-belief and recognise that my skills/experience would be transferable.

Example – We recruited another member of staff to join the office. Although they brought certain skills to the team, I had concerns about their work ethic but was prepared to give them time to settle into Dorrington Academy. As their attitude continued and started to have an impact on others in the team and myself, I needed to share this with Loretta. Loretta was very supportive and the decision was made not to employ them on a permanent basis.

Lesson Learned – A problem should always be shared. Loretta has always reiterated that her door is always open and that she is always willing to offer guidance and support.

Three Times LB has made you want an extra drink

Example – When taking on the role of Office Manager, the school also decided to upgrade their phone, management and finance systems. This was a well needed change but a drastic one considering this was happening together. I was replacing a long-standing employee with considerable experience as well as having to learn new systems.

Lessons Learned – Even though this was a challenging time, it was important to welcome change and see the benefits in the future which I would be part of. Loretta knew it was worth the risk!

Example – Dorrington Academy are believers in bringing their team together and so they like to organise team building events. This year the event was to take part in white water rafting. As a non-swimmer, you can imagine my thoughts when this was shared with staff at the staff meeting. The sheer thought of water scared me so straight away I decided I would not be taking part, even upon reaching the activity location on the day. Courageously, I did take part in the activity and will never forget it.

Lesson Learned – I often wonder what encouraged me to do it but the feeling afterwards was exhilarating. I decided to face my fears and do it anyway. This is a concept Loretta has tried and tested and as she would say "don't ask others to do what you're not willing to do."

Example – Working within the school office can bring something new each day. It is always very busy so one hopes that what you set out to do each day, you will accomplish. This was my intention on a Friday morning until I was told that I would be part of the interview panel for Assistant and Deputy Assistant Head Teacher positions. Interviews went extremely well and ran smoothly but the time taken to come to a decision on the right candidate for the job, was a different story. This was the first time I had the opportunity to sit with the Senior Leadership Team and observe their endeavour to come to a decision. After many attempts to clarify reasons for and against certain interviewees, Loretta left the room requesting that I chair the debate between the deputies as they were not in agreement. Following a long debate, a decision was finally reached.

Lesson Learned – New experiences should be sampled and it is important to listen to everyone's opinion/reason for a decision. However, remember to have the ability to substantiate this and accept that your decision will be considered but not always be accepted.

One thing you will remember LB for

Her ability to motivate her team and remind them that Dorrington's success is not achievable without them.

Her ability to bring humour/laughter into any situation, good or bad. This is really important to her. Let's just say we have had a few!

Her ability to see the good in people and that they are worth investing in.

5

I came to work at Dorrington Academy for Loretta Barratt after
being recruited as a Newly Qualified Teacher. I worked my way
up from Team Leader to Head of Technology to Assistant Head
Teacher. Loretta throughout this journey offered invaluable
advice and mentoring. She helped me in three key areas: First,
she taught me to focus on small details as they are often the
ones that come back later. Second, she encouraged me to keep
pushing towards the end goal even when knocked off course.
Third, she showed me that effective delegation is the key to
success.

She made it clear that even though we were capable of it all, it
was important to let others in.

On the other hand, there were a few times when Loretta made
me want to grab a stiff drink. For instance, when she asked me
to run the annual Christmas market, a market much loved by
the whole community and Loretta herself. The pressure I felt to
get it right was intense but with Loretta by my side I learned
how to manage whole projects, how to consider, spot and
handle health & safety, how to manage difficult staff and boost
morale.

Another occasion was the day she told us to start planning the
whole school trip to Blackpool after a confusing (at least for me)
game of charades, mixed with hangman and a few donkey
noises. The realisation of the scale, the number of children and
the instant issues jumped out at me but I learned not to let the
fear consume me and to tackle it in small steps. Even if that
small step was a midday high tide.

Lastly, one thing I will always remember Loretta for is being unapologetically herself. In my first interview as a fresh hopeful NQT, she asked me where I would be on a zip lining day: at the front cheering everyone on, at the back scared and worried or at school doing some filing. In that moment, I knew I wanted to work at Dorrington Academy. There was something about the way she asked the question and reacted to my response that made the opportunity seem irresistible. Over the years, my first instincts about Dorrington and Loretta have only been proven over and over again. From the out of the box thinking to the unique points of view she has shared; she is truly one of a kind.

6

I came to Dorrington Academy as an NQT in 2012 just after the school converted to an academy. After teaching in Year 3 for two years and being given the time to develop as a class teacher, I moved to Year 6 and was part of the team who developed the curriculum necessary to meet the needs of the new national assessments and curriculum of 2015.

During this time, I was given the opportunity to subject lead Maths across the academy and later on Science. These subject experiences gave me my first opportunities in leadership and I was able to dip my toe in further when appointed Deputy Assistant Headteacher and a year later Assistant Headteacher. My responsibilities included data, particularly supporting other departments with their data analysis such as SEND, pupil premium and end of key stages. As an AHT and later as Deputy

Headteacher, my responsibilities increased and included areas such as behaviour, admissions and pupil premium.

Teaching was not always the dream. Therefore, neither was rising to my current position of Deputy Headteacher but it was an exciting journey! My degree was a 'nothing' degree which left me with few options so I took up landscaping - a trade which gave me insights into the 'real' world and business which my three years at university had failed to do. Additionally, it afforded me the opportunity to work abroad and travel some of the world. However, landscaping was not the dream either and whilst in some far flung campsite near Adelaide, Australia, I decided to look into the prospect of teaching as a career. Upon my return to England, it took another 18 months before I began my PGCE year.

Loretta's links to the PGCE course brought me to Dorrington Academy for an interview in early February and after successfully securing a role, I started as an NQT in 2012 - just after the school had converted to an Academy. I had known when first walking the corridors of Dorrington Academy that it was the place for me: it was diverse, dynamic and energetic. Immediately, it felt like a place that was moving forward with purpose and unashamedly unafraid of trying something new.

From the beginning, Loretta never shied away from identifying what would support and develop me. Towards the end of my NQT year, she observed me teach a lesson in Year 3. She helped me by recognising that I would benefit from support in certain areas and advising that my future lay higher up the school and with the extra responsibility of end of key stage assessments. A year later, I moved into Year 6 and was part of the team who developed the curriculum necessary to meet the needs of the new national assessments. Loretta put her trust in me with this role but interestingly she identified this move far before I had considered it myself. This would be a recurring theme in our relationship. She saw potential in me far before I did. She opened doors I didn't know were ajar and developed skills I did not know I could possess.

As a child I hated maths, despite being quite good at it and seemingly having a mathematical mind, and this lack of passion continued throughout my education. As a teacher, I had to learn to break down what came naturally to me in order to successfully impart knowledge and skills to children. Loretta spotted this aptitude and thus came my first incursion into leadership - subject leading maths. This role and the subsequent position of Deputy Assistant Headteacher taught me a lot. Through my training, I quickly learned that good quality leadership skills can be applied to any context or scenario. Being a competent mathematician did not make me a good leader of maths. If anything, being 'good' at maths had hindered my early teaching in the subject. Instead, Loretta honed my skills in developing people and skills, learning to identify areas for improvement and being brave in introducing concepts to make the required improvements.

The experiences gained in these positions lead to my appointment as Assistant Headteacher. Again, the skills I had developed and sharpened meant that Loretta already knew how I could benefit the senior leadership team. She had seen and recognised that my analytical and mathematical mind could benefit the academy's data analysis processes and support in areas such as SEND and pupil premium.

This is where Loretta helped me with strategic thinking. What skills did I already have? How could they be developed and utilised to the maximum within the academy to the benefit of the children? Most importantly for my development as a leader, I began to ask these questions about others and to plan strategically across the whole academy. She taught me how to audit the school, identifying priorities and budgeting accordingly (the priorities drive the budget). Her foresight in understanding my strengths and developing them into leadership qualities meant I could begin to look strategically across a range of subjects not immediately under my expertise. As a deputy headteacher this enabled me to increase my academy wide responsibilities into areas such as behaviour, admissions and staffing.

The training I have received from Loretta has been invaluable as she is a firm believer in the best way to learn something is to be thrown in and to get on with it. She is always there to offer advice and support but allows you to follow your own instincts. Of course, this can be unnerving and more than once I have required a stiff drink at the end of a difficult day.

Dealing with behaviour issues can be challenging, particularly when parents are unsupportive or unwilling to cooperate so when Loretta asked me to lead with the behaviour management of one particular child, I knew I would be in for a rough ride. Although this child was receiving vast amounts of support, their behaviour meant they had received a number of fixed term exclusions. The child's parents were extremely difficult to speak to and very defensive, turning every conversation into a battle, accusing you of various things and questioning your integrity. Loretta was always there to offer advice beforehand or a quiet seat and debrief following the 'battle'. I learned so much from these situations including being true to your beliefs and the school's ethos and values, ensuring your evidence trail is meticulous, never having a difficult conversation alone and when to end one and move on...they caused me to down a couple at the end of the day too.

Community is a strong thread which runs through Dorrington, and in the community, the academy is renowned for their productions. They are incredible and a step above your usual 'play'. Usually involving hundreds of children and many staff too, they are more akin to Broadway than a school. Being on stage is not my cup of tea – putting myself on display at all is not something I relish. I am very often a closed book so you can imagine my horror at being asked to perform in a scene of 'The Greatest Showman'. I was not the only one and in fact Loretta herself was on stage too as we performed a family friendly scene of 'The Peaky Blinders' much to the amusement and pleasure of the crowd of children and parents.

When first 'strutting' out in my peaky cap and tail coat, the ground refused to swallow me up (I would have jumped in willingly) but suddenly the whooping and hollering of the audience allowed me to come out of myself and into character. I learnt that sometimes you have to place yourself outside of your comfort zone, give a little bit more of yourself as children, parents and staff will respond to this, appreciating your openness, and to also never ask someone to do something you would not do yourself. I am not sure I could have gone out onto that stage without Loretta following me. Cheers Aunt Pol!

Over the course of Loretta's stewardship, Dorrington has developed into an outstanding learning environment with incredible resources for the children and the community. I was fortunate to be given a project to develop a bus into a state-of-the-art sensory room used to support children with many needs including SEN, those dealing with family problems and grief and children who seem to fly just under the radar and need a little something extra. Only one problem in my mind ...getting the American bluebird yellow bus onto site once it had been fitted out with all of our fantastic new equipment. Loretta's charms had convinced the man who had sold us the bus (at an extraordinarily discounted price - it's always worth asking someone to sharpen their pencil), to drive the bus back to us.

However, in order to get it into position I had to arrange for a metal fence to be taken down and a drop of several feet filled in with stone so that the 15 tonne bus would not topple over or become stuck on a prominent ridge. Despite the preparations going to plan, I was still filled with dread as the bus approached the school (typical it should arrive at the busiest point of the day - home time). It would need to be reversed down a single lane with a severe gradient and turned into position over the temporary stone filled ridge. Fortunately, all went to plan and we only nicked the wing mirror once!

This project taught me to always drive a bargain and treat every penny as if it's your own, think outside the box! The bus at £5k offered huge value for money – far cheaper than a classroom build of the same size. The bus enables us to support every child no matter what they are going through. It took a team to put the idea together: from SENDCos to learning mentors and that was another lesson – working collaboratively is key to success. I could not have got the bus kitted out and into position without the team. Collaborative working is at the heart of Dorrington. It is this culture which has allowed me to thrive and be successful in my various roles; it is entwined throughout every layer of the school.

One thing is for sure, life at Dorrington is never dull. I already have a decade of incredible memories to look back on. Picking one outstanding moment is tricky from so many but I will never forget a whole school assembly where suddenly from the top of a scaffolding tower, Spider-Man appeared, whipping the astonished children (and teachers) into a frenzy and enthusing them more than any usual assembly or lesson could do. And that was Loretta – doing the unexpected and thinking outside the box.

She did not just stand at the front in the outfit, she started 8 metres up and scaled down the tower, remaining in character the whole time. It does not matter what the assembly was about now because I can guarantee no child forgot and by the end of the day their parents had the same message too. There was a lesson for me here too. Do not be afraid to do something unexpected , something that will capture the children's imagination and that they will not forget. Be dynamic and energetic but do it for a purpose!

7

As I write this now, I reflect back on the journey I have had in my career to date. None of it possible without Loretta. Everything I have learned and everything I have become I owe to her.

It all started back in February 2010 - the start of my Dorrington journey. I can still remember the day like it was yesterday. I had seen a position for an NQT advertised at the school at university. I was coming to the end of my three year BA (Hons) degree in Primary Education with an English specialism. I had always wanted to be a teacher – always. The realisation of actually qualifying was almost upon me. It was the only job advertised, I still had the majority of my final placement to complete as well as assignments and the university was keen for us to wait until the summer term to apply but that was not in my nature. I have always liked to be organised and have a plan so for me it was a 'no brainer' that I wanted to go and visit Dorrington.

I had registered my interest and had a date set for an informal visit. I had researched Dorrington and felt like I lived on the website – this was so exciting! Obviously, I wanted to make a good impression so that week I went out and purchased my first suit dress with matching heels of course. Something that would later become my trademark.

The day of the visit came, it was after school and there were so many of us touring we had been split into two groups. In mine, about ten of us. I can vividly remember walking up the stairs by KS1 where the whole corridor and ceiling was painted black with all the planets in the solar system. This place is huge I thought! Nothing like I had ever experienced before. When I got home that evening, I called my mum: I have to work there!

Again, I like to be organised so I was wasting no time in writing my letter of application. The following day was a mild and warm Friday and there was no university or placement – perfect! I was living quite locally to the school at the time as my university campus was based in Perry Barr. I had read and reread my application over and over again and printed it and placed it in a brown envelope. I started the 15 minute walk to ensure that it reached the school and I could hand it over in person. Oh the excitement! I opened the main office door, which if I remember correctly was up a few steps. 'Good morning, I'm here to drop off my application for the NQT position.' A lady greeted me and told me that Miss Barratt would be out to see me. I am a very nervous person – (a worrier) but this was hidden with probably me talking too much. I remember Loretta coming out of her office to say good morning to me. I remember us briefly chatting but I cannot remember what was said. The walk home was much quicker than the walk there. That feeling again: I have to work there!

The week passed and I received the phone call to say I had been shortlisted for an interview. Me. Me! How exciting. This was all I wanted. I had to teach a lesson to a year group of my choice so set to work straight away on the plan. English, it had to be. Over the next few days, I planned my reading lesson on inference within an inch of its life. Shopping for the resources was so exciting (and my second suit dress). I spent a fortune and remember arriving on the day of my interview with a trolley full of large blue boxes with green lids (one per table) filled with all sorts of objects. Rubber ducks; gold coins and random shoes to name a few. I set up the resources in my chosen Year 4 class. It felt like everything had left my head, not what I had planned for!

My next memory was sitting outside the PPA room at the time, there were about 15 of us being interviewed. It was my turn. I could see through the window at the panel with Loretta at the head of the table. My gosh, the nerves. I sat down at the opposite end of the table and caught eyes with her. Here we go …. All a blur except telling the reverend to 'give it to me' with one of the questions. What had I done? What did I say that for?

The clock slowly ticked by, hours passed like minutes and at around 5.30pm my phone rang. I was in the kitchen at the time. It was Miss Barratt. She was offering me a job. I had done it! I remember her telling me on the phone that I had shown my personality and really showed the panel who I was. Something Loretta has always taught me. Give the children a bit of you. It goes a long way. Let them in and they will buy into you. That piece of advice I have always tried to give myself as she made me see the value in it so early on. Absolutely she was right, the relationship you develop early on, whether that be with children, their families or staff is so important.

From that moment, Dorrington was in my blood. Thirteen years later, under Loretta's guidance, it still is and always will be. At present, I cannot see myself anywhere else. I love it. Everything about it but it wouldn't be Dorrington without her and I wouldn't be here without her.

My first two years were spent in year 5 where I was able to consolidate my skills and then a move to year 6. After a year there, I remember Loretta explaining to me that she wanted me to lead the year group and end key stage assessments with a new team. Was I ready? Loretta had seen something in me. One of her many talents - enabling the potential in others. Her wisdom pushed me to see things in my own leadership capabilities and aptitudes I had never fully seen, appreciated or understood before. I was not going to let her down.

Next came the addition of Literacy and Reading followed by becoming an Assistant Headteacher and in 2016, Deputy Headteacher. An intense day I will never forget. Again, my success is a byproduct of me being led and trained by Loretta. Being prepared was the key. A message that she has always given me. This still stands now. Always have a paper trail; dot the Is and cross the Ts; be meticulous; rehearse and be organised.

We had seen a change in the National Curriculum with lots of hard work by the team and I was going to start overseeing the end of key stage one assessments. Upper key stage two had been my passion but Loretta encouraged me to see the bigger picture and to think more strategically – to see the Academy as a whole. She is courageous and not afraid to go beyond the expected. She always thinks on a much deeper level in terms of thinking, acting and innovating and was teaching me to do the same. Over time, I have developed more. As previously stated, Loretta has a special wisdom. One day, I hope I can come close to her leadership ability. Without realising it, I learned that the skills possessed by good leaders can be applied to any context at all.

In 2019, one of my most memorable moments came working for Loretta at Dorrington. Now I have to say there have been hundreds, probably thousands but looking across the table at her after the HMI inspector for Ofsted announced that Dorrington Academy was outstanding is something I will never forget. The journey of improvement Loretta had led the school on had been recognised – the first school to receive outstanding against the new Ofsted framework. To say I was proud to be part of her team would be an understatement.

Of course in this thirteen year journey I have, at times, needed to pour a drink! At the time, feelings of being scared, nervous, apprehensive and stepping out my comfort zone but thinking back, all valuable lessons on my journey where actually my skill set was expanding without me even knowing it. Times I have learned the most!

My first show …. Read All About It! How was I going to pull this off? Development of the whole child is integral, a belief Loretta has always had. Costumes, music, lighting, scripts, choirs, props.

Where to start?! Loretta had trusted me to make it happen. I had a pink file full of notes, ideas and quotes. I still have it now.

'Get on the phone, we're not paying that!' Phoning this huge company that had provided the sound, staging and lighting for Glastonbury to say that their price was too expensive and it had to come down. I was terrified! My first experience of finance and budgeting. Something which as the years have passed, I have developed my understanding in far more due to 'doing' if I never had to experience that first phone call I would never have developed the skill of bargaining! Now I cannot remember the phone call but I can remember Loretta's saying … 'Sharpen your pencil'. To my amazement the price came down. Loretta was right (she always is!) What did I learn, every penny counts. You can always save money. More money leads to more opportunities for the children.

In my previous paragraph I mentioned 'doing'. Loretta is a firm believer in 'doing' and there is nothing like being thrown in the deep end and stepping out of your comfort zone. That certainly happened.

Early Years …. Something I had no experience of. A new curriculum and framework was coming into play and I would be overseeing and leading the change. Unnerved – yes. What had I learned from Loretta to date – get stuck in and do as well as the value of reading, researching and being up to date. I read a lot. Researched a lot. Ultimately, the skills I had developed over time working for her would allow me to be successful in this role. The principles of teaching and learning are the same whether you are 3 or 13. Loretta has nurtured my love of this area and helped me to see that. As I type now, I now have a huge passion for the EYFS, it is the foundation to a child's future.

If I had not been thrown in the 'deep end' as such, I would not have the full spectrum perspective I do now of the whole school. Thank you Loretta.

8

As a governor, I have the privilege and honour to have worked with Loretta for over 20 years both at her previous school and Dorrington. When she took over the headship, these schools were 'failing' both academically and financially.

Undaunted by this, she threw herself into radically improving the schools for pupils, parents and staff. Her level of commitment went way beyond what was expected of her and this level of commitment has never ceased to diminish. She has always 'gone the extra mile'.

All her hard work and commitment has been recognised by the various Ofsted inspections and for both schools she has achieved 'Outstanding' when this looked impossible.

We are all unique in our own way, but Loretta is also unique in her leadership and management abilities. She works tirelessly and with infectious enthusiasm and her ambition for the school knows no limit. She has assiduously maximised Dorrington's budget and accessed any external funding that became available. Anyone who only knew the school before Loretta took over, would not now recognise the current buildings and fabric with all its facilities.

When asked what Loretta has done for me I could name many aspects, but three of them would be.:

Firstly, I have to thank Loretta for inviting me to be part of the educational system in the first place. Whilst I have for many years been involved with charitable work, I am grateful for being able to give something back to the educational community so that I can 'pay back' the wonderful education I received during my school years.

Secondly, because of the way Loretta actively runs Dorrington, in such a professional and dedicated manner, she makes my life as a Governor so much easier to cope with. It is always a pleasure to attend the school on Dorrington business.

Thirdly, myself and the other Governors are always welcome to be included and part of many of the activities that take place both during school time and outside school hours. We are a 'team' and it really feels like being part of the 'family'.

When asked on what occasion to do with Loretta I reach for my glass of wine (or two- just leave the bottle), I could outline many times over the years. However, I would just say that the 'danger' point with Loretta is when she says that there is no more to do! Within a very short period, sometimes it is the same day, she would suddenly say she has a new idea that would benefit the pupils and the school. It is a case of 'hang on to her coat tails', we are in for another journey.

Loretta is exceptional by being able to 'think outside of the box' and the interesting aspect of this is that many of her projects derived from this approach are now regarded by other schools as the norm.

Examples of the above would be our psychedelic sensory American yellow bus which ensures that children with learning disabilities succeed in their learning, giving them confidence to tackle new situations and our on site swimming pool facility, where the data for the last term showed an improvement of pupil the can swim from just under 20% to nearly 50%.

When asked about one memorable aspect, you can imagine that there would be many of these over the years! However, I suppose, the one that was so important is the time we became an Academy, giving us more freedom to determine our future. With Loretta at the helm this has certainly been proved right.